Geoff Gillham:
six plays for Theatre in Education
and Youth Theatre

Geoff Gillham:
six plays for Theatre in Education and Youth Theatre

Edited by *David Davis*

Introduction by *David Davis and Chris Cooper*
Forewords to the plays by *Chris Cooper*
Foreword by *Edward Bond*

Trentham Books
Stoke on Trent, UK and Sterling, USA

Trentham Books Limited
Westview House   22883 Quicksilver Drive
734 London Road   Sterling
Oakhill   VA 20166-2012
Stoke on Trent   USA
Staffordshire
England ST4 5NP

First published 2011

British Library Cataloguing-in-Publication Data
A catalogue record for this book is available from the British Library

ISBN 978-1-85856-495-1

Designed and typeset by Trentham Books Ltd, Chester
Printed and bound in Great Britain by 4edge Ltd, Hockley

To the memory of Geoff Gillham and his wife Viet
For Daniel

Acknowledgements

Geoff banged out all his plays on an old typewriter so only hard copies were available. Good friends and colleagues took the ones collected here and word processed them as the first stage of developing this volume. So thanks are offered first of all to those who undertook this work: Jo Underwood, Gavin Bolton, Naomi Doyle, Guy Williams, Adam Bethlenfalvy, Pavla Bier and Liz Brown with a plea to be forgiven if I've missed anyone out.

Many thanks also to Tag McEntegart, Brian Bishop, Mandy Finney, Ian Yeoman, Ceri Townsend and Lina Attel for helping with research and responding to queries about the original productions.

Thanks to Edward Bond who worked professionally with Geoff on occasions and who was pleased to be asked to write the Foreword.

Chris Cooper has, as always, been a stalwart in seeking to promote Geoff's work and memory. Chris organised the processing of the plays from hard copies into Word. It has, as always, been rewarding to work with him.

Finally, huge thanks to Gillian Klein, our excellent editor at Trentham Books. I sent her a copy of *Asylum* to read as a sample play and she let me know that she read it late into the night as she could not put it down. Enormous tribute needs to be paid to her for preserving such a human face in what has all too often become an impersonalised world of publishing.

Thanks as always to my wife Elaine, who knew and valued Geoff and has supported this project from the word go.

Contents

The plays are also available to download as individual playscripts at:
http://www.trentham-books.co.uk/acatalog/Geoff_Gillham.html
and selected by title.
Note that *Bone Cage* and *The Kiss* are combined on one pdf.

Foreword
Edward Bond

In person Geoff Gillham was noticeably thin, a bit angular and pointed – a suggestion of a pair of scissors. It is essential to acknowledge his right and need to be like this – because his smile was sudden and it seemed to come from not only his face but from his whole person. He was a man of contrasts: intense and concentrated but generous and expansive. The contrast came from his relationship to the world. Cruelty and exploitation made him searingly angry. But for the victims he was endlessly generous and, when he could be, comforting. He was angry because he felt the victims' wounds and sufferings. But because his compassion for them was so great and urgent it gave his ideas a precise, accurate definition and a relentless tenacity. It was an understanding beyond sentiment. The vague and indecisive were alien to him. He saw life as an emergency.

There is a double focus in his plays: the figures from fairy tales and myths, the animals that metamorphose into humans, the humans who behave like animals, the laboratories, circuses, wastelands ... He combined these visionary and fantastic worlds with the acute realism and sometimes uncannily precise observation of our everyday world. That is how he saw and understood life. It was the source of his politics. Human existence is made up of contrasts which in history are contradictions. We share the world with millions of others we can never meet and know. They are as concrete and real as we are and yet they are the unknown. But we are unknown also to ourselves – nothing is closer than our own pains and emotions and dreams and yet in some ways they are as beyond our control and as strange as the lives of the other people we can never meet. It is as if we lived in two worlds, two realities – what is in us may be as remote as what is outside us. So our lives are naturally paradoxical and historically contradictory. Politics is the search to resolve these contradictions, to close the gaps – so that we do not blunder about in our own self-ignorance, irresponsibly seeking our own self-interests, and irresponsibly using and abusing others. The two things come together. One cannot be achieved without the other. And if we do not try to achieve them then each one of us is a stranger living among strangers. Then when we set out to build Utopias we end by building prisons.

We think of politics as social organisation, social engineering, making-laws and so on. But as human reality is of the sort I describe, then politics has to be more. There is no text that will teach us how to be human. We are the text and we have constantly to recreate ourselves. We cannot divide text and writer – that is the world of nature, the natural order of things, but it is not our historical condition. To put it aphoristically, we have to teach the text to write and write the text to teach us to write. Only drama can struggle with itself in this way. That is why there is no gap between Geoff Gillham's politics and his plays. They are the same. He could be a politician only if he were a dramatist.

You see this especially in two of his later plays: *Bone Cage* and *Asylum*. They appear to show different, even utterly opposite, worlds. Yet they are as much the same as are identical Siamese-twins. They mirror each other from opposite sides of the divide. They are written by an inspired craftsman who has achieved the power to precisely mirror our situation. That is the reason for the extraordinary accuracy of their language and observation and the exact focus of their imagery. It is the hallucination of suddenly being awake. Geoff Gillham died young but his plays came from long and intense experience. His life was his triumph and his death our tragedy.

Introduction

David Davis

It was as if he could throw a stone in a river and its whole course would change from the place where it struck. (Edward Bond commenting on the life of Geoff Gillham)

Geoff Gillham's death from cancer in 2001, at the far too early age of 56, robbed the TIE (Theatre in Education) world of a great and constantly developing playwright, educator and political fighter for human justice. It has taken far too long to manage to get this volume of his plays together for publication. They are only a handful of the twenty eight plays he wrote.

Background

Geoff Gillham's life work ended, as it began, with pen in hand, or rather dictating a play for someone else to write. Geoff was one of the most important and innovative writers for and directors of TIE internationally. He was not interested in writing plays that young people just watched passively but quickly saw the potential of TIE to actively engage them in productive learning through theatre and drama, making meaning of their lives and the world they live in. Above all, Geoff passionately believed in the power of theatre to humanise and in doing so become a force for change in the world.

Geoff first trained as a teacher but stayed in the classroom for only a year – just long enough to become a fully qualified teacher. He quickly switched to his first love and began his career in theatre, like many brilliant post-war artists, at the Royal Court, albeit as a stage manager! He was later granted an Arts Council bursary as a director at the Lincoln

Theatre Royal. He resigned from this after a short while when he saw the limitations of repertory theatre for the kind of theatre he wanted to create. Geoff moved on to the North-East to found a community theatre which could deal with the real pre-occupations and concerns of a local community. He founded Live Theatre in 1972, whose work continues to this day.

This is where I first met him, when in 1970, as a young man of twenty four, he arrived to take over my job as Head of Drama in Highfield School on Tyneside, while I had a term's sabbatical on Gavin Bolton's two year postgraduate diploma course. This was the start of a life-long friendship and working relationship. It was also, incidentally, an exciting school to be working in. John O'Toole was head of English, Mike Fleming was a newly appointed teacher and Geoff Gillham and I added to lively and innovative English and Drama departments. Dorothy Heathcote lived in sight of the school and on occasion she and Gavin Bolton both worked in the school.

Geoff and I worked in Felling Youth Theatre together for five years. For one of our productions we decided to use Romeo and Juliet as source material. Geoff suggested we meet up in his flat to go through the play together. I tried to put it off as I thought I knew the play. Geoff insisted, so we met up in his council flat in Felling, in a high-rise block looking out over the river Tyne. He had two chairs in his flat, so we did have a chair each, and we sat at his round table filled with plants, (even if Geoff had no money for food he still managed to acquire plants!). He insisted we read the play from start to finish at a sitting. I thought this was a bit much but Geoff insisted. And then I discovered this brand new play called *Romeo and Juliet*. He would pause at every scene and insist we uncover the meanings and the themes held in these particular encounters. Geoff would very patiently and politely wait after every scene to see if I had anything to offer and when it was clear that I hadn't, he would explain to me what was going on in the scene and how it related to the main themes of the play. To this day it is one of the plays I feel I understand best. I don't think I have added anything of my own to it since that first analysis of his.

It was from the influence of Drama in Education (DIE) practitioners, particularly Gavin Bolton and Dorothy Heathcote, that Geoff took the key gains of drama in education into his TIE work. Even though he was working with drama for a comparatively short time, first in school and then as an advisory teacher for Gateshead, he developed important aspects of the theory of DIE. He developed the concept of there being two plays at work in a drama lesson, the play for the class and the play for the teacher. This became one of the most quoted unpublished papers in the history of DIE (Gillham, 1974). Gavin Bolton constantly made reference to it and acknowledged Gillham's original contribution. (In fact I was present at the intense head to head when he first discussed it with Bolton.) In another important article Geoff speculated how important it was for children to have a firm anchor in the base reality in order to enter the imagined reality (Gillham, 1979).

Theatre in Education

Eventually Geoff's journey, strongly influenced by developments in drama in education, led him into Theatre in Education and to what was to become his chosen and beloved art form. It was from this point on that he began to make his most brilliant and inspiring contributions to theatre, and to the lives of tens of thousands of young people. He became artistic director and writer for the Cockpit Theatre TIE Company in London, Action Projects in Education in Cardiff and Harlow Theatre Van. In a lifetime's work he directed and wrote plays for companies such as the Belgrade TIE in Coventry; the Dukes TIE in Lancaster; Spectacle Theatre in Mid Glamorgan; Theatre Powys; Big Brum TIE in Birmingham; Wolsey TIE in Ipswich; Benwell TIE in Newcastle; The Commonwealth Institute London; Wederzijds in Amsterdam; Penygraig Drama workshop in the Rhondda; The Performing Arts Centre, Amman, Jordan and the SCYPT (Standing Conference of Young People's Theatre) Co-operative. He also worked in many countries including Vietnam, Hungary and Kenya. For his work in Bosnia he was awarded the Groz-danin Kikot Award by the Mostar Youth Theatre.

As well as being remembered as a theoretician and a great teacher, Geoff dedicated his life to the development of TIE and the teaching and training of others through the Standing Conference of Young People's Theatre (SCYPT). He became the driving force of this hugely important organisation throughout a period when catastrophic funding cuts to companies threatened the TIE movement and SCYPT itself with extinction. As an internationalist, Geoff was the first to recognise that while TIE was under threat in the UK, progressive artists and educators all over the world were thirsty for its methods and ideas. It was out of this understanding that Geoff led the move to found, through SCYPT, the International Centre for Theatre-in-Education (ICTIE).

The struggle to build the ICTIE took a giant leap forward in August 2000 when artists from 21 countries gathered for the People In Movement Conference on Theatre-in-Education in Amman, Jordan. Geoff was the creative and political spark behind this extraordinary event. It grew from his earlier work in Jordan for which he received the Noor Al-Hussein Foundation Performing Arts Centre Award, presented to him by Queen Noor. Indeed Jordan became his spiritual home: the Arab people, the struggle of the Palestinians, the friendships he made and the work he was a part of creating there were to him a great source of inspiration. And in the staggering beauty of Petra, with its amphitheatre at the heart of this ancient city carved from the rock, he found embodied all that his work stood for. It is worth noting in passing that neither SCYPT nor ICTIE exist as organisations any longer: a sign of the times.

The plays

Each of the plays in this volume, except for *Dressing up, stripping down*, which was conceived as a piece of community/political theatre, would have been part of a TIE programme. There would have been a work pack for the teachers to use and preparation and post reflection with the teachers where possible. The company would have been made up of actor teachers who would work with a class at a time for up to a whole day. The young people would be actively engaged in penetrating and interacting with the play, employing various means including role-play. This separates out Theatre in Education from other forms of outreach work done by theatres or drama centres, where the actors put on a play and then have a bit of discussion with the pupils. TIE is a discreet art form of work first developed at the Belgrade Theatre in Coventry in the late 1960s. It spread throughout Britain in the 1970s, 80s and into the 90s but this original art form was all but killed off by funding cutbacks.

The plays show great variety in form and content. Like all his plays, they exist on the cusp that intertwines the personal and the social. They explore how the social is in the individual and examine the dilemmas, contradictions and responsibilities that flow from this. The area he continually returns to and which his plays revolve around is the struggle to understand and confront the ideological vision given to us by our social and cultural origins.

Gillham's early plays are strongly didactic in form. *Lessons*, illustrates this. As with all his plays, it contains more than it appears to. As well as a critique of teaching in schools, it is a critique of the main ways of inducting the citizens of the future to be compliant and vision impaired. It is also a critique of colonialism and racist and of classist attitudes.

The development of form is shown most clearly in two later plays, *The Kiss*, written to be performed in Jordan, and *Bone-cage*. These are not didactic in form and show a growing influence on his writing which stemmed from his admiration and close attention to the plays of Edward Bond, whom he regarded as the greatest of contemporary playwrights. *The Kiss* examines how young men in particular are weighed down by the traditions they grow up in, no matter how strongly they think they are shaking them off. In this play, as in many of his plays, a major humanising force is a young woman. In *Bone-cage* a young girl is being trundled to the boneyard in a cage, a metaphor for any horrific future place in the world where young people might end up. She is offered the chance to leave – but which is the stronger hindrance to her chance of freedom: the iron bars of the cage or her own bone-cage?

Asylum, which Edward Bond called a 'masterpiece of political theatre', has, in my opinion, a perfect structure. On one level it is a study of alienation in our society, with a contrasting social group, linked by a common destiny, forging human bonds and contacts between themselves. On another level it is a straightforward indictment of the way asylum seekers are often treated.

In a great leap of imagination, all the characters except one in *When sleeping dogs awake* are dogs . By analogy a world is set up that parallels aspects of our own: a world where we are second guessing the true aims of our politicians; where we can choose to remain ignorant of the realities around us; where the working class or the youth can be scapegoated; where the forces of fascism are just around the corner.

Finally, *Dressing up, stripping down* develops almost a pantomime style of tragi-comedy. takes the Hans Christian Anderson fairy tale *The Emperor's new clothes* and works it to his own purposes. Gillham conjures up the world of self-deluding dictators such as Gaddafi travelling overseas, dressed in a full military uniform with acres of medals and with a bodyguard of female virgins and a Bedouin tent to sleep in, while he visits other equally deluded world leaders. It also serves as a metaphor for all political leaders who are naked and think they are clothed. I remember seeing this play in Coventry, performed as a piece of political theatre to comment on the cuts being brought in by local councillors and the arts council. The working class audience loved it.

As Edward Bond wrote in a note accompanying his Foreword, 'I think the last two plays are brilliant (*Asylum* and *Bone-cage*). Extraordinary. Where could his writing go after that? It makes his early death a greater loss'.

A note on edited terms

Trentham's editor, Gillian Klein, asked me to change or delete two terms in two of the plays. In *Dressing up, stripping down* the highly manipulative Chief Minister calls one of the Silesian Weavers 'Little kike'. At the time of writing there was a lot of anti-Jewish racism in the air and Gillham was trying to show that racism is also embedded in political circles. The actual quote is: 'Chief Minister: (to audience) Hear that? Trying to make me feel guilty. Little kike.' (Scene 2). The second term is 'Jewish tailor' in *Lessons*. The line is spoken in Part 2 by the sado-masochistic teacher Susanne. 'Susanne: Don't give me your apologies, you remind me of a Jewish tailor, a week late.' Again, the intention was to show that racism is also present in those who teach young people – the use of tailor immediately brings to Susanne's mind the racist stereotype of Jewish. In discussion with Chris Cooper we have both accepted the argument that these terms might be viewed, not as originally intended, but as terms of abuse insufficiently contextualised. We have therefore chosen simply to delete these terms.

End piece

Geoff began his professional life directing the world premiere of Samuel Beckett's Breath in Glasgow in 1969 and ended it directing a national tour of the British professional premiere of Edward Bond's *The crime of the twenty first century* in 2001. Geoff probably had the pancreatic cancer eating away at him unknown throughout the time he worked on this, his last production. He knew he was ill but thought he had an ulcer. He would not stop for medical treatment because he knew that his work on the play might be cut short. He remained obstinately at the helm till his last days.

> *We must learn never to be surprised, but always reserve the right to be shocked.* (Geoff Gillham)

Chris Cooper

I had heard about Geoff, heard a lot about him, read his articles in the *SCYPT Journal* at college and at work, before I met him in person in 1988 in Lancaster, at an editorial board meeting of the *Theatre in Education Journal* (*TEJ*) I had tagged along to. I can't say I was very impressed by what I saw at first sight. I think I imagined a giant of a man. I wasn't prepared for a small sinuous cross-legged figure nursing a cup of coffee in mantis-like hands. First impressions can of course be misleading, and heaven's knows what he made of me.

I quickly realised Geoff was a remarkable man and came to learn that he was indeed a giant in our chosen field of work. He was my teacher and we built a professional relationship and enduring friendship based on our interests in theatre in education, young people and political trust.

In order to give more context to the plays in this volume, let me outline how we in SCYPT defined theatre-in-education.

The basis of the work is the use of theatre as a tool for social learning. By learning, I mean using the art form to enable children and young people to know and create themselves and their own values through imagined experience. We are not teaching them what to think, because theatre cannot teach like this. As Edward Bond would say, we can learn where the continent of Africa is, but no one can teach us who we are.

Only we can know that. This is the role of theatre and drama in our culture, to know the 'self' and come to know it as social and historical *being*, in order to be more human.

> This is the job, the purpose, the domain of the arts in education. And, because such things concern the *processes* of social and human *interaction*, the domain particularly of drama and theatre in education, real understanding is a process of coming to understand: we cannot 'give' someone our understanding. Real understanding is felt. Only if the understanding is felt can it be integrated into children's minds, or anyone's. Resonance is the starting point of the integration process. The resonance of something engages us powerfully; that is, affectively. But, significantly, it also engages us indirectly with that which it resonates. Resonance is not authoritarian; yet it's an offer you cannot refuse! (Gillham, 1994)

A TIE company employs actor/teachers working with a small group or one class at a time. This is critical to the work which is highly participative and requires the greatest possible teacher-student ratio. The actor-teacher is a unique hybrid, combining all the specialist skills the title implies. It is this, alongside working with small groups of young people, that most distinguishes TIE from any other form of theatre, including young people's theatre.

Each programme often has participatory work before a performance, in between episodes or 'theatre moments', and after. Often the participatory element is integrated even further into the structure with a more fluid boundary between the two different modes of audience and active participant. The participation will often relate to the use of a role and there is an always a task, a purpose to their participation. Being able to engage in this way enables the participant to bring their whole selves to the TIE programme: they are not watching it but are *in* it. In this way the TIE programme has all the characteristics of learning in real life.

> But the TIE experience diverges from other life activities in that it is fiction and not 'life'. As fiction, it condenses life experiences; it's not haphazard or chaotic in the way life is, and brings these experiences under control, as with materials in a laboratory.
>
> The TIE experience, like drama in education, is lived like 'ordinary life' and is at the same time 'not life' but fiction. This dialectical characteristic enables children to 'learn right' – not learn right answers, but 'learn right' in the sense of – learn to be, become, more human not less. (*Ibid*)

The best theatre work in TIE also seeks to place the whole 'self' in the site of the plays presented. In many ways the process is the same, and demands handing over responsibility for making meaning of the situation to the audience/participants. This is achieved by employing dramatic devices to get behind the ideology that constrains and determines both thought and action, and brings us imaginatively into the site. This approach to theatre is very much informed by Edward Bond, the most important influence on Geoff's practice as a dramatist. The main function of 'Bondian' theatre and drama is to put *us* on the stage. Geoff's later plays reflect this understanding incrementally: as his writing progressed, it showed more and more the influence of Bond's approach to theatre.

Geoff and I worked closely together for four years on SCYPT committees, some of the most important years of my life. The preparation of SCYPT Conference 1991 was the high point in our professional relationship in SCYPT. Committee wanted a conference that in form and content truly embodied all the historical gains of SCYPT but also projected our thinking into new developments. As the Conference drew nearer it was mandated to Geoff and me to finalise the structure. What emerged was a ground-breaking structure for a whole conference task around a fictional brief to develop the treatment for a short film about theatre, called *Imagining the Real*. Although I liked to moan about his obsessive attention to detail, I loved the intensity of the experience, as we hammered out the finest detail of the conference structure over five days in Geoff's house in Canton, Cardiff, from early in the morning until late at night. I was in awe of his relentless energy and appetite for learning and his endless patience with me. But Geoff was the real driving force behind that conference just as he was the driving force behind so many of the developments within SCYPT that helped to establish TIE as a discrete art form in its own right.

Geoff's own need to be more consciously human was reflected in his consistent drive to the social, not just at home, but internationally. It is hard to over-emphasise the importance of this to his work and is very much part of his legacy. Not all the struggles were creative, particularly in IDEA (International Drama and Theatre Education Association). But his ability to learn from every experience, to pick up the pieces and find the new at every turn so as to go forward was part of what made Geoff who he was. He struggled to see everything in its movement and change, including himself. I shall never forget talking to him in Budapest late one night in 1997, after a typically miserable general council meeting of IDEA. I had not seen Geoff that low since the outbreak of the first Gulf War. To break the mood I decided to tease him about his refusing the offer to travel on a bus with the Mostar Youth Theatre for a meeting in Zagreb the next day. The timetable made the trip a ridiculously arduous 36 hour journey if he was to arrive back in Budapest in time for his flight back to the UK. I insisted, however, that the real content of his decision not to go was that he was getting old and set in his ways. 'Do you *really* think so?' he demanded. He didn't say much for the next hour and we went our separate ways in the early hours. I awoke next day to find that Geoff had left on the bus for Zagreb at 6 o'clock that morning.

In 1997 we shared our most profound artistic experience together when I worked as an actor in the first production of Edward Bond's *Eleven Vests*, directed by Geoff, at Big Brum Theatre in Education Company. The artistic experience brought about a qualitative development in our friendship. We were forever bound by that experience. I know working on that play radically transformed the way I thought about art and politics – about life! For Geoff it was the next stage of a process that had begun with directing Bond's first play for Big Brum, *At the Inland Sea*. I remember his greeting my reticence about the first production with an impatient 'Don't be so conservative. He's developing a new form of theatre!' And so too was Geoff, through his own work on *Bone-cage*, which dovetailed with his work on *At the Inland Sea* and was influenced by it. The process of preparation for directing *Eleven Vests* and writing and directing *The Kiss* dovetailed too. The tragedy is that he never had the time to fully explore his new knowledge about theatre through his great talent as a writer.

Geoff was courageous, fiercely principled, brilliant, inspiring, generous, complicated, frustrating, wise, loyal, sometimes overbearing, and occasionally wrong. But whatever difficulties our working relationship suffered it was never less than one hundred per cent honest. And that's how I remember him – as honest and as complex as his plays.

I once asked Geoff what he thought the secret is of being a playwright. He replied that it is the art of finding something smelly and not being frightened of putting your nose right in it. He was never afraid to do that, however uncomfortable the reality was of where that took him and his audience. It was the artist's duty to show the world as he saw it. And through his work he has enriched the lives of countless numbers of young people throughout the world, either directly or indirectly through those he taught. We owe him a huge debt. Geoff's plays are a remarkable legacy and it is to be hoped that they will be discovered by a new generation of young people and artists.

References

Gillham, G (1974) Condercum school report for Newcastle upon Tyne LEA (un-published)

Gillham, G (1979) 'What's Happening when Children are Experiencing Drama', in *Schooling and Culture* 4

Gillham, G (1994) 'What is TIE?', *SCYPT Journal*, 27

ASYLUM

Foreword by *Chris Cooper*

Asylum (running about 60 minutes) was written in 1999 and first pre-miered by Big Brum Youth Theatre on 13 July 2001. This was only a month after Geoff's death on 15 June and was attended by Geoff's wife Viet, his family and many friends and colleagues. The power of the performance of this outstanding play was a fitting tribute to the man and all we have lost with him.

The production was subsequently performed at School No.4 in Mostar, Bosnia-Herzegovina on 26 August 2001, as part of the Mostar Youth Theatre Festival: XXII International Festival of Authorial Poetry, and was given a special award for its contribution to youth theatre.

The play takes the asylum system as its specific focus but is about so much more. The alienation that so many people, particularly young people, feel is evident in every encounter and stilted exchange. It is as if hardly anyone has a common language to share what they feel and think. Take the Immigration Officer relaxing with his school teacher wife at home:

> **IO2:** *(still eating)* How about some sex after?
>
> **W2:** *(looking at him briefly)* Why?
>
> **IO2:** (still eating) No big deal.
>
> *She continues marking*
>
> Haven't done it for a bit. Thought you might fancy it.
>
> **W2:** *(still marking)* We'll see. Got to finish these first.

Once again we are reminded that Geoff was greatly interested in people's behaviour and how people show who they are through what they are doing and how they are doing it.

This was very much a play about Britain. Twelve years on this is equally true. Asylum is a play for our times, one that needs to be played and seen by more people.

It was specifically written for young people to perform. With a cast of twelve, it is ideal for youth theatre productions. Note that the three central female characters in the play are critical to its dramatic structure. They almost frame our experience, as if we see the scenes they are in through their experience. These roles – similarly the Girl in *Bone-cage* and *The Kiss* – present a wonderful opportunity for a young actor to explore.

Technically the play is relatively easy to realise and any challenges, such as Tenant One throwing himself through the window, does not require great resources, just ingenuity and imagination. The play however would lose a huge amount of its drama without the use of light and blackout which is self evident in scene one and scene five.

David Davis notes in his introduction that the play has a perfect structure. There is a great deal that could be said about this but I'd like to note just one or two things here.

The overall structure corresponds in many ways to Frytag's analysis of classical Greek and Shakespearian drama (*Die Technik des Dramas,* 1863) which states there are five acts (or scenes in this case) – exposition, rising action, climax, falling action, and revelation/catastrophe .

Asylum has five scenes. The first contains essential exposition for the narrative development of the play, though not just in the traditional sense, as it offers a whole lot more about the content of the play through the form the scene takes. The second scene provides 'rising action' that juxtaposes the alienation and abuse of an asylum seeker with the alienation in the Immigration Officer's life. In doing so it probes the deeper content of the play while setting up the climax that comes in scene three with the arson attack on the house shared by asylum seekers. The 'falling action' of scene four allows us to process what has gone before while another tragedy begins to unfold, the revelation/catastrophe that is revealed in a superb scene five. As with life, which is what Geoff's drama is about, there is no resolution in revelation, or catharsis, or end, but we are left poised in another moment (an echo of the final moment of Beckett's *Waiting for Godot*, an echo which subverts the futility at the end of the latter's play).

There are some powerful theatrical devices at work throughout the play and I mention two of them here. In scene one, Woman 1 is translated by an interpreter. The text indicates 'AL' (another language) but Geoff made it clear in emails to the director that that while 'AL' indicates the translation, he intended that all the text should be spoken in English. This made for a very powerful device in the production – the subtle difference between what is said and what is translated, what is omitted and what isn't, and once again the speech rhythms, or what Geoff called the speech acts (see introduction to *The Kiss*) become very significant.

The use of blackout and lights up is used throughout the play not just to show the passing of time but to dramatise the agony of the Woman's situation. It is like a prolonged silent scream.

This 'masterpiece of political theatre', as Bond has called it, is brought to wonderful dramatic fusion when the three central women in the play, hitherto separated, are brought together in the park in scene five.

Asylum was first premiered by Big Brum Youth Theatre on 13 July 2001.

Cast

Immigration Official	Rob Brew
Woman	Charlie Dunn
Second Immigration Official	Iqbal Mohammed
Interpreter	Katie Baxter
Second Woman	Natasha Francis
First Tenant	Martin Hunyh
Second Tenant	Tanya Conlon
Third Tenant	Justin Murphy
Fourth Tenant	Kerrie Pullen
Third Woman	Danielle Latham
First Young Man	Sunny Mahay
Second Young Man	Louis Murran
Directed and Designed by	Ceri Townsend
Assistant Directors	Richard Holmes and Steve Nolan

Scene One

An interview room. A table. Three chairs. A white screen upstage. A camera on a tripod faces the screen. On the table, a phone. Otherwise, nothing.

An immigration official shows the Woman into the room.

Immigration Official: In here.

The Woman advances a few steps into the room. She stands still, looking at the ground. She is dressed in a robe in black and dark colours. A loose headscarf covers her shoulders. She holds a polyester jacket in her hands. The immigration official (IO) is dressed in a plain dull navy suit with a matching shirt and tie. A security pass is attached to the top pocket of his jacket. He carries a clipboard with a few papers attached to it.

(Putting the clipboard on the table) Put your coat down and go and stand in front of the screen, would you please.

The woman,who is kneading the jacket with her thumbs and index fingers, looks at him briefly, and then mumbles something inaudibly in another language with her eyes lowered.

There. Screen.

The IO goes over to her and takes the jacket from her. She takes a half step away from him as he gets near her and flinches when he takes the jacket.

(Pointing) Screen. Go and stand in front of it. *(Putting the coat over the chair)* Understand? Over there. Take your picture.

He nods towards the screen. She moves towards the screen. He moves towards the file on the table. Sees she is not in the necessary position.

Right against it.

The woman does not move. Looks at the ground. He goes towards her. She retreats a step or two and backs into the screen.

Don't have to be that close.

He goes to the clipboard and removes a piece of card with access numbers on it: 1/7352/F/00/4. He puts the card on the screen in a slot near her hand. The Woman flinches. He takes her firmly but not roughly by the shoulders to place her in the right position for the camera. An involuntary shiver ripples through her body as he touches her.

6

(*matter of factly*) Not going to give you one. Just moving you. Wife'd give me hell. (*satisfied with her position*) Going to take your picture. (*nods at the camera*) With that.

As he walks away towards the camera, the Woman covers her nose and mouth with headscarf and looks away and down. A small puddle of urine appears at the Woman's feet.

Immigration Official: (*at the camera*) You'll need to look at me. (*gesturing, mime*) Headscarf. Take it off. Thing round your head. Off. The thing. Got to see your face – turn towards me. Oh God – (*going over to Woman*) I've got other people to do you know. Not just you – (*sees the pool of urine on the floor*) Oh no. Wet herself. Just my fucking luck. Why didn't you say? You can go to the toilet you know – it's not a bloody police state. Could've made yourself understood, surely.

He looks at her face for a response. She is still looking down and away from him, the scarf round her face.

Ah what's the use. Come on, let's get it over with.

He turns her head firmly but not roughly to face the camera. The Woman has frozen.

(*tugging gently at the scarf*) You going to take it off or am I?

No response. He sighs slightly then pushes the headscarf off her head. Her face looks as if she is dead.

Not difficult, uh? Now keep looking at the camera.

He points at it. Then he goes to the camera and looks through the viewfinder.

OK, that's good.

A flash from the camera.

And another one...

Another flash.

Good. Alright.

He walks over to her.

Profile

Turns her to the right, side-on to the camera. He walks back. Looks through the viewfinder.

That's fine.

A flash.

And another...

Another flash.

Not like being shot at dawn. OK.

He walks over to her.

(*turning her to face left*) And the other...

He lifts her chin a little.

That's fine. Stay like that.

He goes back to the camera and looks through the viewfinder. A flash from the camera.

Immigration Official: Good stay like that. One more.

Another flash. He rewinds the film, removes it from the camera, and puts the film on the table, writes her access number on an envelope he has on the clipboard, puts the film in it and seals it. He goes over to the screen and removes the card from the slot. The Woman remains frozen. He returns to the table. Dials three numbers on the phone and puts the film envelope in the clipboard as he waits.

(*Phone*) Yeah. Hi. Alan here. Hi. Finished the m/s. She's all yours. Gonna need an interpreter though. (*Brief wait*) Not a word far as I can see. Yeah, cheers.

He puts the phone down and goes out, taking the file with him. The Woman relaxes a little but remains where she is. Black-out. Lights up briefly. She is as before. Black-out. Lights up. She walks towards the chair where her jacket is. She reaches her hand towards the chair back, but doesn't touch it. Brings her hand back to her body. Black-out. Lights up. She reaches for the chair back and supports herself with her hand on it. Black-out. Lights up. A second IO enters carrying a clipboard with papers. An Interpreter is with him. The Woman immediately removes her hand from the chair and steps away from it. The 2nd IO is dressed similarly to the first. The Interpreter, a woman, wears the female equivalent uniform with a knee-length skirt. She wears make-up and nail-colouring. The 2nd IO sits behind the table and glances at the form on the clipboard.

Second Immigration Official: She can sit down. (*takes out a pen*)

Interpreter: {*another language – AL*} (*indicating the chair near the Woman, and sitting down herself in the third chair*) You can sit down.

Woman: {*AL*} (*to Interpreter*) Please. I've done nothing wrong. I come to see my cousin. Not –

Second Immigration Official: What's she saying?

Interpreter: She says she's come to see her cousin.

Second Immigration Official: (*to Woman*) I'm going to ask you some questions and you must answer them clearly and truthfully – (*to Interpreter*) Tell her to sit down.

Interpreter: {*AL*} You must sit down.

The Woman sits.

The officer is going to ask you some questions. You must answer them clearly and truthfully. You understand?

The Woman nods. Then looks at the table. The IO takes a passport and a paper from the clipboard and looks at them for a while.

Second Immigration Official: (*holding up the documents*) These are forgeries. Why do you have forged travel papers?

Interpreter: (*translating as he speaks*) Your documents are forged. The Officer wants to know why you have forged travel papers.

Second Immigration Official: It's an offence to travel without the necessary legal documents. You have to apply to your government for a passport. Then you have to go to our consulate in your country of origin to get a visa to come here. Why didn't you do this?

Interpreter: (*translating as he speaks – AL*) It's a crime to travel without the necessary legal documents. You have to apply to the government for a passport. Then you have to go to the British consulate at home to get a visa to come here. He wants to know why you did not do this.

She finishes a little after the IO.

Woman: {*AL*} In my bag. (*The Interpreter translates*) My cousin's address. In London. I stay with –

Interpreter: She says she has her cousin's address in London, it's –

Second Immigration Official: Did she understand my question?

Interpreter: I think so. {*AL*} The officer asked you a question – you have to answer it.

Woman: {*AL*} I haven't done anything wrong. I will stay with my cousin.

Interpreter: {*AL*} You have forged documents (*pointing to them on table*). The officer wants to know why you didn't get the correct documents from the government and from the British Consulate?

The Woman looks down at the floor.

{*Eng.*} I put the question to her again. She was talking about her cousin.

Second Immigration Official: (*to Woman*) Well?

Interpreter: {*AL*} Answer the question.

The Woman puts her hand over her face.

Second Immigration Official: If you don't answer the question, we can send you back home on the next plane.

Interpreter: {*AL – translating as he speaks*} He says if you don't answer the question we can send you back home on the next plane.

She finishes a little after the IO.

Second Immigration Official: Answer the question then.

Interpreter: {*AL*} You must answer the officer's question.

Woman: {*AL*} Please. They hurt me again.

Interpreter: She says they will hurt her again if she's sent back. (*She shrugs her shoulders to the IO*)

Second Immigration Official: (*Putting finger on the documents and tapping them*) Did you buy these?

9

Interpreter: {*AL*} Did you buy your papers?

Woman: {*AL*} No. Real papers.

Interpreter: {*Eng.*} No. She says they're genuine.

Second Immigration Official: That's shit! (*to Interpreter*) Translate accurately. (*to Woman*) Don't shit me. Don't tell me they're genuine when you know that's shit.

Interpreter: {*AL*} He says that's shit. Don't tell him shit. Don't tell him – (*The Woman begins feebly to shake her head*) – they're genuine when you know that's shit.

The Woman stops shaking her head and looks to the Interpreter and then to the IO pleadingly.

Second Immigration Official: If you knew how many... (*to Interpreter*) Don't translate that.

The IO scribbles a note on the form.

Woman: {*AL*} Please don't send me back. Police hurt me again.

Second Immigration Official: (*Still writing*) What did she say?

Interpreter: She says the police will hurt her again if you send her back. She's begging you not to.

The IO finishes his note.

Second Immigration Official: (*to Woman*) In your luggage you have the equivalent of about seven pounds in cash. Do you have any other money with you?

Interpreter: {*AL translating as he speaks*} You have money worth about seven British pounds in your luggage. Do you have any other money with you?

She finishes a little after him. The Woman shakes her head.

Second Immigration Official: Not very much is it?

Interpreter: {*AL*} He says this is not much money.

Woman: {*AL*} I can get more for you – my cousin has money.

Interpreter: She thinks you want money from her! She's offering money.

Second Immigration Official: It's not for me. We don't do that here. You have to be able to show you can support yourself in this country.

Interpreter: {*AL*} The officer doesn't want your money. You have to have enough money to support yourself in this country.

Woman: {*AL*} Thank you sir. People in Britain – good. Kind. Thank you, sir. May God send his blessings to you and your family.

Interpreter: (*translating as she speaks*) She's thanking you. She says people in Britain are good and kind. She says – she's asking God to bless you –

Woman: (*overlapping the Interpreter – AL*) My cousin in London will support me. My cousin has money –

Interpreter: (*translating*) She says her cousin in London will support her and has money.

Second Immigration Official: That's what they all say. (*to Woman*) You don't have a letter from your cousin.

Interpreter: (*translating as he speaks – AL*) He says you don't have a letter from your cousin.

Woman: {*AL*} I have address. My cousin's address and telephone number. You have. In my bag. Please – you telephone him –

Interpreter: (*translates as she speaks*) She says she has her cousin's address ... and telephone number. It's in her bag. She asks you to ring him –

Second Immigration Official: Is her cousin expecting her?

Interpreter: {*AL*} Is your cousin expecting you?

Woman: {*AL*} No. I had no time to send him a letter. But it doesn't matter to him. He will let me stay in his house. You telephone him –

Interpreter: (*translating as she speaks*) She says ... she hasn't contacted him but that, er, it will be alright to stay in his house, for her to stay in his house, and we can telephone –

Second Immigration Official: (*to Woman*) Anyone can answer the phone and say whatever they want. You need clear proof that you will be financially supported.

Interpreter: {*AL*} Anyone can answer the phone and say what they want to say. You need clear proof that you will be financially supported.

Second Immigration Official: You don't have any proof. Isn't that right?

Interpreter: {*AL*} You don't have any proof. Isn't that right?

Second Immigration Official: It's not my job to find all this out. You have to provide the proof. Letters, bank statements.

Interpreter: {*AL*} It's not the officer's function to find all this out. The proof must be given by you. Letters, bank proofs.

Second Immigration Official: You have to have a good reason for being here, and you don't have one do you?

Interpreter: {*AL*} You don't have a good reason for being here do you?

Second Immigration Official: If you did, you would have sorted all this out, got all the necessary legal paperwork before you left your country of origin, wouldn't you?

Interpreter: (*Interpreter translates while the IO makes another note on the form – AL*) If you had good reason you would have collected all the necessary documents before you left your country of origin, wouldn't you?

Woman: {*AL*} I couldn't. I had to leave –

Interpreter: (*as the Woman is speaking*) She says she couldn't do it before she left. She had to leave –

Woman: {*AL*} – I can go to my cousin. He will show you everything.

Interpreter: (*to IO*) She says she can go to her cousin. – (*to Woman*) What do you mean, show everything?

Woman: {*AL*} Permission to stay in his house. A letter. He come and speak to the gentleman. Show he has money. In the bank. I bring it.

Interpreter: (*after she has finished speaking*) She's still going on about her cousin. That he would give her a letter, bank statement. He would bring it in person or she would ...

Second Immigration Official: You had to do all this before. Not after. That's the rules, you understand?

Interpreter: {*AL*} You can't do this after you arrive here. You have to do it before you leave your country of origin. That's the law.

Woman: {*Eng – to IO*} Please... (*to Interpreter – AL*) I can't go back.

Interpreter: It's what she said before: she says she can't go back. (*the Interpreter shrugs her shoulders to the IO*)

Second Immigration Official: Is she married?

Interpreter: {*AL*} Do you have a husband?

The Woman looks down to the ground. The Interpreter looks at the IO.

{*AL*} – (*Insistently*) The officer wants to know if you have a husband.

Woman: {*AL*} (*Still looking down*) Yes.

Interpreter: She said yes.

Second Immigration Official: Where is he?

Interpreter: {*AL*} Your husband, where is he?

The Woman puts her hand over her face.

{*AL*} Where is he?

Woman: (*mumbling through her hand*) I don't know.

Interpreter: (*shrugging*) She doesn't know.

Second Immigration Official: (*a little ragged*) Well, is he in her country?

Interpreter: {*AL*} Is he back home?

Woman: (*as before*) I don't know where he is.

Interpreter: She doesn't know where he is.

Second Immigration Official: (*still ragged*) Is she separated or what?

Interpreter: {*AL*} Are you separated?

Woman: (*as before*) He had to run away. They wanted to kill him. I don't know where he is.

Interpreter: (*translating as she speaks*) He had to run away ...They wanted to kill him.

She doesn't know where he is.

Second Immigration Official: Is he here in Britain?

Interpreter: {*AL*} Is he here in Britain?

Woman: {*AL*} No. I heard he was in the mountains. But that was five months ago.

Interpreter: No he's not here –

The IO makes a note.

Second Immigration Official: But he's alive...?

Interpreter: She thinks so. She's not heard from him for five months. She said he escaped to the mountains in the north of the country.

Second Immigration Official: (*making a note*) I see. (*after finishing*) Does she have any children?

Interpreter: {*AL*} Do you have children?

Woman: {*AL*} (*looking at the IO*) My husband did nothing wrong –

Interpreter: (*translating as she speaks*) She says her husband has done nothing wrong – she's not answered your question –

Woman: {*AL*} He's not a criminal. He tried to organise the people – on the tea plantation – into a union –

Interpreter: She says he's not a criminal. Er ... she says he was organising a union er for farm labourers.

Second Immigration Official: OK. I need to know if you have children.

Woman: {*AL*} My husband – good man. He – village school teacher. Honest man.

Interpreter: Saying her husband's a good man. Teacher. Honest. {*AL*} The officer needs to know if you have any children.

Woman: {*AL – to Interpreter*} Is it alright?

Interpreter: {*AL*} He understands what you said. (*pause*) Now he wants to know about your children.

Woman: He understands not a criminal. Not bad man.

Interpreter: {*AL*} Yes (*to IO*) She's wanting to know if you understand about her husband. I said, yes you did.

Second Immigration Official: What about children?

Interpreter: {*AL*} How many children do you have?

Woman: {*AL*} Four.

Interpreter: She has four.

Second Immigration Official: (*making a note*) I need their full names, sex and date of birth. Do it with her will you. Take a lifetime trying to spell their names.

He passes the clipboard over with the pen on it, stands up, and stretches his back. While the Interpreter fills in the form with the Woman. The IO picks up the phone and dials 12 numbers. He waits.

Interpreter: {*AL*} Give me the name of the oldest, then the next oldest to the youngest...

The questioning continues while he is on the phone, inaudibly.

Second Immigration Official: (*phone*) It's me. How was your day? Alright? – Listen, I'm on the last one now. Be home in about an hour OK. – No. I know. I'm sorry, loads of them on the SA nineteen-o-five. You know what it's like. (*listens*) No I'll get a Chinese on the way back – no problem. D'you want anything? OK. Bye

He puts the phone down. The Interpreter passes the clipboard over to him. He looks briefly at it.

Second Immigration Official: (*to the Woman*) OK, now listen to me. You are an illegal immigrant – (*the Interpreter begins to translate*) – your papers are not in order – you have broken British law, d'you understand? I don't make the decision about your case. That's made by the Secretary of State. I shall make a report of this interview and send it to him, you understand?

Interpreter: {*AL*} He says you are an illegal immigrant ... your papers are not in order ... you have broken British law ... he doesn't make the decision whether you can stay – it's made by the government. He will make a report of this interview and send it to the government person in charge, you understand?

She finishes a little after the IO. The Woman looks blankly at him.

Second Immigration Official: While you are waiting for his decision, I could send you to prison, d'you understand? Because you are an illegal immigrant.

Interpreter: (*AL – translating while he speaks*) While you wait for his decision you could be put in prison ... because you are an illegal immigrant.

When the translation comes through, a look of terror suddenly appears on the Woman's face.

Second Immigration Official: I am not going to do that –

Interpreter: {*AL*} He said he could send you to prison – he's not going to.

The Woman covers her face with her hand.

Second Immigration Official: Are you listening to me?

Interpreter: {*AL*} Listen to the officer.

The Woman takes her hand from her face, but does not look at them.

Second Immigration Official: I am telling you what I could do – (*the Interpreter begins to translate as he speaks*) so that you make sure you follow the instructions on this sheet.

He hands her a piece of A4 paper from the clipboard to. She holds it on her lap, not reading it.

Interpreter: {*AL*} He's telling you what he could do so that you are sure to follow the instructions on this paper.

Second Immigration Official: It's in your language so there's no excuse. (*the Interpreter begins to translate*) If you fail to follow them, you can be imprisoned. D'you understand? You must stay at the address on that sheet and report to the nearest police station once a week at the time shown.

Interpreter: {*AL*} It's in your language so there is no excuse not to follow the instructions on the paper. If you do not do so, you can be put in prison. Understand? You must stay at the address on that paper and report to the nearest police station –

The Woman begins to shake and is trying to overcome the shaking.

Interpreter: – once a week at the time printed on the paper.

Second Immigration Official: Do you understand me?

Interpreter: {*AL*} Do you understand what the officer has said to you?

No response. The Interpreter and the IO look at each other.

Second Immigration Official: (*to the Interpreter*) What's the matter with her?

The IO looks at his watch.

Interpreter: {*AL*} Are you alright?

Woman: {*AL*} (*weakly*) I do nothing wrong

Interpreter: {*AL*} At the police station they just check you. (*to IO*) I told her they just check her at the police station. I think she's frightened to go.

Woman: (*as before*) I do nothing wrong.

Interpreter: {*AL*} You have to go – or it's prison OK? (*to IO*) I told her she has to go or she has to stay in prison.

Second Immigration Official: OK, does she have any questions?

Interpreter: {*AL*} Do you want to ask the officer any questions?

No response.

Do you want to ask any questions?

Second Immigration Official: Tell her she must collect her SAL at the desk. Can I leave that with you? I'm late as it is.

He gets up and leaves

Interpreter: {*AL*} Come with me.

The Woman looks at her for a moment, then hesitantly gets up. She's very fatigued.

Bring your coat. We have to go to another office.

The woman picks up her jacket and follows the Interpreter out.

Black-out.

Scene Two

The Second Immigration Official's living room. A table with a stack of school books on it. Habitat-type sofa. A chair at either end of the table. Two more matching chairs pushed in on either side of the table.

The Second Woman enters with a mug of coffee. She puts it on the table amongst the books, sits down, and lights a cigarette from a packet on the table. She picks up the coffee and takes a few sips of it with her cigarette in her hand, contemplating the exercise books she has to mark. Then she puts the mug down and takes one of the books from the pile, picks up her red biro and begins to read the book. She puts occasional marks on it, correcting spelling, grammar, etc... She works very quickly without any sense of hurry.

Second Woman: (*under her breath*) Idiot.

She crosses out something in the book and scribbles a note. She continues to read a moment longer, scribbles a note at the bottom of the pupil's work. She closes the book, starting a new pile, and brings another one from the pile. As before. The second IO comes in carrying a small polythene bag with his Chinese take-away in it.

Second Immigration Official: (*kissing the top of her head*) Sorry I'm late.

Second Woman: (*finishing off the book with the briefest of comments as she speaks*) Did you get something to eat?

Second Immigration Official: Ah-ha

He puts the polythene bag at the other end of the table.

Second Woman: Don't put it there – may be greasy underneath.

She puts the second book on the pile, and leaves the cigarette burning in the ashtray as she speaks.

Second Immigration Official: It's OK

Second Woman: (*getting up*) I'll put it on a plate.

Second Immigration Official: 's OK, just a fork will do...

She exits with the polythene bag

(*calling*) Where are the boys?

Second Woman: (*off*) Upstairs

Second Immigration Official: Oh (*calling*) Just going to change

He exits. Second Woman comes in with a place mat, fork and salt. Sets them at the table. Exits. After a moment she returns with a plate with the Chinese meal and chips.

Second Woman: (*calling*) On the table.

She takes a chip and then moves back to her place. She picks up the cigarette and stubs it out. She then picks up the pen and begins work. The Second Immigration Official enters wearing a loose tracksuit and comfortable shoes.

Second Immigration Official: They're on the computer.

He sits down at the table, salts the chips and begins to eat.

Second Woman: (*still marking*) How was your day?

Second Immigration Official: (*eating*) Alright. Usual thing. Have we got anything planned for the weekend?

Second Woman: (*as before*) I said we'd call in on your mum.

Second Immigration Official: (*as before*) I was thinking of taking the boys fishing.

Second Woman: (*as before*) Got to do the shopping Saturday.

Second Immigration Official: (*as before*) That won't take all day.

She finishes the book, brings another from the pile, opens it and sips coffee.

What d'you think? Could do the shopping Saturday morning, see Mum in the afternoon, then we've got all day Sunday. Get up early.

Second Woman: (*marking again*) Fine.

She lights another cigarette

Second Immigration Official: (*eating*) I'll have to renew the permit.

Second Woman: (*marking*) Permit?

Second Immigration Official: (*as before*) Fishing.

Second Woman: (*marking, she tuts briefly, crosses out something – to herself*) Kids don't understand a thing. Don't listen half the time.

She writes a note on the book.

They got exams in four weeks' time and he doesn't know who Archduke Ferdinand was! Why do we bother, honestly? Can't even spell Sarajevo.

She puts a line through a word and closes the book and takes another one from the pile. He continues to eat.

Second Immigration Official: How much longer you going to be on that?

Second Woman: (*briefly looks at the pile*) An hour, bit less maybe.

He continues to eat. She continues marking. Some time.

Second Immigration Official: (*still eating*) How about some sex after?

Second Woman: (*looking at him briefly*) Why?

Second Immigration Official: (*still eating*) No big deal.

She continues marking.

Haven't done it for a bit. Though you might fancy it.

Second Woman: (*still marking*) We'll see. Got to finish these first.

Second Immigration Official: (*as before*) Don't push yourself.

He pushes the plate a little away from him – there's still food left – gets up and sits on the sofa. Picks up a holiday brochure that is on the sofa and flicks through it.

Second Woman: (*as before*) D'you want some tea?

Second Immigration Official: (*still flicking through the brochure*) No, I'll do it myself in a sec.

Pause

You want to go away?

Second Woman: (*as before*) What do you mean?

Second Immigration Official: (*indicating brochure*) Holiday.

Second Woman: (*as before*) Came through the door.

Second Immigration Official: Well you were looking at it! I could sort it out at work. No bother getting freebies. Just say where you want to go. Irene would sort it.

Second Woman: (*as before*) I'll think about it.

Second Immigration Official: (*after a moment, getting up*) Going up to see the boys. See if they want to go fishing on Sunday.

He exits. Second Woman puts the book she is marking on the pile, and looks at the remaining books to mark. She looks at the Second IO's plate. Looks in her mug and decides it's too cold to drink the remainder. With the cigarette in her mouth, tipping her head slightly to avoid the smoke she picks up the mug and the plate and takes them out to the kitchen. She re-enters, picks up the brochure and puts it on the table. She picks up the place mat and salt.

Second Woman: (*on her way to the kitchen, calls*) Do you want that tea?

No reply. She exits to the kitchen. Blackout.

Scene Three

A room on the first floor of a house. Practically no furniture. On the floor are old mattresses, blankets, sleeping bags. A washing line with clothes on it stretches across the room from fixings on the walls. There is a paraffin heater in the centre of the room. Each sleeping area is separated from the next. There are five in all. Each has a few markers of the occupants' territory: suitcases or travel bags, some of which double for small tables; utensils; magazines; a few personal belongings. Despite the obviously crowded conditions, an attempt has been made to keep the room clean and tidy.

On the left, a young man is lying on a camp bed. He is fully clothed, wears a tight fitting hat and fingerless gloves. He has a cushion from a chair as a pillow, and apart from his arms and head he is covered by a sleeping bag. His position resembles that of a corpse lying in state. He has a headset on, the metallic external sound of which is audible. The cassette, together with a few tapes, is on the floor next to him.

Centre, is an area belonging to a couple. There is a mattress with an old piece of carpet to the left of it with an old pillow on the top. A sleeping bag stretches across both, with a couple of coats on top of it – making a kind of double bed. In the mattress side of the bed is a woman. She is hardly visible beneath the sleeping bag. She is unwell and has a wracking cough, the sound of which is frequently muffled by the sleeping bag.

Next to them, to the right, near the door to the hallway, there are two or three cushions covered by a piece of cloth forming a bed, with a blanket neatly folded on top of it. This is the Woman's bed. Her jacket, covered in another piece of material, serves as a pillow. Her bag is next to the bed. Next to this – on the floor – is a photo, in a simple frame, of her children. A second photo shows the portrait of a man – her husband.

Downstage of the Woman's bed and the washing line, pointing into the room, is a piece of foam covered with a piece of material. A sleeping bag has been left on it unfolded. Personal things are left strewn about. A dirty plate with a fork on it. A few items of cosmetics indicate this area is normally occupied by a young woman. This is the only area that is not tidy.

There is a moment where we hear the cassette and the woman coughing. Then a man enters carrying a mug of broth.

Third Tenant: (*to Second Tenant*) New couple using the kitchen. Just moved in this evening. (*holding the mug for her*) Here. Must be in the rooms downstairs. He packs them in. Like dates.

Second Tenant: (*turning a little towards him*) I don't want it.

Third Tenant: Try.

Second Tenant: I can't keep it down.

The doorbell rings downstairs.

Third Tenant: That'll be the drop. Late. (*looking at his watch*) Nearly twelve.

He puts the mug down and gets up to go.

Try and have some.

He exits. Second Tenant props herself up and looks at First Tenant.

Second Tenant: Ah-yi-yi

She reaches for the mug and has a coughing fit. She lies back. Third Tenant re-enters lugging a package of free newspapers and a couple of packets of leaflets.

Third Tenant: Are you alright?

Second Tenant: It's so cold in here. So cold in this country.

Third Tenant: No more paraffin. Get some when I get paid for this.

Second Tenant: Why do they make us live like this...

Third Tenant cuts a package open and begins to collate them, putting each of the leaflets in each newspaper, making a pile.

Is she still in the bathroom?

Third Tenant: (*collating throughout*) Yes. Do you want me to ask her to let you go in?

Second Tenant: No I can wait.

Pause.

Poor woman. Do you think she's alright? Hardly says a word to anybody.

Third Tenant: Cleaning helps her. Keeps her mind off things.

Second Tenant: Reminds me of the foreign maid we had – what was her name? – the one before the last one, Samalla – she would hardly say a word, slip in and out of the room like a shadow, you'd go out of the room and she'd have cleaned it before you came back in. She reminds me of her. Disappears during the day to look for her cousin – walks the streets looking for him, every day knocking on doors – then she comes back and cleans everywhere. Sleeps. Just a shadow, poor woman. Hopeless. So many people in and out, gets dirty as soon as she's finished.

Third Tenant: Useful she does it.

A pause. Second Tenant coughs again.

Third Tenant: Try and drink some of that. Just a sip.

Second Tenant:(*after a time*) I was thinking about our house back home. Who they've moved in. One of his thugs. Sprawled on our couch. Putting his filthy boots all over the cushions –

Third Tenant: Don't –

Second Tenant: – picking the oranges you planted in the courtyard –

Third Tenant: – it doesn't matter –

Second Tenant: And your piano...

Third Tenant: Let your mind rest. You won't get better if you fret over things.

Second Tenant: I'd rather they walked on my face. Such a beautiful house.

Third Tenant leaves his collating and goes over to her and soothes her forehead.

Third Tenant: Don't fret. They're only things.

Second Tenant: Look at us now.

She has another coughing fit. He holds her tenderly. The coughing gradually stops.

You're such a good man. I'm not complaining.

Third Tenant: I'll see if she's finished.

He exits. After a little he returns. The Woman slips in after him like a maid. Shy or embarrassed – it is difficult to tell. She is holding an old cloth and a bottle of bathroom cleaner. She waits by the door. Second Tenant gets out of bed. She is clothed. She gathers her things together while Third Tenant goes back to collating. She gets a toilet roll from among her things discreetly. As she gathers her things she speaks to The Woman in broken English, heavily accented. She also uses mimetic gestures to make herself understood. The Woman nods but not as one who understands.

Second Tenant: (*English*) Thank you. I sorry. Always Grushka go there when she come from rest'runt. (*exiting*) I sorry.

Third Tenant: (*Eng*) You did not find your cousin today? (*with gestures*) Cousin. Today – not find.

Woman: (*Eng*) No. Next day.

Third Tenant: Inshallah.

He continues to do the collating. The Woman hovers a moment. Then exits, unnoticed by Third Tenant. Another woman enters. She is pretty, fashionably dressed, with a long coat covering a short skirt.

Fourth Tenant: (*Eng, with an accent*) What's she doing on the landing?! Standing there with a bottle of cleaner in her hand.

She looks over to First Tenant.

Hi Rudi

No response.

Third Tenant: (*Eng.*) My wife in the bathroom.

21

Fourth Tenant: Oh...

She picks a coat hanger up from her bed and hangs her coat on the washing line. Third Tenant is continuing to collate.

Fourth Tenant: One of the customers asked me tonight if I was a student over on a working holiday – this weather! – I'm sure he was chatting me up – I said no so he said my English was good. Thought I was from France. Good that, yes?

Third Tenant: Yes.

Fourth Tenant: Two months ago, they'd ask where I was from, was I in Britain learning English.

Third Tenant: Your English very good now

Fourth Tenant: (*correcting*) Your English is very good now. Have to have the verb.

Third Tenant: Yes – verb 'to be' no in my language.

Fourth Tenant: Your English is good.

Third Tenant: My mind thinks my language.

Fourth Tenant: I need to change.

Third Tenant: My wife nearly finish.

Fourth Tenant: I was thinking of her. She'll go in after. Be one o'clock before I get to bed.

She sits down on her bed – the foam bed.

I shall be out of here soon. They'll let me stay. Get my own place then. Or meet a fella maybe. Good one – doesn't have to be handsome .... Get my stamp. Wouldn't have to do the eatery then. Could get legal work. Not like this. Smiling at the customers, putting up with them looking at you because you want a good tip. Have a life. Don't you think?

Third Tenant: (*collating*) Yes.

Second Tenant enters carrying her stuff and underwear she's just washed. She's very frail. She puts her stuff down by the bed, begins coughing as she heads towards the washing line to hang the underwear. Third Tenant is about to stop collating.

Fourth Tenant: I'll do them. Let me.

She takes the underwear from an embarrassed Second Tenant and pegs them on the line. Second Tenant, still coughing, gets into bed. Third Tenant looks across to her but continues collating. Fourth Tenant finishes pegging and looks across to Second Tenant.

(*to Third Tenant*) She's not well.

Third Tenant: (*with gesture*) Can't keep anything in stomach.

Fourth Tenant: Can't you take her to a doctor?

Third Tenant: After Monday maybe.

Fourth Tenant: That's three days away!

Third Tenant shrugs his shoulders.

Second Tenant: {*AL2*} What are you saying to her?

Third Tenant: {*AL2*} Doctor.

Second Tenant: (*Eng. to Fourth Tenant*) Me fine. Doctor... (*She waves her hand dismissively*)

Fourth Tenant: Look after yourself, yes?

Second Tenant: {*Eng.*} He good man

Fourth Tenant: Yes.

Fourth Tenant exits and re-enters immediately.

She's gone back in! Instead of cleaning the bathroom and the kitchen all the time she'd be better practising English. Been here nearly three weeks she only speaks a few words!

Third Tenant: Difficult.

Fourth Tenant: I know but you don't learn if you don't speak! You have to learn their language if you want to fit in. She doesn't try! Just cleans all the time!

Third Tenant: Why don't you ask her to let you go there...

Fourth Tenant: I don't want to trouble her.

Third Tenant: I think she clean because she hurt. Make better her. Clean help her mind.

Fourth Tenant: I don't know.

A pause. Then Fourth Tenant goes over to the end of First Tenant's bed.

Hey Rudi! Why don't you say hello when I come in?

No response.

Third Tenant: He got a deportation order today. They sending him back.

Fourth Tenant: (*To First Tenant*) You've got nowhere!!

No response. Third Tenant continues collating. She kneels down next to First Tenant and holds his hands, but not moving them. The Woman enters.

Rudi, I'm so sorry. Can't you appeal?

No response.

(*to Third Tenant*) He can appeal can't he?

Third Tenant: (*still collating*) Made up their minds. Not win. Put him in prison while he wait.

The Woman is watching from the door, still holding the cloth and bottle of cleaner.

Fourth Tenant: You'll have to disappear. They'll come for you. You have to disappear. How long d'you have? Two weeks? You have to disappear.

No response. She gets up from him.

(*to Third Tenant*) We have to talk to Siaka when he gets back from work in the morning. He could get him fixed up at his place, couldn't he? They're always wanting packers, always people coming and going (*looking to the empty bed beside First Tenant*) He said! Someone there could find him somewhere to stay. Sure they could.

She looks to First Tenant. He looks like a dead man. She suddenly seems helpless. After a moment she starts to collect things for the bathroom. She knocks things over in her agitation. She lastly takes her pyjamas from the bed and exits past the Woman, who hasn't moved. Third Tenant continues to collate. First Tenant is as still as ever. The Woman puts the cleaning things down by her bed, quietly, like a shadow. There is a desolate screaming and sobbing, offstage. It is the Fourth Tenant. The Woman stops and listens. Third Tenant stops a moment. Glances towards the door, then commences collating again. The sobbing and screaming continues.

Woman: (*Eng.*) I go to her...

Third Tenant: It stop soon. No worry. Nothing help. It happen sometime.

He makes a vague gesture that indicates 'something from another time'.

... she hear about Rudi, she remember ... (*the gesture again*)

It becomes quiet outside. The Woman nods, semi-understanding his words

........She OK soon.

The Woman looks at Tenant 1. Then at Third Tenant again. Fourth Tenant re-enters – in pyjamas, carrying her clothes. There is no sign of her earlier distress. She puts the clothes on her bed. Exits. She returns with wash things and washed underwear. She pegs up the wet knickers and bra on the line and then hangs the clothes on her bed neatly on a hanger, and hangs them next to the coat. She pushes the dirty plate to one side and gets into bed and closes her eyes.

Woman: (*to Third Tenant*) I help you?

Third Tenant: If you want.

She joins him collating. Some time. There is a crash of a window smashing somewhere in the house.

Male: (off) Fuckin' immigrants out!!

Male 2: (off) Go back home you fuckers!!

While this is happening, the Woman and Third Tenant stop collating and look towards the door. Fourth Tenant sits up.

Fourth Tenant: What's that?

Noise can be heard downstairs and growing panic. Muffled shouts of 'fire', 'attack', etc ... Third Tenant goes to the door and looks down the stairs.

Third Tenant: Quick. Fire. Downstairs.

There is no panic. Fourth Tenant gets out of bed. Third Tenant goes to Second Tenant and wakes her, gets her out of bed. First Tenant becomes aware of the sudden change of movement as the Woman moves towards him.

Woman: (*Eng.*) Fire. Must –

First Tenant jumps off the bed at great speed – the cassette is dragged after him as he runs left at the window and smashing it as he jumps through it. The Woman screams as does. Fourth Tenant who sees it.

Fourth Tenant: He's gone through the window!!

Third Tenant: Quick get out!

He starts to bundle everyone out having covered his wife with a coat. Fourth Tenant seizes her coat from the line and puts it over herself as she leaves. The Woman sees the photo of her family and tries to pick them up. Smoke billows through the door. She catches the photo of her children but drops the other as Third Tenant grabs her to drag her out of the door.

No time! Come!

They are gone. Smoke fills the room. Shouting from the other tenants getting out can be heard indistinctly. Blackout.

Scene Four

Living room in a council flat. Sofa. Clothes drier with, mostly, a child's clothes on it.

Offstage are heard the voices of two young men coming into the flat. They are high on drink and excitement.

First Young Man: (*off*) We are the mighty!! We are the mighty!! WE are the mighty!!

Second Young Man: (*off joining in*) We are the mighty!! We are the mighty!!

First Young Man: (*off*) Come on you wankers! We fucked you, you wankers!!

Second Young Man: (*off*) We are the mighty!! Burnt your fuckin arses off!!

The two young men enter the room, jubilant. Second Young Man is carrying the remains (two) of a six-pack of lagers. They are really hyper.

First Young Man: See him come crashing through the window. Thinks he's fuckin James Bond!

Second Young Man: Fuck! Crash! Fuck! Fucking crash!

First Young Man: Smoke pouring after him! Out the fuckin window!

Second Young Man: (*tossing a can to the other*) D'you see them others – hurtling out the front door! (*opening the can*) Like rats out of a dead 'orse's arse when you hit them with a spade. (*the can sprays*) Fuck! Did you see 'em?!

First Young Man: That was a fucking hit! (*opens can*)

Second Young Man: We are the mighty! We are the mighty! We are the mighty!!

First Young Man: (*joining the chant*) We are the mighty! We are the mighty!

They both collapse on the sofa, drinking.

Did you see him though?! Come out sideways. First fucking floor!

Second Young Man: Pity it wasn't the top!

The wife of First Young Man enters. She is in pyjamas.

Third Woman: Can't you keep the racket down? – I've only just got Terry off.

First Young Man: Sorry Shaz. Not thinking –

Third Woman: (*seeing the gash on his forehead*) What've you done to your head?

Second Young Man: Fell over a wall –

First Young Man: (*feeling the blood with his hand and looking briefly at it*) 's nothing.

Second Young Man: – when we ran for it! He's pissed!

First Young Man: I ain't pissed!

Second Young Man: You're pissed you wanker! You fell over a fucking wall!

First Young Man: (*play-fighting on the sofa*) I ain't.

Third Woman: Can't you two shut up?! Terry! And mind the sofa!

First Young Man: (*hitting the other on the head*) Yeah, shut up you!

The fighting stops.

Should've seen it Shaz. Boney and me done a burn out of the immigrants down in Churchill Road. Burning rag through the letter-box, then a brick through the window to let 'em know. You should've fucking seen it. Come tearing out in their pyjamas –

Second Young Man: One of them didn't even have his pants on – probably on the job –

First Young Man: – yelling –

Second Young Man: Fucking showed him!

Third Woman: You stupid –

First Young Man: Out the front door! 'Nother one threw himself out the window! First floor! Yowwwwwwwww! Bang!

Second Young Man: They'll have to fuck off home now, back where they came from!

Third Woman: You fuck off home!

First Young Man: Take it easy Shaz...

Third Woman: You stupid fuckers – both of you –

First Young Man: Why you – ?

Third Woman: What if some of them are dead?! What if you killed any of them?!

First Young Man: None of them'll be dead, what you talking about?

Third Woman: How do you know?! –

First Young Man: None of them –

Third Woman: You didn't stick around to –

First Young Man: Course not –

Third Woman: – find out –

First Young Man: Most that guy'll have's a twisted ankle and a few cuts –

Third Woman: Who says? You a doctor now are you?

First Young Man: Oh fuck off Shaz...

Third Woman: Need your head examined...

Second Young Man: They're fucking Pakis and Gypos – what's the matter anyway? –

Third Woman: You – fuck off, get out of my house.

Terry: (*off, a young child's voice*) Mummy!

Third Woman: (*to Second Young Man*) Now you've woken the fucking kid. Fucking get out!

First Young Man: Don't tell him to get out – he's my –

Terry: (*off*) Mummy!

Third Woman: (*to First Young Man*) You go too if you want!

Second Young Man: (*getting up*) 's OK Stomp. See you tomorrow.

First Young Man: (*to Second Young Man*) No need to –

Second Young Man: I'm off.

He exits.

First Young Man: Fucking satisfied?!

Terry: (*off*) Mummy.

Third Woman: Who's going to see to him? You or me?

She exits

Second Young Man: (*off*) We are the mighty!

First Young Man: (*laughing*) Wanker...

Third Woman: (*off*) No you can't have a drink. Go to sleep. Or there'll be trouble.

First Young Man swigs the lager.

Third Woman: (*entering*) He was out of bed.

She plonks down on the sofa next to First Young Man.

What we fucking going to do now?

He puts his arm round her for a smooch.

I don't wanna.

He continues.

Stop it will you.

He stops.

What you gonna say if the coppers come round?

First Young Man: They ain't gonna come! They don't give a flying fuck about the immigrants. They hate them an'all. They aint gonna do anything.

Third Woman: You set the bloody house on fire didn't yer?! Could've killed someone for all we know –

First Young Man: Didn't kill anyone –

Third Woman: You don't know! It's not like giving one of them a beating. Fire, they have to do something! Specially if anyone's hurt.

First Young Man: No one saw us!

Third Woman: You're so psyched up you fall over a wall and smash your 'ed open. You can say for a fucking certainty no one saw you! Fuck that!

First Young Man gets up and picks up the can left by the other.

And what's to say Boney can keep his mouth shut! Probably told half the estate by now – woke 'em up to tell 'em!

She gets up and makes to exit.

First Young Man: Where you going?

Third Woman: (*exiting*) Kitchen. Get a fag.

First Young Man: (*calling*) Bring us one.

He sits down on the floor with the can. She returns, taking a cigarette out of the packet. She sits down on the sofa and lights the cigarette.

Did you bring us one? Chuck us one.

Third Woman: (*ignoring him*) If the police come I'll tell 'em you were here with me watching the telly. They won't believe us. Depends if they wanna put someone away for it. Ring Boney in the morning and tell him to keep his fucking gob shut.

First Young Man: Gis a fag.

Third Woman: What you do it for? Got a kid, 'nother one on the way. You're just … stupid. Don't get a job –

First Young Man: Ain't any jobs.

He lies back on the floor.

Third Woman: Other boys get 'em. You don't try.

First Young Man: Build the factories in Botswana or some fucking place.

Third Woman: Other boys get 'em! When did you last go for something?

First Young Man: What's the point!

Third Woman: Just waiting to get banged away again. Kids not having a Dad half the time. I want a home for chrissake. Not this stuff. What yer do it for?

He has his eyes shut, sleeping. The lager can is held on his tummy with both hands.

Talking to myself.

Terry: (*off*) Mummy

Nothing happens.

Mummy

Third Woman: (*calling*) Go to sleep Terry. It's way after midnight.

Slight pause.

Terry: (*off*) Mummy.

She gets up, stubs out her cigarette, turns out the light, and exits. Blackout.

29

Scene Five

Some weeks later a public park. Sound of children playing. A broken bench. Graffiti on it. It is cold and daylight is beginning to go.

Woman is seated on the bench. After a while Third Woman enters, pushing an empty push chair.

Third Woman: Alright if I...

She sits down on the bench a little away from Woman.

Bench is a bit wonky isn't it.

(*calling*) Terry, come off there! Play nicely! (*to Woman*) Terry by name, terror by nature!

Woman nods and smiles faintly.

You're not from round here are you.

Woman smiles and nods.

Ain't seen yer.

Silence. Third Woman watches the children.

Look at him! Doesn't care, does he?

Pause.

(*Not looking at Woman*) I'm in a hell of a mess. Just put his Dad away for six years. Got Terry there and another one on the way. What am I supposed to do?

She looks at Woman who smiles faintly.

Don't mind me talking to you do yer?

Woman smiles and shrugs vaguely.

'E'll be ten by the time he gets out. Could go back to me Mum's – she said I could – I think she'd like the company – but I'd go crazy. That or in the flat on me own with two kids. Feel like I'm in prison myself. My Mum said I should leave 'im now – 'e's no good. Not wait. Misery all my life. She said I could hang around and wait for him to come out and then after a couple of weeks he

30

could just walk out on us. Find another girl. It happens, I know. You keep 'em going while they're inside, when they come out you ain't who they thought you was. Fuck you a few times, then they're fed up with you. Off with someone else.

Pause.

Kids won't know 'im. Terry will hardly remember him, and this one won't know 'im at all.

Pause.

I won't leave him though. You can't can you – not when they've banged him away.

Pause.

What a fucking mess, eh?

Silence.

Well no point moping. (*pause*) Got to be going. Gotta get 'is tea.

She gets up.

(*calling*) Terry! Come on, get off there now.

She starts moving off.

(*still calling*) Going 'ome.

(*to Woman*) See yer then.

Woman: (*nods and smiles – Eng.*) Goodbye.

Third Woman: (*After looking at her a moment*) Yeah bye.

She exits. Some time. Blackout. Lights up. Woman hasn't moved. Blackout. Lights up. The Woman hasn't moved. The sound of a park-keepers whistle. No response from the Woman. Second Woman enters. She is in a warm coat and carries a travel bag. She glances briefly at Woman without stopping. Having passed, she stops. Turns back to Woman.

Second Woman: They've blown the whistle.

Woman looks to her, not understanding.

Have to leave. Closing up.

Woman nods and smiles faintly. Second Woman hesitates a moment, then exits. The sound of the whistle again. Darkness closes in. The Woman does not move.

BONE-CAGE

A play for children, and adults

Foreword by Chris Cooper

The play (running about 25 minutes) was first performed in Lancaster on 19 February 1996, by the SCYPT Theatre Co-operative. This was formed by four unemployed members of SCYPT financially supported by the Lancaster and Morecambe Trades Council which had enjoyed the production of *Dressing Up, Stripping Down* (See Working with the SCYPT Cooperative – Rowan Padmore, SCYPT Journal 32, 1996). *Bone-cage* has since enjoyed student productions and most recently a two repertory run (2008-2010) in Budapest, Hungary, with Kerekasztal (Roundtable) TIE.

From the viewpoint of someone who experienced the first production, *Bone-cage* is a remarkable play. It touched and disturbed me in a way I had never experienced before. I remember my own disbelief that it had lasted a mere 25 minutes. Kharon's nightmare alone seemed to last forever. Until then I had never so intensely wanted a play to end (for the right reasons!) so much and at the same time continue.

To be more objective, it seems that the play articulated, and continues to articulate something very profound about our culture. It is a play about what it means to be at home in a world that cannot house you, about desire, freedom and the liberation of action, about reality for young people in a post-human society.

Bone-cage also marks a qualitative development in Geoff's writing, and reading it makes you painfully aware of the talent and potential that has been lost. It departs completely from Brecht and we can sense the influence of Bond and, what's more, a moving towards the articulation of what Geoff saw as his own art form.

The play offers so much for actors, trainee actors and young people to work on. There are only three roles, which makes it ideal for a Company, but the text would be perfect to work on simultaneously in groups for young people or trainee actors, as long as there is the central image of the cage to work from, whether this is physically realised or socially imagined.

The play radiates from this central metaphor/image and pivots on the key objects in the piece; the smoking cigarette, the rag, the knife, the keys and the leash round the girl's neck, tins of food and water, sparse but essential to and very active in the site of the play for the meanings they evoke.

The cigarette which 'produces an unusual amount of smoke' when Kharon puffs on it presents us with an important dilemma. In the first production the actor playing Kharon smoked real cigarettes, but this is not acceptable today. Resolving it is not, however, primarily a technical question. The image is central to the play – combined with the image of Kharon pulling the cart behind him, the clouds of smoke from the cigarette resonates the trains to Auschwitz. How any company deals with this problem will have a profound effect on the meaning the audience takes from the play.

Also fascinating to consider are the notes Geoff made about the acting of Bone-cage:

> Bone-cage (as with all my more recent work) proceeds from a physical image. This is the art-form of sculpture. We do not ask of a sculpture, what is it thinking? For it is stone, wood, bronze, etc. we look at its form, its texture, its volume and space and the interplay of these elements. A sculpture conveys *meaning* through its form not the thoughts of its figures. It is possible that we, the viewers, *may attribute* to the figure(s) *thoughts/feelings* but these are ours, not its. The opening image of Bone-cage (to the point where the Man stops and smokes) is a sculpture – but made out of human beings instead of bronze etc. One might consider Rodin's *Burghers of Calais* or Ana Maria Pacheco's *The Journey*. Sculptures with dramatic and narrative tension. The actors could be (although I don't recommend it) thinking about the 2.30 [horse race], for all it matters if the *outer form* of the sculpture is right. Less provocatively, they would be best thinking about the train waiting in a station on the way to Dachau. That is, about the meaning of the sculpture – then they will attend to the right thing: making the image (sculpture) as pre-

cisely as possible for the audience to view and read meaning/acquire resonance (*Some thoughts on the acting of Bone-cage* – Geoff Gillham, 27 October 1996, unpublished)

There is an interesting convergence here between Geoff's theorising and Bond's concept of playing the situation and not the character, and allowing the audience to ascribe their own thoughts and feelings to the situation. Added to this development of form is how the text develops the language of poetic realism.

> The Netislik hunter, Orpingalik, was recorded as saying, 'Songs are the thoughts which are sung out with the breath when people let themselves be moved by a great force, and ordinary speech no longer suffices.' That's profound. Again the recognition of the qualitative transition from one art-form (speech) to another (song). Music does what words alone cannot do. (Significantly, in *Bone-cage* this art form and dance appear.) But Orpingalik's words are at the root of all I have written in these notes: sculpture – dance (action) – speech-acts – song. The unity of quantity and quality – measure. Let the actors explore these transitions and transformations. This is a matter of form. By tracking the outer form we can arrive at the inner content (ie its movement, unfolding). This will avoid the subjective idealist 'grabbing at meaning, or imposition of meaning upon the play/performance.' (Ibid)

Form into content, content into form.

The play was first performed in Lancaster on 19 February 1996.

Cast
Ian Yeoman
Rowan Padmore
Michaela Dunne

Facilitator
Daley Donnelly

Director
Ian Yeoman

Schools Liaison
Sue Shewring

Design Assitance
Kate Greenway

Set Construction
Mike Smith

CHARACTERS
The Man (Kharon)
Girl 1
Girl 2

Road. Rugged terrain.

Darkness falling.

The Man enters hauling a small iron four-wheeled truck on which there is a cage. On the roof of the cage there is a tarpaulin covering baggage. A small flag with a coat of arms on it sticks out horizontally from the back. The cage appears to be empty apart from a pile of rags. The Man wears heavy clothes. He wears gloves with half-fingers partially covering severe burns. A cap and a muffler make it difficult to see his face which is severely disfigured, perhaps from an accident.

He has a cigarette in his mouth which produces an unusual amount of smoke when he puffs on it.

The Man comes to a stop.

Stillness. The cigarette still in his mouth, he puffs at it a few times at regular intervals. Some time.

Man: Stop 'ere.

The Man decouples himself from the cage truck and goes round to the side of the cage, unlocks it with his keys and opens the door. He draws a bag from under the tarpaulin on the roof of the cage. The pile of rags moves. The Man takes the bag back to where he was and sits down. A Girl comes out of the cage. She is dressed in the rags and is filthy. She has a shaggy rope around her neck. The Man takes food and a water bottle from the bag, stubs the cigarette and begins to eat. At some distance the Girl squats to urinate. The Man takes no notice of her. The rope is slack and extends back to the cage where it is tied off. The girl finishes and is beginning to readjust her clothes.

(*eating*) Aren't you doin' the other?

Girl 1: Don't want to.

Man: Your life. Not openin' it 'gain for ya before morning.
Know that.

The girl stands and begins to walk back to the cage. As she does, the sound of a very low-flying jet fighter rips the air. The Girl cowers on the ground. The Man looks up at it.

Man: (*not to her*) Same one. Exercises.

The Man continues to eat. After a moment the Girl gets up and makes to go away.

37

Where you goin'?

Girl 1: Want to –

Man: No.

The Girl heads back to the cage.

Warned ya.

The Man finishes eating, drinks from the bottle, puts a cigarette in his mouth and lights it: he always holds the cigarette with his mouth, never his hands. The Girl by now is back in the cage, having pulled in the rope slack. The Man passes the remains of his food through the bars to her. She eats hungrily while he pours water into a plastic beaker. He passes it to her. He smokes.

Yer stinkin'. Know that?

Girl 1: Sorry –

Man: Stinkin'.

Girl 1: Yes.

Man: Gimme tha'.

The Girl finishes the water and passes the beaker to the Man.

Girl 1: Thank you.

The Man puts it away in the bag, together with the bottle. He goes to the bag and puts it on the roof under the tarpaulin. He closes and locks the door and exits. The Girl lifts her dress and tries to clean her bottom with a dirty rag. She disposes of the rag underneath the cage. She sings softly to herself:

How wide and how endless Is the mighty sea.

Moon will rise, sun will set, wind will blow free.

Rolling on, rolling back, breaking in foam.

Sea-waves roll, sea-waves break, where is their home?

Sailing a ship on the wide open sea

To lands –

She breaks off. The Man returns, still smoking.

Man: Chou asleep ye'? Light's nearly gone. Don' wanna come in there and make ya.

The Girl lies down to sleep.

Prayers.

The Man reaches down a groundsheet and a rolled-up blanket from the roof of the cage and walks round to where he was. While he is doing this the Girl gets up and kneels, hands together. The Man pays her no attention.

Girl 1: Dear god. Please keep safe our birds of peace. Please look after Kharon and help me not to sin. Amen.

She lies down but does not close her eyes. The Man lights another cigarette with the previous one which he then stubs out. Pause.

Man: You asleep ye'?

Pause.

Know you're no'.

The girl does not move. Pause. A jet-fighter passes over as before. The Girl squeezes herself down on the floor of the cage. The Man looks up at the plane. When it has gone:

(*not to her*) Time was.

After a moment he puts out the cigarette.

Go 'a sleep now. Wake ya when it's time ta.

He settles down on the ground sheet using the rolled blanket as a pillow and goes to sleep immediately. His breathing can be heard with a slight regular catching snore. Stillness. The Girl half sits up and quietly tries to retrieve the rag from beneath the truck. A second girl enters. Like the first, she is dressed in rags. The Girl retreats into the cage, glances at the Man, then watches Girl 2.

Girl 2: (*softly*) Want the rag?

Girl 1: (*ditto*) No.

Girl 2 has reached under the truck and holds out the rag to Girl 1. She does not take it.

Girl 2: Seen ya before. Watchin' ya.

Girl 1: Yeah?

Pause. Girl 2 is still holding out the rag.

Girl 1: You'd better go away.

Girl 2: Why?

Girl 1: Better.

Girl 2: Don't you wanna clean yerself. Here.

Girl 1: (*taking the rag*) How long yer been watchin'?

Girl 2: On the way.

Girl 1 begins to clean the top of her legs.

Girl 1: 'E wakes up 'e'll kill ya.

No response. Girl 1 finishes cleaning and puts the rag away from them both but not outside the cage. She looks at her hands.

Girl 2: Keeps yer like an animal.

Girl 1: No 'e doesn't.

Girl 2: I think 'e does.

Girl 1: 'Sup to you.

Slight pause.

Girl 2: Where's 'e takin' yer?

Girl 1: The Yard.

Girl 2: Wha' Yard

Girl 1: Don't know.

Girl 2: Where is it?

Girl 1: Don't know.

Girl 2: Wha' kind of yard?

Girl 1: Don't know nothing.

Girl 2: (*after a moment*) Aren't you afraid?

Girl 1: Don't know.

Girl 2: You don' know much do ya!

No answer.

Does 'e bea' yer?

Girl 1: No.

Girl 2: Be' 'e does.

Girl 1: Why d'you arst then.

Silence, except for the Man's breathing.

(*factually*) Why donsha go away?

Girl 2: Wan' me to?

Girl 1: Dunno.

A moment.

Girl 2: Watch.

Girl 2 dances in front of the cage. Not hurried or slow. It is beautiful, with open and flowing movements. She 'la' – sings to herself as she does. It is vaguely the same tune as Girl 1 was singing earlier.

Girl 1: (*watching her*) 'F 'e wakes up...

Girl 2 continues a moment, then comes to an end.

Girl 2: Did ya like it?

Girl 1: Dunno.

Girl 2: Jou wanna?

Girl 1: No.

There's a disturbance in the Man's sleep. The two girls watch him. Both very still.

Girl 2: (*whispering*) 'S 'e dreamin'?

Girl 1: (*ditto*) Be'er go.

Girl 2: Why?

She moves across to the Man to look at him. Girl 1 keeps her distance from him in the cage. Extremely still.

Man: (*talking with someone in his dream*) ... No – 'ere 'ere 'ere 'ere ..... don' be like tha', come 'ere... why won' yer – ?

Girl 2: Who's 'e talkin' to?

Man: Show some int'rest can't ya... Look wha' I give ya! ... Dug the foundations with these broken bones. Used m' blood to mix the cemen'. Decora'ed the

walls with cinders for ya. Four walls for ya. Isn't this enough for ya? Come
'ere... Show some gra'itude can't ya? Bought i' for the price of me face. Show
some can't ya? Four walls! .... nonononononolookno – 'Thin these four
walls wha' I say goes! ..... Yes i' does. Don't – .... I am. No. 'Thin these four
walls I am! (pause) Be''er. Be''er.

The Man gets up, moves to the cage, a hand reaching out.

I love ya. I love ya. Yer know tha'.

*The Man reaches the bars. Girl 1 moves to him bringing her face into contact
with his hands – but is rigid.*

Girl 2: Why yer – ?

Girl 1: I 'ave to or 'e comes in.

Man: (*feeling her face and hair with his hands*) I'd be nothin' 'f I didn' 'ave you.
Say yer love us. Say yer need us. Say you wan' the king! (*he chuckles at what
he's said*) Nothing will go beyond these four walls ... . nothinatall. Tall walls.
(*kissing her gently on the front of her neck beneath her jawbone*) Make them
taller if yer wan' ... tall walls ... no problem ... four walls tall ...... (*looking into
her face, smiling*) .... mm?

The Man leaves her and goes back to where he was and lies down.

Tall walls .... OK, four walls tall ....four ...

He continues to sleep. Girl 1's rigidity ebbs away.

Girl 2: You alrigh'?

Girl 1: Yeah.

Girl 2: 'S 'e of'en like tha'?

Girl 1: Sometimes 'e dreams 'e's on fire. 'Is clo'es. Tears at 'em. Can't put it ou'.

*Girl 2 goes to girl 1 and takes her hands through the bars. The Man's breathing
can be heard again.*

Wha'cha doin'?

Girl 2: 'Oldin' yer 'and.

A pause.

Why donsha come with me? (*no response*) Could get yer ou' of here.

Girl 1: Why?

Girl 2: Wha 'cha mean?

No response. Girl 1 releases her hands.

Donsha wanna ge' ou'?

No response. The Man's breathing becomes more pronounced a rattling sound.

(*touching Girl 1*) Donsha wanna?

No response.

Doncha?

No response.

All I go' 'a do is ge' 'is keys, open the door.

Girl 1: No.

Girl 2: Why no'? You 'ate i'.

No response.

I'm ge"in' the keys.

Girl 1: (*cold fear*) No.

Girl 2 moves to the Man. She tries to put the tips of her fingers into the opening of his trouser pocket. The keys are inaccessible.

(*watching*) 'F 'e wakes up...

Girl 2 takes no notice, concentrating on the task in hand. She rolls the Man over a little to provide access to the pocket. Holding him with one hand, she puts the other into the pocket. There is a slight disturbance in the Man's sleep. He stops snoring. Girl 2 waits a moment. Then she digs down into the pocket searching for the keys. She finds them and draws out her hand. The keys are held between her index and middle fingers. She lets his body return to its original position. She stands, looks at him a moment as the rattling sound begins again.

Girl 2: (*smiling to Girl 1*) No' difficult!

She walks back to the cage, unlocks it and opens the door leaving the keys in the lock. She gets out a pen-knife, leans into the cage to cut the rope.

Girl 1: (*out loud*) No!

Both girls look to the Man. Then whispering:

Girl 2: Why no'?

Girl 1: Don' wanna.

Girl 2: Wha's yer name, you 'a'e i'!

She puts the knife back in her pocket.

Girl 1: No I don'.

Girl 2: Look. The door's open. All you go' 'a do is come with us –

Girl 1: No.

Girl 2: (*pointing upwards, showing her*) – See that dark shape against the sky. See tha', like a cliff-thing. Tha's the Scar. We're livin' up there. You can be with us. There's others.

Girl 1: Wha' yer mean, scar?

Girl 2: 'S wha' i's called. Its name.

A moment.

Well?

The Man's sleep is disturbed. He moves and briefly murmurs, indistinctly.

D'you wan' 'im to wake up and find us?!

Girl 1: Look, go away.

Girl 2: Wa's your life like? Animal in a cage.

Girl 1: Don't wanna go with ya. This is my 'ome.

There is a moment: neither understands the other.

'E takes care of me, 'e looks after me. I belong. 'E keeps me safe.

Girl 2: Safe from wha?

Girl 1: Don' ya know wha' I mean? My 'ome. Yer know wha' an 'ome is, don' ya?

No response. Girl 2 turns away from Girl 1.

Why yer tryin' to make us leave? (*tears well up*)

Girl 2: Ain' makin' yer. Jus' unlocked the door.

Girl 1: Donchou wanna home?

Girl 2: Not like tha'!

Girl 1: Doncha though?

Girl 2: Course.

Girl 1: Well then.

A pause. Girl 2 begins to go.

Where ya goin'!

Girl 2: Back to the Scar.

Girl 1: No. Yer gotta lock the door first! 'E'll know. Put the keys back in 'is pocket!

Girl 2: (*turning to Girl 1*) Ain' lockin' yer up.

Girl 1: Please! I can't lock the door and get the keys back! You gotta.

Girl 2: Call out to 'im.

She takes the pen-knife out of her pocket and puts it down in the cage.

If you don' use it chuck i' over there in the scree. Come back for i' in the mornin'. Cost a lot to ge' another one.

Girl 2 exits. Girl 1 does not move. The Man's breathing with the slight regular catch in it can be heard again in the stillness.

Some time.

A jet-fighter suddenly passes over very low as before, ripping the air. As it does, Girl 1 cowers down in the cage glancing at the Man as she does. The Man does not stir. When the sound is disappearing:

Man: (*not waking, clearly*) Ours.

The Man's breathing is heard again immediately. After a moment, Girl 1 reaches for the rag she discarded in the corner of the cage and brings it to her face. She holds it there.

THE KISS

Foreword by Chris Cooper

The Kiss (running about 50 minutes) was first performed in the autumn of 1997, at the Performing Arts Centre of the Queen Noor Hussein Foundation in Amman Jordan. Translated as *The Moment* in Arabic, the play was commissioned for 11th and 12th grade students (16-17 year olds).

Geoff's brief was to write a play about the challenges facing youth in Jordan in the era of globalisation. As the translation of the title of the play into Arabic suggests the pivotal moment of the kiss between the Boy and Girl on stage was breaking a taboo in the Arabic culture. But it was a bridge too far. As Lina Atel explained in recent correspondence about the production, 'We are a conservative society and there is no kissing on stage. So we replaced the kiss with a long passionate moment of both characters hugging each other! and hence decided to change the title from *The Kiss* to *The Moment* as it was a turning point in the dramatic action of the play. Geoff was gracious about this and accepted the change out of respect for our culture and theatre traditions.'

But it is important to note that while the play has a culturally specific site, it is not a play specifically about Jordan or the 'Arab world'. It also raises much about the process of globalisation and identity. The play dramatises experience from the viewpoint of the young and invites the audience to makes sense of the world for themselves. As the Girl says:

> **Girl**: I was confused. You have to be allowed to be confused, be able to say it and then look at your confusion, not have everyone telling you what you should think, what you should do. And then maybe you can sort it out and not be confused.

The central metaphor of the play is concerned with a journey, like *Bonecage*, from the old to the new and, like *Lessons*, it is in many ways a play about learning. But the difference in approach between *The Kiss* and *Lessons* is startling. It illustrates another journey for the writer.

The journey from the Old City, through the Droughtlands to the new City, like Christian's journey in Bunyan's *Pilgrim's Progress*, retains universal significance that is as relevant and resonant in 2011 as it was in 1997. That the play has never had a production in the UK is to be regretted and we hope its publication will give it the production by or for young people that it deserves.

The play's sites reflect the simple structure of the play and it requires few resources to create – only attention to detail (such as the delightfully resonant stage direction: 'Caught on one or two of the thorn-bushes are the tattered and weather-degraded pieces of black and blue polythene') which changes subtly in each scene. Each site is very powerful. The Old City is like the developed world as it is today. The New City is the future. The Droughtlands is the space between now and the future, a zone of being lost and of becoming, a zone of proximal development.

There are five actors and, like *Bone-cage*, the play makes real demands on the actors. *The Kiss* was the play Geoff wrote after *Bone-cage* and it picks up where that play left off.

The characters in the play often don't say what they mean and what they do mean is often expressed negatively by *how* they express themselves. Speech rhythms become important.

> In a sense all this is at the heart of the *method* of my playwriting. I'm interested in people's *behaviour* most of all – hence the mass of detailed stage directions. People (in life) show who they are, what they're doing, through their feelings, in their actions. We are accustomed (even more so in theatre) to focus on what they say. I tend to treat what they say (and therefore *how* they say it) as behaviour, ie speech-acts. It's important too that the actors are aware of this method of the play. They're accustomed to 'leaping at' the 'character' as though this were a fixed essence. Whereas for me what's interesting is how people change. The play itself is a lot *about* this. To what extent we are made, and to what extent we make ourselves in the process of living – the relationship of one to the other. (GG Letter to Lina Attel 28.7.97)

Geoff does something very interesting with the characters in this play. We can see aspects of ourselves in the Boy and Girl as they develop and change. And briefly to return to learning, we see a totally different approach from the one used in *Lessons*. This reflects the influence of Bond and his own development as a writer. The struggle to know is firmly located in the logic of imagination.

> I've conceived the Old Man and the Barefooted Boy as personifications of the requirements of the Boy's and Girl's imaginations (I'm not sure about the Woman....) This is not to say they are imaginary. They are real people and at the same time they are personifications of what exists in their imaginations! Our imaginations do in fact function like this – we imagine the real. An audience is being asked to consider, are these people real or are they phantoms (jinn)? and the play never clarifies this question, because they are *both*.

We can hear the voice of the artist and the pedagogue united (Geoff had been studying Vygotsky's *Imagination and Creativity of the Adolescent* before he began work on the play).

The end result of this combined thinking is a funny, tragic, profound and beautiful play by a very fine writer.

The Kiss was first performed in the autumn of 1997, at the Performing Arts Centre of the Queen Noor Hussein Foundation in Amman Jordan.

Characters
The Boy
The Girl
The Old Man
The Bare-footed Boy
The Woman

A note on textual lay-out
Stage directions in italics and separated off from the speech, it indicates that the actions take place without overlap of speech, unless otherwise stated.

Stage directions contained in left brackets] indicate simultaneity with speech.

Stage directions in round brackets (...) indicate the author's clarification.

When a character tails off in speech leaving a thought uncompleted, this is indicated thus: .....

When a character is interrupted by another, or breaks off him/herself abruptly, this is indicated thus: –

or: – .

Scene 1:
At the Outer Limits of the Old City

City limits. Dry, stony ground. Scrub and a few leafless thorn-bushes, dried thistles etc. No green. Caught on one or two of the thorn-bushes are the tattered and weather-degraded pieces of black and blue polythene. To one side there are two corroded metal posts sunk into mounds in the ground some three feet apart. One of these is about eight feet in height and leans somewhat from the vertical towards the other. Bolted to it near the top is a bent metal signboard designating the city limits. It is pitted and dented – perhaps it has been used as a target. Words indecipherable. Of the other post, only eighteen inches or a couple of feet remains. The top is sharp and jagged as though and animal had some time ago tried to tear it out with its teeth.

Silence.

The Boy and the Girl enter. They are dressed in ordinary contemporary western-style clothes. They carry a small amount of baggage and wear small back-packs like those sometimes used by students for school. They are holding hands.

After a moment, a freeze

The Boy: (*to audience*) At the outer limits to the Old City.

End freeze. They walk another few steps, looking around for something. They stop. Drop hands.

The Girl: It's just stopped.

The Boy: Hang on here a sec.

He puts down the bag in his hand and exits where they came from. She waits, looking as before. The Boy enters.

Nothing. Just stops.

Pause.

The Girl: What we going to do?

She looks ahead. The Boy walks round to look at the sign-board. She puts the bag in her hand down and joins him. He looks around.

The Boy: You'd think there'd be tracks at least.

The Girl: We've come out the right way.....?

The Boy: Yeah.

After a moment – to himself.

Definitely the right way..... You'd think there'd be something.

He looks back where they have come from. Looks ahead.

The Girl: (*taking the bag from his shoulder*) Here, give me that. We can just have a think for a moment.

She puts the bag with the others.

Why aren't there any tracks?

The Boy: Not enough people go this way I s'pose. I dunno.

The Girl: (*looking back*) Funny the road just stopping.

The Boy: Ran out of money.

He slaps the post several times without much force, then rubs the palm of his hand on it. Looks at his hand. Brushes the hand against his clothes.

What d'you want to do?

The Girl: What do you want to do?

The Boy: I asked you first.

The Girl moves to the Boy, touching him.

Do you want to go back?

The Girl: No. We can't.

The Boy: We can.....

The Girl: No.

She puts her arms around his waist and hugs into him. He puts his arms around her, and gently hugs her, closing his eyes. They stand motionless for a little while. He opens his eyes and the Girl moves out of the embrace and takes his hand.

(*looking ahead*) Which way shall we go?

The Boy: (*looking around and back*) There's someone coming. We could ask him.

They drop each other's hand.

Maybe he knows the way. Give us directions.

An Old Man enters. He is dressed in shabby contemporary western-style clothes except for a kaffiyeh, and wears blue rubber flip-flops. He has a bag over one shoulder. He walks with the aid of a stick. He looks very frail. He comes from the same direction as the Boy and the Girl came. As he enters, he is looking at them but without particular interest. The Old Man slightly raises and lowers his head in greeting to the Boy as their eyes meet, and continues walking.

Hallo there. How are you?

Old Man: Ah, well. How are you?

The Boy goes over and shakes hands with the Old Man in greeting.

The Boy: I'm fine – thank you.

Old Man: Headed into the Droughtlands are you?

The Boy: Yes.

Old Man: Ah-ha.

There is a pause.

Do I know your father.... Your grandfather...?

The Boy: My grandfather passed on about six years ago. My father lives – (*pointing vaguely*) on the other side of the City.

Old Man: (*with a slight nod*) Aah.

Slight pause.

I might have known your grandfather.

He ponders. The Boy looks across briefly to the Girl. He smiles to her. She returns the smile.

The Boy: We were wondering if you knew the way to the New City. There are no tracks.

Old Man: Ah-ha.

The Boy: Even the general direction would help.

Old Man: You're going there?

The Boy: Yes.

Old Man: It's a long way.

Slight pause.

Why do you want to go there?

The Boy: Work.

Old Man: D'you know anyone?

The Boy: No.

Old Man: You'll need money – have you got any?

The Boy: Not much. But I'll get a job.

Old Man: Ah-ha.

The Old Man takes the bag from his shoulder, sits down on a flat stone. The Boy looks again to the Girl, raises his eyes to the heavens. She returns his look with an acquiescent smile.

You'll have to go through the Droughtlands to get there.

Slight pause.

The Boy: Have you ever been? To the New City....?

Old Man: No, but I know a thing or two about it. (*for the first time, to the Girl*) Have you got provisions?

The Girl: Yes – and we have water.

Old Man: Well prepared then.

Slight pause.

The Boy: (*slight laugh*) Except we're not sure of the way.....

The Old Man says nothing.

We thought there'd be tracks.

Old Man: (*reaching for his bag*) Why don't you share something to eat with me? You'll have been walking since first light to get here from the other side of the City. I've food here.

He begins to bring things from his bag: bread, a plastic pot of yoghurt, some goat's cheese, a small tin of olive oil, a small jar of mixed herbs and spices.

The Boy: No – thank you – really – we need to be going.

Old Man: You haven't eaten I bet and you want to keep what you've got there.

The Boy: It's very kind of you but –

Old Man: What is your hurry! It'll give me pleasure to share it with you.

The Boy looks to the Girl. She is laughing quietly, hiding her mouth with her hand.

(*not looking at her*) She can come over. She doesn't need to wait. (*to the Boy*) Here, sit here.

The Boy sits down on the ground as the Old Man lays out food on the ground. The Girl comes over, sitting to the side and at a little distance from the Old Man and the Boy. During the following, the Old Man deftly readies the food for eating: shaking some of the yoghurt onto an enamel plate, pouring a little olive oil to the side of it, tipping some of the herbs into the lid of the jar, etc.

When I was your age I didn't have to go somewhere else to work. Work in the Old City. Market. Driving animals. Making furniture. Anything. You couldn't get a job?

The Boy: Well –

Old Man: Nothing like that?

The Boy: Not really.

Old Man: Terrible. What's happened, uh.

He gestures to the food, then takes some bread. The Boy does likewise. They both begin to eat. The Boy gestures to the Girl. She leans across and takes bread as the Old Man speaks.

(*to the Boy*) Are you married?

The Boy: No – but we're going to as soon as I get a job and find somewhere to live.

Old Man: May not be as easy as that.

The Girl: I can work too.

The Old Man dips a piece of bread in the oil and then the herbs.

The Boy: (*to the Old Man*) No – there's plenty of work. Good jobs too. Not like at home.

Old Man: (*to the Boy but indicating both of them*) What do your fathers say about this?

The Boy: About what?

Old Man: About going to the New City. Getting married.

There is a pause.

The Boy: It's our decision.

Old Man: (*after a moment*) Ah-ha....

He pushes the cheese towards the Boy.

Here. Have some.

The Boy takes a piece.

There's nothing in the Old City for the young.

There is silence. The Boy gestures to the Girl to eat. Everyone eats. The silence continues.

The Boy: Do you live around here?

Old Man: Yes. By the slaughter-house. (*gesturing vaguely, bread in hand*) You'll have passed it on your way. (*dips bread in yoghurt*) I used to be in the centre. Not anymore.

The Boy: Yeah?

Old Man: I go in once in a while. Have a look. Bad. Changed. Not surprised you want to leave. Who wouldn't.

The Boy: We didn't want to stay. Nothing. Prison with hard labour.

The Old Man nods.

What's the point in that!

Old Man: (*with a slight nod*) Aah.

The Boy: Don't get me wrong. I don't mind working – you know what I mean? But not in a dead end. I want to be able to do things. Worth working then. Not like here.

Old Man: Money's not everything.

The Boy: No, I know. I'm not saying it is.

In the New (*the Old Man speaks over*) City, when we –

Old Man: Everyone thinks money's the important thing. World will never be right if you think like that. Further away. Secret's here.

He bangs his fist intently on his heart.

You follow me?

The Boy: Yes I think so.

Old Man: We have to renew the soul – not sell it to your New City.

The Boy says nothing.

You'll do what you want, of course.

The Old Man turns to his bag and feels in it.

I have some fruit here.

He brings out a small blue plastic bag containing a few small oranges. He passes one to the Girl.

Here, have one.

The Girl: Thank you.

Old Man: *(to the boy)* I'll do it for you.

The Girl has taken the orange and holds it in her hand on the ground. She does not eat it. The Old Man begins to peel the orange for the Boy, passing segments as he speaks. Red juice trickles from his fingers as he does so.

A stranger came to a man's house. The stranger had nowhere to go. So the man welcomed the stranger into his house. The stranger had a dog. The man told the stranger he was welcome but the dog would have to be tethered in the yard, outside. Of course it wasn't long before children began to throw stones at the dog and the neighbours complained about the noise of the dog barking. The yard filled with the litter of the dogs' faeces and its uneaten food. The neighbours told him – the man – they didn't want the dog there. It was unclean. The man replied, 'I don't like it any more than you – but what can I do? He's my guest. The dog belongs to him.' So nothing was done. The man didn't go into his yard anymore. The filth and stench made his stomach turn. But he said nothing to the stranger. For his part, the stranger took to bringing the dog into the house while the man was at work. When the man realised this was happening he asked the stranger if the dog had been in the house while he was out. His guest always denied it: 'You asked me to keep him outside. See for yourself – he's tethered outside in the yard.' And the man fell silent. But soon he could not bear returning to his house at night. Eventually the man moved out. Not only had he lost all his friends because of the dog: he no longer felt he belonged in his own home. So he moved out and went to another town.

A moment.

The Girl: We want to live!

Old Man: (*looking at her*) Of course you do.

The Girl: No I mean, *live*.

Old Man: (*still looking at her*) What do your parents say about you leaving?

The Girl: (*factually*) They won't notice. My father said he had too many girls.

Old Man: ⌉ Ah-ha.

The Girl: ⌋ (*sotto voce, to the Boy*) Don't you think we should go....?

The Boy: (*to the Old Man*) Yes. We do need to get going now. Thank you for the food.

The Girl: Yes, you're very kind.

The Boy: Could you tell us the general direction we have to go.

Old Man: (*to the boy*) Please stay. Why the haste?

The Boy: (*getting up*) No – we have to go –

The Girl is getting up.

Old Man: Why? Because she says so?

The Boy: No! We do! We wanna get as far as we can before nightfall.

Old Man: Stay a bit longer, uh?

The Old Man stands, with the aid of his stick.

We haven't finished our conversation....

The Boy: Please – just tell us the way. We –

Old Man: I'm not telling you the way to hell! Go there without my help!

The Boy: I –

Old Man: I haven't told you what can be done about the Old –

The Boy: ⌉ We're going!...

Old Man: ⌋ – City – if people like you had a mind to it!

The Boy: I'm sick of the Old City. I don't want to. (*to the Girl*) Come on.

Old Man: Needs cleansing –

He takes hold of the Boy's clothes.

– only the youth can do that. Needs strength, will. –

The Boy shakes the Old Man off and turns towards their bags. The Girl follows the Boy's lead.

– Don't TURN YOUR BACK ON ME!

The Old Man hits the Boy with extraordinary force a glancing blow with his stick.

The Girl: ⌉ Look out!

The Boy: ⌋ Shit!

The Boy retreats. The Old Man comes after him, beating him with the stick, speaking at the same time. Some blows connect, others miss.

Old Man: New City. Devour. Everything. You. Every one – else. Sell your birthright. Soul.

The Boy comes towards the Old Man and tries to get hold of the stick. The remains of the food is trampled in the process of the scuffle.

The Boy: Stop! You'll – . Aah!

Old Man: Night clubs. Alcohol. Drugs. Loose – . Gambling. Is that what you want?!

The Boy: No! –

> *The blows continue. The Boy, unable to get the stick, moves away to try and collect the bags. The Old Man pursues him, treading in the food.*

(*to the girl*) – Come on. Get the bags.

Old Man: You filth. I could have taught you – something. –

The Boy turns and manages to get hold of the stick but the Old Man will not let go of it.

– Together. What we could've done. But no – Found ourselves again – listen to that filthy harlot instead –

The Boy pushes the Old Man away and sharply tugs the stick from him as he does, and throws it away. The Old Man has a seizure at the same moment, totters back and collapses amongst the food. He flails with his arms, somehow trying to get up. He cannot, but manages to reach up the mound supporting the short post. He clutches the post momentarily, then jerks away from it as though he received an electric shock from it. Then, he lies still, strange sounds coming from his mouth for a moment or two. Then he is silent. There is a long stillness as the Boy recovering his breath, and the Girl, look at the Old Man on the ground.

The Boy: (*to the Girl*) What's.....?

After a moment they both go to the Old Man and crouch over him – looking to see if he's alive.

He's....

The Girl: I think he's had a heart attack.

The Boy: (*to the Old Man*) Stupid. (*pause, to her*) D'you think he's dead....?

The Girl: Yeah.

The Boy: Sure?

She says nothing.

Oh, god.

He drops his head onto the Old Man's chest. Almost immediately he lifts it again.

D'you think anyone saw?

They both look around – he, getting up to look back to the road from the Old City.

No one around.

A moment.

What shall we do?

The Girl: I dunno.

The Boy: Didn't mean to do it..... (*looking to the Old Man*) he attacked us.... he was trying to stop us going to the New City.... wouldn't tell us.... he had no right....

Silence.

The Girl: I know. I saw.

The Boy: What we going to do....?

The Boy begins to shake. The Girl goes over to him. Holds him.

What we going to do? He was mad.

The Girl: Alright, lovely, alright.

The Girl looks towards the body of the Old Man.

We'll have to – .

She looks around.

Help me.

She moves to the body. And begins to drag it. The Boy comes over.

The Boy: Here let me.

He takes the body from her and begins to drag it.

The Girl: Put it out of sight somewhere. Make it look like he had an accident on his own.

She begins to collect up all the trampled food and shoves it in the Old Man's bag. The Boy exits with the body of the Old Man. The Girl looks around – ensuring that not even a piece of orange peel remains. She notices the stick, goes and picks it up. She returns to the Old Man's bag and picks it up. She is having a last check of the area as the Boy returns. A strand of saliva droops from his lower lip.

The Boy: I've been sick.

The Girl: It's alright. Take these. Put them with him.

He exits with the stick and the Old Man's bag. She ruffles the ground with her feet.

The Boy enters.

You alright?

She moves towards their bags.

The Boy: Yes.

She collects up their bags.

(*in a daze*) No, I can do it.

The Boy takes the bags he carried before.

Which way shall we go?

The Girl: Let's just go.

The girl takes his hand and they exit towards the Droughtlands. Silence. Stillness.

Scene 2:
The Droughtlands

Droughtland. Dry, stony ground with scrub, leafless thorn-bushes, thistles etc., as before. No green. No polythene waste.

The Boy enters. A moment later the Girl enters.

The Girl: Slow down! I can't keep up!

A freeze:

(*to the audience*) The Droughtlands.

End freeze. The Boy stops and turns to the Girl. She smiles at him as she catches up.

D'you know where we are?

No response. The Boy is scanning the horizon.

All looks the same. Nothing but thorn-bushes.

The Boy: (*still looking*) Nothing. Goes on for ever.

The Girl: Is it alright if we have a drink?

The Boy: Sure.

The Girl begins to get a bottle of water from her bag.

(*to himself*) Should've brought one of those – what d'you call them? –

The Girl: Not exactly cold..... (*taking the cap off.*)

The Boy: – compasses. (*puts down his bag*) And a map. (*taking the bottle which the Girl is passing.*) Didn't think we'd need one. (*drinks*) Thought there'd be a road. (*passes the bottle to the Girl*)

The Girl: Weren't to know.

The Boy: (*for her*) Not too much.

He continues to look to the horizon including, briefly, where they came from, as she drinks some water.

The Girl: (*putting the cap on the bottle – to him*) I keep seeing his face.

The Boy: It's best not to think about it.

The Boy glances to the Girl. She puts the bottle away in her bag.

58

We need to move. OK? (*picks up his bag*) Can't stop yet. Wanna get as far as we can.

The Girl: (*a burst*) But we DON'T KNOW WHERE WE ARE! So how can we know WHICH WAY TO GO!

She cries. The Boy looks to her.

Sorry......

The Boy: No, it's OK. It's OK.

Pause.

The Girl: (*still tearful, looking at the Boy, – an explanation*) I keep.....

The Boy: (*going over to her*) It's OK.

He holds her to him, bag still in hand.

The Girl: Don't you?

The Boy: We have to not lose sight of the New City. Where we're going, uh?

The Girl: Maybe we should've told someone.

The Boy: We couldn't.

The Girl: We just left him there. Killed him and just left him.

The Boy: We didn't kill him. Went berserk – had a heart attack. We didn't do anything. Crazy – worse than my father. Went berserk.

The Girl: Yeah....

The Boy: (*putting bag down*) Come on lovely.... stop it now, don't think about it. It'll paralyse us.

She looks at him.

The Girl: D'you think?

The Boy: Yeah. We have to put it behind us. It was an accident.

The Girl: Was it?

The Boy: Yeah. It was.

The Girl says nothing.

Look, thinking about him's not going to bring him back. He's dead. We have to put him behind us. It's history. Can't change it.

The Girl: No, I know.

She becomes a little tearful. He holds her close again.

Sorry.

The Boy: It's OK. (*after a moment*) Everything'll be alright when we get to the New City. Away from all this.

He releases her a little to look at her.

OK?

She nods to him.

Feel OK to go on?

She vaguely nods.

The Girl: Do you love me?

The Boy: Yes! What a stupid question.

The Girl: No I mean really.

The Boy: Yes! We're going to marry in the New City aren't we. Have kids.

He hugs her to him. She hugs into him.

The Girl: Sometimes I feel really afraid.

They remain still for a few moments. He hugs her closer. After a moment, she draws her head up to look at him. He's not looking at her. She takes his cheek in her hand and turns his head to her.

I really love you.

He looks at her a moment, then slightly moves his face away from eye-contact.

(*dropping her hand*) Are you alright?

The Boy: Yeah. (*letting her go*) We need to go. (*looking in the direction they were going*) We should just keep going straight. (*looking to her*) Hit a road maybe.

The Girl hasn't moved.

Yeah?

The Girl: Whatever you think's best.

The Boy picks up his bag. As he is doing so, a bare-footed Boy enters from the direction they were about to go. He is about the same age as the Boy, but he looks younger – perhaps as a result of malnutrition. He is dressed in western-style clothes with a faded green tee-shirt. The skin of his feet is leathery and calloused. The Bare-footed Boy is aware of the Boy but is looking at the Girl. The Girl, without expression, watches the Bare-footed Boy for a moment before indicating to the Boy to turn. The Boy turns and sees the Bare-footed Boy.

Bare-footed Boy: Are you lost?

The Girl: ⎤ Yes.... (*the Girl looks to the ground, and doesn't look up*)
The Boy: ⎦ No, not really – (*a slight laugh*) yes! We're headed for the New City. Are we going the right way?

B-f Boy: Yeh, more or less. (*turning and pointing to the distance*) See that low rise? (*the Boy looks*) You wanna head for that. When you get up there you'll be able to see it in the distance. Sky-scrapers. Just keep on walking.

The Boy: Thanks. OK well.... thanks. (*to the Girl*) Let's get going.

The Girl: (*flurriedly feeling in her bag and quickly drawing the water-bottle from it, dropping the bag in the process, and holding the bottle out to him*) Would you like some water?

The Boy looks sharply at the Girl. The Bare-footed Boy looks at the Boy, then to her.

B-f Boy: (*slight gesture of declining*) No thanks.

The Girl: Oh.

The Girl looks down holding the bottle to her chest.

The Boy: (*to her*) OK?

A brief moment. The Boy is about to go.

The Girl: (*to the B-f Boy, again looking to him*) Do you live out here?

The Boy: We have to go.

The Girl: (*to the Boy*) Maybe he could tell us something....

The Boy breathes out slightly audibly.

(*privately*) He's alright....

The Boy: We've wasted enough time.

He puts his bag down at his feet.

We have to keep moving.

A silence.

(*to the B-f Boy*) You on your own?

B-f Boy: Yeah.

The Boy: Where you headed?

The Girl slips her back-pack off and puts the bottle on the ground beside it as the conversation continues, watching the Bare-footed Boy as she does so.

B-f Boy: Nowhere in particular.

The Boy: (*after a moment*) We're headed for the New City.

B-f Boy: Yeah.

The Boy: Have you ever been?

B-f Boy: Once or twice, few times.

The Boy: What's it like?

The Girl: Don't you have any shoes?

B-f Boy: (*to the Boy*) Er – . (*to the Girl*) Shoes?

The Girl: Yeah, don't you cut your feet or –

B-f Boy: Not really.

The Girl: (*looking down*) I didn't mean to embarrass you...

B-f Boy: I know. You didn't.

The Girl glances up, then down again.

The Boy: So what's it like? The City.

B-f Boy: A stomach made of reflecting glass.

The Boy: Eh?

The Girl: (*looking up*) I don't understand.

B-f Boy: They don't make anything there. Not a thing. All comes from the slave camps.

The Girl: Slaves....?

The Boy: (*to the Girl*) Wait a sec. (*to the B-f Boy*) It's a big city isn't it? – how do people make their money?!

B-f Boy: Picking up a phone. Pressing a few keys on a computer terminal. (*a slight laugh*) Running the city.

The Boy: There are jobs...? I mean you can get a job.

B-f Boy: Some.

The Boy: Yes.

B-f Boy: Depends what you want.

The Bare-footed Boy casts a glance at the Girl who has been looking at him since she last spoke.

The Girl: I didn't know there were slave-camps near the New City....

B-f Boy: Couldn't exist without them.

The Girl: (*to the Boy*) Did you know?

The Boy shakes his head.

That's.....

She looks to the Boy.

The Boy: You mean they wear chains?

The Girl looks at the Bare-footed Boy.

B-f Boy: It's not chains that makes a slave. It's being owned.

The Boy: So they don't.

A brief pause. The Bare-footed Boy turns, takes a few steps away and crouches down with his back to them, picking up and inspecting stones.

The Girl: What do the slaves do?

The Bare-footed Boy turns but remains crouched, a stone in his hand.

B-f Boy: Everything. Grow their food, make their clothes, assemble their computers and mobile phones, make their weapons. Bussed in to clean their streets, serve in their restaurants and hotels.... everything.

He gently lobs the stone in front of him.

The Girl: (*looking at the B-f Boy*) I....

She looks to the Boy.

What shall we do?

The Boy: What d'you mean?

The Girl: Well.... I don't know but....

The Boy: What d'you want us to do?! Go back! There's injustice everywhere. You could spend your life trying to get justice – and still never get it and you've wasted your life. You end up old and with nothing.

There is a pause – the Girl looking at the Boy. Then she looks to the Bare-footed Boy. He is looking at her without expression.

(*to the B-f Boy*) I'm right aren't I?

The Bare-footed Boy looks at the Boy without expression for a moment and then looks to the ground.

I'm right.

The Girl walks across to a thorn-bush and feels its prickles with her hand.

B-f Boy: (*to the Girl*) When the rains come you wouldn't recognise it. Green everywhere. Boof! All of a sudden – millions of tiny leaves. Every shade of green. Flowers too. Amazing.

The Girl: Why don't they just run away?

B-f Boy: What to?

The Girl: (*a slight shrug*) Freedom.

B-f Boy: It's not like that. If you live in a prison you can dream of escaping or you can dream of destroying the prison which means understanding why the prison is there and working out how you can do it. I *used* to dream of escaping, but here in the Droughtlands I realised that escaping wasn't the problem or the solution. Escaping is another form of imprisonment.

A moment. Then the Girl walks back to the Boy and puts a hand on his arm.

The Boy: (*to the Girl*) What?

She squeezes the Boy's arm.

What? You want to go?

She slightly shakes her head, then looks to the Bare-footed Boy who hasn't moved.

(*to the B-f Boy*) I don't quite understand. You live out here....? You a runaway slave....?

B-f Boy: (*a slight laugh*) No, I'm a slave. Live in one of the camps.

The Boy: (*also a slight laugh*) Well – what you doing out here then? Don't they keep a watch on you?

B-f Boy: Sure! Armed guards everywhere. Concrete walls, razor-wire on top. But there's always way and means – find the moment.

The Girl: Why do you do it? Isn't it dangerous – if you're caught?

B-f Boy: Not particularly – as I say, find your moment. I like it here.

The Girl: And you go back?!

B-f Boy: (*slight laugh*) Yeah! (*factually*) My father and mother are slaves. My brothers and sisters... friends. My grandparents were slaves. I'm a slave. That's how it is.

He picks up a stone from in front of him. Then he looks at the Girl without expression.

The Girl: (*like water flowing into sand*) Just after we'd set out from the Old City we killed this old man –

The Boy: Don't tell him that – it's – be quiet – you... (*he shakes the Girl off his arm.*)

63

The Girl: – and I don't know why it happened. He was horrible, well he gave us food but, but he wouldn't give us directions to the New City even though he knew it because he wanted us to cleanse the Old City, get rid of everything he didn't like, go back to the old ways, had these oranges, but we can't can we, tried to make us – I'm sure he was in pain, so much hate, just a poor old man and now he's dead and I don't understand why. (*a slight laugh*) Sorry.

The Bare-footed Boy, who has been looking at her throughout, remains as expressionless as sand.

The Boy: (*after a moment – to the Girl*) Are you satisfied? He's a complete stranger. Why did you tell him? You can't tell people. We have to keep it to ourselves. It's ours. What did you go telling him for?

The Girl: I don't know. I'm sorry.

The Boy: 'Sorry'. (*turning his back on her*) Ours.

The Girl: I didn't know you – . (*to the B-f Boy*) You're not going to tell anyone else?

B-f Boy: There are old men like him in the camps. Old men like him are born all the time.

The Girl looks at the Bare-footed Boy for a moment, then looks at the Boy whose back is still turned to her. She walks round to face him.

The Girl: I'm sorry. I didn't know it was so important to you –

The Boy: Us. Us.

The Girl: Alright, us. I didn't realise. It was thoughtless of me. I'm really sorry.

The Boy makes no response to her. The Bare-footed Boy lets the stone fall in front of him and stands up and makes to leave while the Girl speaks.

I don't know what I can say to – . (*turning to the B-f Boy*) No, don't go.

The Bare-footed Boy stops. He looks at her. The Girl looks down, then almost immediately looks again at the Bare-footed Boy.

I....

The Boy: (*without turning*) We need to go.

The Girl: I....

The Girl walks over to the Bare-footed Boy. She stands in front of him, reaches out her arm and touches him lightly just beneath his eye with her fingers. The Bare-footed Boy is looking at her but makes no reaction. The Boy turns and looks at the other two. The Girl takes a step forward and taking the Bare-footed Boy's head gently in her hands kisses him on the mouth. The Bare-footed Boy responds, kissing her and lightly putting his hands on her sides. They give and receive each other's tongues in the kiss. The kiss continues while the Boy tries to take in what he's seeing with gathering anger.

The Boy: What the – ?!

As soon as he speaks the Girl and the Bare-footed Boy turn to face him. She reaches out her hand to the Boy.

I'll kill you! (*running at them*) Get out of here you bitch, whore you –

The Girl and the Bare-footed Boy run away as fast as they can, and exit.

(*continuing*) – I'll kill you both! (*picking up a handful of stones and dust and hurling it after them.*) Bitch! Bitch! Bitch!

He is crying with anger and hurt, and crumples up on the ground. Supporting himself on one arm, he stares in the direction the Girl and the Bare-footed Boy ran in. The Old Man enters from the direction the Boy and Girl entered. He seems shrunken. His face is grey and colourless. His clothes have decayed and blackened, except for the blue flip-flops. He walks with the aid of his stick. No bag. The Boy has his back to him. The Boy does not turn when the Old Man speaks.

Old Man: (*evenly*) Come back to the Old City. She was a whore from the start. Carry me on your back – I know the way.

The Boy: Your stench is terrible....

Old Man: Ah-ha. (*with a shrug*) I can't help that.

The Boy: I don't want to go back.

Old Man: Women are not worth it. Even when they're faithful they're faithless in their hearts.

The Boy: (*to himself*) Bitch.

Old Man: Should've gone after her. Beaten the sin out of her.

The Boy: (*to himself*) I wouldn't have her back if she came on bended knees.

Old Man: You gave her too much rope.

The Boy: (*getting up*) You can say that again.

Old Man: No good comes of women.

The Boy glances at the Old Man indifferently, and starts collecting together the bags.

You think it will be better in the New City? It isn't. All the women there are whores.

The Boy tries to load himself with the bags as the Old Man speaks.

Everything's for sale. You have money? Sell your soul! Is that what you want my friend?

The Boy: (*putting the bags down again*) Go to hell.

The Boy opens the bag which the Girl carried on her back and starts pulling out the few clothes etc. that belong to her and dumping them beside the bag.

Old Man: (*continuing*) If you don't – you'll die. What's life for then, eh?

The Boy: (*putting back a small radio-cassette which he has taken out*) I'm not listening to yer. (*closing up the bag again*)

Old Man: You want to be a cog in the machine of the New City? Go ahead.

The Boy throws a glance at the Old Man.

If you don't, then come back with me to the Old City. Purge it – make *it* new. Make it somewhere we can be proud of again. Not ashamed. Then you'll be somebody. Not a nothing.

The Boy begins to load himself again with the bags, notices the water-bottle amongst the Girl's clothes, hair-brush, etc, goes and picks it up and puts it in the Girl's other bag while the Old Man continues to speak.

You think you can kill me and then leave me behind, forget me... no... no I will always be there –

The Boy: That's what you think.

Old Man: (*suddenly loud*) You owe me! (*normal again*) That's history, boy, always there –

The Boy exits towards the New City.

– always waiting to be paid. (*calling after him, not angry*) Never turn your back on me

– I'll climb right up on it!

He turns away. Stillness. Then the Old Man looks at the discarded clothes. He turns over a garment or two with his stick without much interest. He walks slowly over to the mound and sits down, resting the stick against him between his arms which rest on his legs. He looks around, then drops his head and falls asleep. Silence. Stillness.

Scene 3:
At the Edge of the New City

Dry, stony ground with scrub, leafless thorn-bushes, thistles etc., as before. No green, no polythene waste. To the side there is a tall zinc-alloy pole painted a gloss beige about twelve feet in height sunk into a mound in the ground. There is a remote control security video camera mounted at the top focused towards the Droughtlands.

A woman enters from behind the camera-angle. She is about 40 years old. Very beautiful. She is dressed in a comfortable leopard-print skirt just above the knee, a loose silk blouse, discreet gold-chain necklace, and gold earrings. Her hair is fashionably loose. She wears iridescent lilac snake-skin high-heel shoes with gold-chain T-bar which shows her feet and red-painted toenails. She looks towards the Droughtlands.

Woman: (*to audience*) At the edge of the New City.

She looks again at the Droughtlands, waits without impatience. A silence. The camera pans slightly and tips down a little, accompanied by a soft whirring sound. After a moment the woman walks over to the pole and turns in the direction the camera is pointing. The Boy enters from this direction. The camera 'follows' him, again with a soft whirring sound. It stops. The Boy looks very different from before: He is totally exhausted. As well as all the baggage which is falling off him, he is carrying the Old Man on his back in a kind of fireman's lift. The Old Man is completely inert. He has lost his stick and one of his blue flip-flops. The Boy's clothes are torn by thorns, his shoes are falling apart. There are scratches and traces of blood from them on his face and hands. The Boy stops. He struggles to bring the water-bottle out of the bag, without putting anything down. He opens the bottle, drops the cap, and drinks the remains of the water. He throws the bottle towards the thorn-bushes. He drops himself to the ground. The camera whirs and 'centres' him, then stops. The Boy looks up towards the sound, but sees the Woman. The Boy panics: he tries and fails simultaneously to get up, push off, or hide the corpse. He makes no sound. He is like an animal that has been injured and brought down by a predator and is still caught.

It's alright. We know what it is.

After a moment, he is still.

The Boy: I can't – .

Woman: It's alright.

A pause. The Boy looks at the Woman.

If we let you in there'll be none of that... (*indicating with her head towards the bottle.*)

The Boy: (*looking towards the bottle, back to her*) Er...?

Woman: Yes.

The Boy struggles to his feet, the corpse still firmly locked on his back, some of the bags being released. He struggles across to the bottle in the thorn-bushes – the camera following him – picks it up, collects the cap on his way back, and puts both in a bag on the ground. Camera stops. He looks towards her. She smiles at him very embracingly. No trace of falseness. He smiles back gratefully. A pause.

The Boy: I've come from the Old City and... is this the New City?

Woman: How old are you?

The Boy: Twenty.

The Woman looks amusedly at him.

Eighteen – . Seventeen.

Woman: Don't be ashamed. It's a lovely age. (*a brief pause*) Energy. You know what you want. (*a brief pause*) And you want to come in.

The Boy: ....Yes.

Woman: Everyone who enters the City has an equal chance to make good. Man or woman. Black or white. Arab or Jew. Work is offered to everyone who is permitted entry. If you have money and wish to start your own business, that is your own affair.

The City does not interfere in how you use your money. You are given eight weeks to settle in. If after that you are not happy or you find you don't fit in, you will be offered a place in one of the satellite towns nearby. We have no unemployment. Anyone who has the talent can rise to the top. (*a brief pause*) There's no crime. We have no prisons: they are schools of crime. Anyone who commits a serious crime – murder, rape, armed robbery, burglary – is humanely, and privately, executed. Such things are very rare. Lesser crimes are punished by exclusion from the City. There are no second chances. Everyone knows this, and agrees to it before they are permitted entry. Our children are taught it from the cradle. Our streets are safe. (*a brief pause*) If you think you may wish to live in our City, you will be given a booklet, which you may keep, which contains all our laws and customs. You may of course ask questions, and one of our officers will do his or her best to answer them to your satisfaction. (*briefest pause*) If you then decide you wish to make an application to live in our City you will be invited to provide various details about yourself and to sign a statement indicating your willingness to conduct yourself according to the City's laws and customs. You will then be given your identity – electronic card, papers, so on. We have a minimum of bureaucracy or red tape. All the formalities can be completed within an hour. (*she pauses, smiles at him*) Then, by the look of you, you may wish to take advantage of the washroom facilities provided for new admissions at the immigration centre before going on to your new home!

The Boy: (*after a moment*) Is it alright.... if I ask you something?

Woman: Naturally. (*smiling embracingly*)

The Boy: Well – you know what you said about crime.... What if someone's done something before. Before coming to the New City?

Woman: You mean, him?

The Boy: Yes. –

Woman: It does not concern us. All that concerns us is that you tell us, and give your permission to make independent enquiries into your history. Once this is done, you can forget it. In fact you are urged to forget your past. It has no place in the New City. The past creates unhappiness.

The camera moves with the whirring sound to view the Droughtlands. She looks to the camera and then to him.

You have friends?

The Boy: No.

Woman: Well there's someone.

She smiles, then looks in the direction of the Droughtlands. The camera pans slightly and tips down a little. The Girl enters looking much the same as she did except that now she has bare feet which have become scratched. She is looking up to the camera as she enters. She sees the Boy and the Woman. She stops, as does the camera. Then the camera 'moves' to the Boy who having seen her, has sat down not looking at her. The camera 'returns' to the Girl. It stops.

The Girl: You have him with you then.

The Boy: (*not looking at her*) I didn't want him.

The Girl: I know.

A pause.

I want you to come with me to the camps.

The Boy glances back towards her, then –

The Boy: You've got bare feet.

The Girl: Yeah, it's better somehow.

The Boy: Still with him then.

The Girl: It's not like that.

The Boy: Like what?

The Girl: You know.

A pause.

Why don't you turn round and look at me?

A pause.

Come with me to the camps.

The Boy looks across to the Woman who is looking at him without expression. He then returns his gaze elsewhere.

The Boy: I'm going to live in the New City.

The Girl: It'll kill you.

The Boy: You sound like him (*indicating with his head the Old Man on his back*).

The Girl: I don't mean like that. I just mean.... We could have a real life there.

The Boy: What, as a slave!

The Girl: (*a sudden burst*) No, that's what you'll be THERE! (*pointing towards the New City.*)

The Boy: Ha.

The Girl: (*quiet again*) I can't explain properly what I mean. But I know. (*pause*) Please look at me.

The Boy: You betrayed me. Twice. First about this (*indicating the corpse*), then kissing that kid. I'll never forgive you for that.

The Girl: I didn't betray you –

The Boy: Ha!

The Girl: – It may have felt like that. I needed to talk about it. I was confused. You wouldn't talk about it!

The Boy: We talked about it!

The Girl: Not properly. I was confused. You have to be allowed to be confused, be able to say it and then look at your confusion, not have everyone telling you what you should think, what you should do. And then maybe you can sort it out and not be confused.

The Boy: You didn't look confused when you kissed him.

The Girl: No, I'm talking about before!

The Boy: I dunno what you're talking about.

The Girl: (*after a moment*) Please don't do this.

The Boy: What?

The Girl: Avoiding.

The Boy makes no reaction. The Girl looks at the Woman, who has neither moved nor displayed any reaction to what has been said. The Woman smiles embracingly. The Girl looks back to the Boy. The Old Man's head turns to the Girl stretching his neck round like a tortoise.

Old Man: (*to the Girl*) He doesn't want to come with you to the slave-camps. Don't you hear him! Nothing there for him.

The Girl very slightly retreats.

(*to the Boy*) Take me back to the Old City..... eh? With or without the whore.

The Boy: No.

The Old Man's head slowly drops to where it was. He is inert once more.

(*to the Girl*) You never kissed me.

The Girl: I wanted to.

A pause. The Girl walks in an arc to where she can see the Boy's face. The camera pans to follow her with a whir. The Girl and the Boy look at each other. The Boy looks away.

Please come with me to the camps.

The Boy shakes his head. He looks at her again.

The Boy: You could come with me.

The Girl: I couldn't.

The Boy continues to look at her a moment longer. Then, he passes one hand quickly over the other in the gesture that means 'finished'. He begins to stand up. This rouses the Old Man. The camera pans with a whir to the Boy.

Old Man: Are we going back?

The Boy: (*still getting up*) No.

Old Man: Where are we going?

The Boy: Into the New City.

Old Man: (*beginning to struggle on the Boy's back*) I don't want to go to the New City! I WANT TO GO TO THE OLD CITY! We have work to do!

The Boy stops trying to get up.

The Boy: Pack it in will you!

The camera pans to the Girl. Stops a moment. She is still. She is watching the Boy and the Old Man – but distant. The camera pans back to the Boy and the Old Man.

The Old Man has calmed.

(*to the Woman*) What can I do about him? I can't get him off.

Woman: They will do it for you in the immigration centre if you are accepted. It's a straight-forward operation. (*briefest pause*) He will be painlessly removed and incinerated hygienically. –

The Girl: (*to herself*) No.

The Woman puts her fingers through her hair, then tosses her head.

Woman: – D'you want to show me you can take him there....?

The Boy: I can take him.

The Boy begins to struggle to his feet. The Old Man begins to struggle on the Boy's back. The Girl watches the Old Man.

(*to the Old Man*) Won't make any difference.

Old Man: Traitor! You owe me!

The Boy: (*nearly to his feet*) I didn't promise you anything, old man.

Old Man: You killed me!

The Boy: (*factually*) It was an accident, you know that.

The Boy is now on his feet and begins to walk towards the Woman.

Old Man: Now you're going to kill me again!

The Old Man's kaffiyeh falls off in the struggle. The Girl moves rapidly forward – the camera panning rapidly towards her – and picks up one end of the kaffiyeh at the same time the Old Man grabs the other end. This causes the Boy to jolt to a halt.

Give it to me, bitch! Thief!

The Girl: No.

Old Man: Give it to me! It's MINE!

The Boy: What's – ?! Let go, will you!

The Girl: (*to the Old Man*) They're going to destroy you – can't you see?

Old Man: You think I'm afraid of death?!

He tugs at the kaffiyeh, once.

The Boy: Why d'you have to do this?! Let him have it. It's his.

The Girl: (*to the Old Man*) I'm not letting go. Now listen to me, please. Come with me to the camps – don't waste your death in there. They will destroy you. There are old men in the camps. You will have friends. We will look after you.

There is a pause. Then the Old Man spits at her. She recoils but does not let go of the kaffiyeh.

Old Man: You kill me, then you want to take me with you!

The Girl: I don't want you to die in pain. I want you to die without that.

Old Man: (*after a moment*) I don't feel pain – whore.

There is a silence. The Girl drops the kaffiyeh. The Old Man hurriedly hauls it in and holds it tightly to his chest. The Boy does not move.

Woman: I thought you were going to show me what you could do.

The Boy: Yes. (*to the Girl*) Won't you come with me? We've come all this way.

The Girl shakes her head. The Boy looks to the Woman.

(*to the Woman*) She could come in, couldn't she? You wouldn't stop her – would you?

Woman: She will be given the same opportunity as you. I told you, we don't concern ourselves with the past. She need only give us a description of this boy and anything else she can tell us about him. Why should we stop her? The choice is hers.

The Boy: (*to the Girl*) See?!

The Girl: (*to the Woman*) I'm not telling you ANYTHING.

Woman: (*smiling embracingly*) As I say, it's your choice. No one's forcing you.

The Boy: In the New City we could forget all this. We could really do something. You and me. We could make something of ourselves, could make a fresh start. Leave everything else behind. It would be us.

The Girl walks away, the camera 'following' her with a whir.

(*to her back*) I'm not begging you.

The Girl: (*turning, tears in her eyes*) I don't want you to.

The Boy: (*looking at her*) Last time.

The Girl shakes her head. Then looks to the ground. The Boy continues to look at her.

Silence.

Woman: (*to the Boy*) Have you decided?

The Boy: (*looking towards the Woman*) Yes.

Woman: (*smiling embracingly*) I'll show you to immigration then.

She puts out a hand to him, as if to take his hand. She doesn't move towards him. The Boy starts to walk towards her. The camera pans to the Boy. The Old Man begins to struggle and scream. Although having difficulty in walking, the Boy takes no notice. The Girl exits towards the Droughtlands. The camera swings to view her. It stops. Then it pans back to the Boy who is still heading to the Woman's hand. The Old Man becomes more and more like a child thwarted by an adult.

Old Man: (*during the above*) No, I don't want to go! Don't want to go! Don't want – ! No! Don't want to g——o! No——o! (*ad.lib.*)

As the Boy reaches the Woman, she smiles sympathetically to the Boy, as if to say 'they can be trouble, can't they.' She drops her hand and exits to the New City. The Boy follows and exits. The Old Man's weakening screams can still be heard a moment. Then there is silence. The camera pans to the Droughtlands, slowly scans left and right, centres and then stops. Silence. Stillness.

WHEN SLEEPING DOGS AWAKE

Foreword by Chris Cooper

When Sleeping Dogs Awake (running at 2 hours) was devised and rehearsed with Geoff Gillham as writer/director at the Belgrade TIE, Coventry, and toured to 10-12 year olds in June and July 1988 (there were also evening community performances as part of the project too).

The play came out of a process examining systemic and 'street' racism. More specifically it explores what racism is, where it comes from, what it looks like and how it works. It also takes account of the history of imperialism and the post-colonial period.

Although the influence of Brecht is still present, it is much less so in this play than in Lessons. *When Sleeping Dogs Awake* represents a significant development from Geoff's earlier work, away from a more didactic form of theatre towards showing rather than telling. The use of metaphor is of particular importance.

From the first production two things remain fresh in my memory, my enjoyment of watching it and the actors' enjoyment of playing in it. When revisiting the play it is impossible not to get drawn into the interplay in the text between the 'dog-ness' of people and the 'human-ness' of dogs. I will never forget the absolute seriousness with which Bernard, the thoughtful though rather austere St Bernard, replies to Whip, the irritating Chihuahua: 'And don't call me Bernie'. This kind of playfulness, which cleverly inverts the truism that dogs begin to look like their owners, is the source of much delight and invention.

Once again the use of humour is central to the piece but, as with all Geoff's plays, it takes us into a deeper engagement with the serious content on offer. The play begins with a killing and ends with the dogs facing extermination at the hands of humans; the tragedy being that some of the dogs, including Bernard, have found a rope to tie themselves up with in the desperate and vain hope that it will win them favour with the Warden. This is a perfect example of the way to dramatise the Belgrade TIE's focus on how material conditions affect thought and actions and how people frequently hold ideas contrary to their real interests.

> **Warden**: They're over here in the central area. Some of them have tied themselves up for us! Over.
>
> **Goldie**: It's too late, Flick.
>
> **Flick**: We didn't understand in time.
>
> **Goldie**: Sorry.

The play is written for ten actors. It is easy to see why the play is ideal for youth theatre productions. It resonates with the Britain of today as it did with its audience 25 years ago, because the form of the play allows the content to resonate. It is use of metaphor and particularly the central metaphor of dogs that really opens up the relationship between being and consciousness contained in the image of dogs putting themselves on leads at the very point of being destroyed. The image highlights the relationship of dogs to their owners; the significance of the lead; the nature of their training in different situations; the way they are separated from each other; their social instinct, their trust in their owners. It would be possible to break down the action of play through these examples alone and extend the metaphor in the rehearsal room, in order to come at the content of the play.

The play takes place in the same location, a disused shopping precinct where the steady dripping of water from the roof serves to underline the sense of desolation and abandonment. Here the dogs live in the play's present and re-enact moments from the past. And although the original production had an elaborate set, the form of the play is flexible enough for the site to be recreated in other less ambitious ways.

To my mind a good production of the play will stand or fall by how the company uses the metaphor and how the actors portray the dogs. This is a challenge that any director, designer and above all actors should relish. It is not a question of costuming (in the same way as in *Lessons*) but of the interplay between dog-ness and human-ness. Perhaps the emphasis should be less on how the dogs look and more about how they behave.

Bernard: We have to learn self-control. We must choose to control our natures. Instead of actually wearing a lead, we should each walk around imagining we've got a lead on.

Whip: Sounds stupid to me.

Bernard: I do it! Each of us can chose between good and evil. You can't blame circumstances Flick. It's down to us, individually. God gave us the choice.

The play was first performed by the Coventry Belgrade Theatre in Education Company, Coventry in 1988.

Cast

Bernard, a St Bernard	Brian Bishop
Whip, a Chihuahua	Doreene Blackstock
Goldie, a Labrador	Sally Ellis
Flick, an Alsatian	Maxine Finch
Pug, a Pug	John Hazlett
Target, a Collie	Lindsay Johnson
Bounder, a Husky	Simon Nagra
Precious, a Poodle	Anthony Ollman
Lucky, a Spaniel	Melanie Sharpe
Dog Warden, a Human	Elliott Turner
Director	Geoff Gillham
Designer	Elliott Turner
Lighting Designer	Paul Bright
Stage Manager	Steve Miller
School Liaison Worker	Nigel Gilkes
Administrator	Maria Gee

Stray Dogs – may be played by male or female – indicated in text by she or he or him or her but gender is randomly selected for ease of reading and will depend on casting.

ACT ONE

A disused shopping precinct. A group of stray dogs are at rest. Some are sleeping. The dogs are Flick, Precious, Whip, Lucky, Bernard, Bounder, Goldie. Water drips from the roof. Silence.

Precious: Flick. . . (*no response*) Flick....

Flick: What?

Precious: Do you think the humans will ever pull this precinct down?

Flick: Stop worrying and go to kip.

Precious: Will they though?

Flick: Humans never do things quick. Spend their time arguing.

Precious: Oh.

Whip: (*trots over to Precious*) I heard they're bringing the bull-dozers tomorrow.

Precious: Oh no. (*panicking*) Bernard, they're going to bash it down. We'll have nowhere to go. Help! Wake up everyone! They're going to pull the shopping precinct down. (*no-one does*)

Bernard: Pipe down, Precious. She was having a joke with you.

Precious: Oh no. You rotten dog, Whip! You got me really worried then. My heart missed a beat.

Whip: Shame it didn't miss a lot more.

Precious: What you mean? (*pause*) Oh. Hey!

Flick: Leave off both of you. Whip, stop winding him up.

Precious: No fun being a stray dog. Be alright when my owner finds me.

Whip: She lost you deliberate.

Precious: No she didn't.

Whip: Did.

Flick: I said, leave off.

Precious: Didn't. (*Flick scowls. Precious lies down.*)

Whip: (*whispering*) Did.

Precious: (*whispering*) I'll get you later.

Peace returns. Pug arrives. They sense something's wrong.

Bernard: What is it Pug?

Pug: Bullet's dead.

Whip: (*incredulous*) Bullet? Blimey.

All look at each other.

Flick: How?

Pug: He was one of the best. No-one could put one over him. Not any of the humans, not any dog. One of the best was Bullet.

Flick: What happened Pug?

Pug: Killed. Murdered. Should have seen him. Lying by the bins behind Alma Road.

Precious: Oh no. (*starts running around*)

Bounder and Flick: Lie down Precious.

Lucky: What we gonna do!

Flick: By a human?

Pug: No. It was a dog.

Whip: What did he look like?

Pug: No question of that. A wild dog. A savage.

Whip: Was there lots of blood and stuff?

Lucky: Shut up Whip. Making me feel sick.

Whip: Was there though?

Pug: Throat ripped out. Fur all over the place. (*pause*) Had his eyes open. Like he was looking at me.

Bounder: Who done it Pug?

Pug: Don't you know?

Precious: Wasn't me. I was asleep.

Flick: Did you see him?

Pug: Don't need to have. (*Pug looks around*)

Bernard: This is terrible.

Whip: Who you looking for Pug?

Pug: You know don't you? (*Whip smiles*) That Target!

Flick: Now wait a minute...

Pug: Where is she, eh?

Goldie: Target couldn't have done that!

Pug: Who you trying to kid!?

Whip: Target done it.

Precious: (*like something unpleasant*) Urr...

Bernard: You can't go accusing dogs.

Pug: Come off it. Got to be her. She's the only savage round here.

Bounder: That's rubbish Pug.

Pug: 'Taint rubbish!

Bounder: Yes it is.

Lucky: Target wouldn't do that.

Pug: Should have seen the state of Bullet. Go and see if you don't believe me.

Whip: It's definitely her.

Bernard: Nothing's definite.

Bounder: Target wouldn't hurt a fly.

Flick: No. Bounder's right. Target's not that kind of dog.

Pug: Well, where is she then? Anyone seen her today?

Silence

Pug: No. See!

Lucky: She might have gone off... to...play in the park.

Goldie: Yeah. Target likes playing there.

Pug: All day?!

Precious: I don't want to go to the park.

Whip: Let's go and find her, eh Pug?

Flick: Now wait a minute.

Target enters, blood on her clothes, face and hands.

Pug: Now perhaps you'll believe me.

Silence

Lucky: Murderer! Murderer!

Pug: Animal.

Precious: You'd better clear off Target. Go on, shoo.

Flick: Shut up (*to Target*) How could you do it?

Pug: Little runt. Evil little beast. Shouldn't ever have been allowed into Goodlands in the first place.

Target makes to attack Pug. Other dogs come in between.

Yeah go on. You try it. Kill me like you did Bullet.

Bounder: Say you didn't do it.

Target: I did. And I'm not sorry.

Pug: Bet you aren't. Condemned out of her own mouth.

Flick: How could you do it?

Target: Easy.

Target moves towards Flick and thrusts him down onto the floor. She and Flick demonstrate the killing of Bullet.

He was lying by the bins. Sleeping. He'd been gorging himself. I knew what I was going to do. So I crept up on him. Slowly. 'Till I got very close. Like this. Then I grabbed him. Teeth in his neck. He woke up. Struggled. But I wouldn't let him go. I wouldn't let him go. Then he stopped moving.

Target gets up

He had it coming. If you had to run and hide every time Bullet appeared – you would've done it too. Every time he saw me there was some insult.....

Bernard: Bullet did that to everyone. That was his way.

Lucky: Yeah. He called me a wimp once.

Bernard: But you can't go around killing every dog that insults you.

Target: What was I supposed to do then?

Pug: Not come here in the first place.

Target: I was born here!

Pug: Don't give me that stuff. Nothing but an animal.

Bounder: Come on Pug, she was provoked.

Pug: Provoked! Whose side are you on, eh!?

Bounder: No-one's. I was just saying...

Pug: You a Target-lover are you? And Bullet still lying there, crying out for justice! If you'd seen his eyes you wouldn't be talking that twaddle. I seen 'em.

Lucky: Yeah, come on. Let's put her on trial.

Pug: Trial! She's guilty. She's already admitted it. I say she wants stringing up.

Bernard: Now just hold on Pug...

Pug: What you say? Precious? Whip? Lucky? Flick...

Bounder: No. You'd better get going Target.

Target: No I'm not leaving. I've had enough of running, kow-towing,

Target goes for Pug – restrained by others.

Bernard: Let's not get carried away...

Pug: Look at her. Ever seen a rabid dog. Well there's one, I'll tell you. They're all the same. You can't keep the beast in them down. It always comes out in the end. Humans know what to do with rabid dogs. Short and sweet.

Flick: Now stop this.

Pug: What is this! You all turning Target-lovers?!

Several dogs: No. Not us. Let's finish her. etc

Whip: (*presenting a rope*) Here you are Pug.

Flick: Put that away Whip.

Whip: No. Why should I?

Bernard: We don't want to get carried away.

Pug: Why are you protecting her Flick? I don't understand you. Nor you Bernard. Bullet was one of us. Right? He was our friend, wasn't he?

Flick: That's not the point.

Pug: Yes it is. But this Target isn't. She's not one of us. She's not Goodlandish is she?

Target: Yes I am.

Pug: None of us would do anything like what she's done, would we? We aren't like that. Look I'll tell you about the Targets of this world.

Bounder: You've told us before. Many times.

Flick: All right Bounder.

Pug: But you still haven't got it, have you! (*to all*) They aren't like us. When we discovered Shortlands, them Targets were just living wild, fighting each other; they didn't know anything. They didn't even know how to eat out of bowls. So the Goodlands humans had to teach them everything. Go on. I'll show you. You lot be the natives.

Lucky: What do we have to do?

Pug: Just bark at each other. Have a scrap or something....

They do.

Then the Goodlanders came. (*Flick/Precious*) and they tried to civilize them.

Target: This is rubbish. Where'd you get all this from?

Pug: It's in the history books. I read it, so shut up. The Goodlanders were great. They were brave and they were dead kind to animals, specially dogs and that. But Target's ancestors were pagans – they even ate each other when they were hungry.

Target: This is.....

Bernard: Let him have his say, Target.

Pug: Yeah, she don't like the truth.

Target: You wouldn't know the truth if it got up and bit you.

Pug: Don't you threaten me.

Whip: Get on with it Pug.

Pug: So eventually they tamed them.

Bounder bites a human.

But it was always there. Despite all the civilizing in the world. Anyway in the end, we gave them Goodlandish identity tags. Biggest mistake we ever made. Oh yeah they were grateful then. Cock-a-hoop. Cos they knew what they were going to do. Sly little beasts. Cos now they weren't satisfied with being

Goodlandish, they started to want to come over here. Thousands of them. It'd have been alright if it had just been one or two. But no. Thousands of them. I mean we were the sapheads – they were actually welcomed to Goodlands. Pat on the back, plates full of liver, the works. Course the humans wanted them, cheap to keep and that. You could keep two of them for one of us. So they got all the best owners, all the best kennels, Pal – with extra marrowbone. And what did we get, the proper Goodlandish dogs?? – Nothing. On the scrap heap, having to scavenge round back doors and that. 'Oy what about me?' Then they start thinking they're it, think they own the place, swanking around on posh leather leads, nice collars. And they keep coming. More and more of them till we're getting swamped with them. Goodlands used to be a lovely place before they came – now it's a cesspit. All because of them (*pointing at Target*). It's as bad as where they come from. They don't appreciate it, not like us. I mean take yesterday. I was outside the butcher's, round the back like you're supposed to, waiting in line for the bits – I'd been there at least 35 minutes. Butcher slings a bit out to us and one of these Targets comes up behind and rips it off me. Takes the food out of my mouth. And me an old dog. I mean that's not on is it? And now this with poor young Bullet. We're not in the jungle here. But the beast will out. They're just animals. Nothing but savages. All of them. And my Goodlandish heart cries out for justice. Justice!

Whip: (*after a pause, claps*) Good one Pug.

Precious: My owner's still looking for me anyway.

Lucky: Justice! We want Justice!

Target: You're sick Pug. Really sick. And you Lucky.

Pug: Don't like the truth, do you!

Target: That's not the truth. It's false from beginning to end.

Precious: Big words now. Hah!

Whip: What word?

Precious: False.

Whip: That's not a big word.

Precious: Isn't it?

Whip: No.

Precious: I thought it was.

Flick: Let's get on.

Precious: Yes. (*tongue out at Whip*)

Flick: Which bit are you saying is false?

Target: All of it. It's all lies.

Bernard: Be specific.

Target: Well for a start. They didn't fight each other. All the dogs used to live in a pack. My mother was a pup then. They used to do everything together – they used to roam the land freely together, hunt together and feed together. I'll show you. Precious, you pretend to be a gazelle – dead nervous, likely to take fright at the simplest thing.

Precious: Oo, I don't know if I'll be able to do that.

Flick: Try.

Precious: All right.

The dogs stalk the gazelle as a pack and bring it down to kill it.

Pug: Look at that, born killers.

Target: No. They only killed what they needed to live. No more. And when they'd fed, they'd groom each other's fur and then sleep together for warmth at night. Then the Goodlanders came.

She indicates Flick and Bernard as the humans. They demonstrate.

They saw the land was good and wanted it for themselves. For food, for the trees, for the stones beneath the earth. So they drove my mother and the other dogs off the land and fenced the land off. The dogs fought them. But the Goodlanders were much stronger and besides...... . they had guns.

One of the dogs is shot.

The dogs had never heard a gun before. So they retreated to the poorest land which the humans had no interest in. And the humans took everything from the land, and exploited it for their needs alone. While my mother and the other dogs began to starve. Weakened, they crept back to the fences.

Bernard: 'Look at those mangy dogs. They're back again.'

Target: Then they had an idea...

Flick: 'Supposing we could train those dogs... Like the ones back home...'

Bernard: 'They're killers Arnold.'

Flick: 'I know. But why not get them to kill for us..,'

Bernard: 'I say, Arnold. What an excellent notion. Save us the job of getting our food.'

Target: And that's what they did. They trained us.

Flick: 'Take the young ones, the healthy ones – we can train them easier.'

Capture of dogs. Offering bowls of food and putting them on leads.

Target: Those they didn't take, starved. So the Goodlanders trained then to do what they wanted.

Hunt. The gazelle is captured. The dogs pulled off.

Bernard: 'Again.'

The same. The dogs obey commands better than previously.

Target: After a while my mother and the rest learnt how to do what the Goodlanders wanted. They used our skills at hunting – but now to serve them.

Perfect hunt. Scraps thrown to the dogs, who fight over them.

And that's how they learnt to fight each other. At night the Goodlanders would lock the dogs up on their own. Their coats got dull and the dogs got thin.

The dogs are tied up.

Pug: Propaganda! Do we have to listen to this sob story stuff? I've heard it all before. All lies.

Bernard: I'm sure it happened sometimes Pug.

Target: (*to Bernard*) Rubbish, it happened everywhere!

Pug: Ha!

Bernard: Now don't go to extremes. I'm trying to help you.

Target: Oh yeah! (*going on with story*) After a time things got very bad. As dark fell the humans would sit on their verandas eating, smoking, drinking and telling civilized jokes...

Bernard: 'Have you heard the one about the Target dog who got lost in a wood?'

Flick: 'No, Rodney. What happened?'

Bernard: 'Didn't have a leg to stand on.' (*laughter from both*)

Target: ... while the dogs remembered the days before the Goodlanders arrived and the chains chafed their necks...

Flick: 'Wonderful place, Goodlandish Shortlands, wouldn't you say.'

Target: ... and the dogs began to get angry...

Bernard: 'First class.'

A dog gives a low growl and strains at the leash.

Flick: 'Not like home though.'

Bernard: 'Oh no.'

Ditto, a second dog.

Flick: 'Did you hear something then?'

Bernard: (*listens*) 'No. Did you?'

Ditto, a third dog.

Flick: 'There it is again.'

Bernard: 'I didn't hear anything.'

Ditto, a fourth dog.

Flick: 'You are sure the dogs are all tied up.'

Bernard: 'Well I... hope so.'

Target: Then one day a dog bit a human. Of course the dog was punished. But the Goodlanders knew it would never be the same again... It was time to leave. There was a big ceremony with much smiling...

The humans put down a food bowl. The dogs sidle up, smiling.

...and much patting of heads... and much talk of dogs being Goodlanders' best friends... but they were pleased to get out of Shortlands alive and the dogs were pleased to see the back of them. And so the Goodlanders went back to Goodlands.

Bounder: So how come you came here?

Target: Well, the dogs were pleased they'd gone but they soon realised the humans had taken everything and ruined the rest. The hunting grounds were barren, the woods had gone. There was nothing left. They'd left the dogs a desert. Then my mum saw a notice saying, 'Dogs wanted in Goodlands. Good homes offered. Must be good with children.' So she made the long journey here. Do you remember there used to be a shop along there?

Pointing down the precinct.

Precious: Oo yeah. Lovely smells. You used to nick biscuits and things from there, Whip.

Lucky: So did I.

Goldie: And me.

Whip: You didn't. You never dared.

Goldie: I did.

Whip: Goldie. You talk too much. Button it.

Precious: Lovely smells.

Target: I'm talking about my mother!

Bounder: Yeah, shut up you lot.

Target: Pug. You can be in this bit. You like humans so much.

Lucky: I'd like to be human.

Whip: Typical.

Bounder: (*to Lucky*) Why don't you shut up.

Lucky: No. Why should I?

Bounder: Cos I say so.

Lucky: Big deal.

(*Bounder makes a move at Lucky. Lucky winces.*)

Flick: Let's get on with it eh?

Whip: Yeah come on. Shut up you lot. Pug?

Target: In the shop. Whip, you can be my mother. Precious you come in to buy her.

Precious: All right. 'How much is than nice little doggie in the window?'

Pug: (*to Target*) How much?

Target: Three pound fifty.

Pug: 'Three pound fifty.'

Precious: 'Ooo. That's cheap. Hallo you're a pretty little thing aren't you. (*to the pet shop owner*) Not going to die on me or anything?'

Pug: 'No. Fresh in. Lovely little bitch.'

Precious: Pug. You shouldn't use bad language.

Pug: That's a proper word.

Precious: Is it? Are you sure?

Pug: Yeah. Get on with it.

Precious: 'You're a lovely little bitch aren't you. Nice nature. Ah look at that. She loves me, don't you. And I love you. (*to the pet shop owner*) Doesn't cost too much to keep does it? Don't want one that eats me out of house and home...'

Pug: 'Oh no. Very cheap to keep.'

Precious: 'I'll have her. (*pays money*) I'm going to call you Dolly.'

Pug: 'Do you want her doctored?'

Target: He never said that, Pug. That's you.

Pug: Well he should have done. (*flare up between them*)

Precious and Whip carry on while the flare up is sorted by Flick, Bounder and Bernard.

Precious: 'Do you want some food, Dolly? You're my dog now. Isn't that nice.'

Target: As time passed though my mother's owner began to change.

Pug: Here we go. Wicked and bad Goodlanders strike again.

Target: ... She couldn't afford to keep her.

Precious: 'I'd like to give you something but money's a bit tight at the moment. Maybe tomorrow. No I'm sorry I haven't got anything. Go on. Go away. Shoo! Shoo! (*Dolly whines outside*) Oh dear. (*lets her in*) I still haven't got anything. I'm sorry...'

Target: So my mother's owner decided to get shot of her.

Precious: 'Let's go for a nice walk shall we? In the park. The park. (*jangles lead*) Come on then... Fetch. Bye Dolly. Sorry. Can't keep you no more...' (*Belts off. Dolly barks, whines and whimpers.*)

Target: My mother gave birth to me behind a shed on the allotments. Here in Goodlands.

After a pause.

Whip: Brings tears to your eyes doesn't it Pug?

Target: I'm not asking you to feel sorry for us. I'm just saying that's how it was. OK?

Whip: Look at Goldie. She's crying.

Goldie: (*hiding tears*) I'm not.

Pug: I don't see how all this justifies you killing Bullet. S'got nothing to do with Bullet. Totally irrelevant.

Target: It's got everything to do with it!

Pug: No it hasn't. You still aren't a proper Goodlandish dog. Nothing can change that.

Lucky: No. You still murdered Bullet.

Target: It was self-defence.

Pug: Self-defence! Don't give us that! You decided to kill him. You consciously set out to do him in when he couldn't defend himself. These Targets are destroying our way of life. Civilized behaviour? They don't even know the meaning of the words. I tell you unless we put a stop to it now, we'll be finished. We'll become the minority, and civilized behaviour will go right down the pan. You (*to all of them*) want to have that on your conscience? (*the others not sure*) Look, we're not angels, nobody's saying that – but we have rules. Don't we? We have ways of going on and ways of not going on. These lot don't understand that. Be nice to them, they stab you in the back. Got to keep to the rules or what do you have? Anarchy. That's what.

Bernard: Pug's right there. Rules are rules.

Lucky: Anyone want to go to the park? I'm bored.

Precious: Yeah come on.

Flick: No one's going to the park till we've sorted this out.

Lucky: I want to go to the park.

Whip: What's anarchy Pug?

Pug: Doing what you like. Dog eat dog. Terrible.

Target: Yeh? And what about when Bullet attacked me, day before yesterday? Was that in the rules?

Pug: He didn't attack you.

Target: No!?

Pug: He was just having a joke.

Target: Is that what you call it! And you lot, what did you do?

Lucky: Nothing, we didn't do anything.

Target: No, you just stood and watched it happen. I didn't hear anyone talking about 'rules' then!

Lucky: That was different. I want to go to the park.

Target: Right here it happened in this shopping precinct.

Lucky: I hate this place. It's a real dump.

Precious: I don't remember. I don't think I can have been here the day before yesterday.

Target: Yes you were. You were there. (*she positions them all*) Flick. You be Bullet. You know what he was like. Pug you weren't there – you were with him when he arrived. I was playing with Goldie and Lucky.

Lucky: 'Let's go to the park. We could paddle in the pond. Then chase around shaking water all over the humans.'

Goldie: 'Yeah.'

Target: Then Bullet arrived....

Flick: (*sees Target – but ignores him*) 'Funny smell around here. Don't you think Whip? Bit like a second-hand clothes shop where the damp's got in. Someone peed themselves have they? What you think Goldie?'

Goldie: 'Yes.'

Flick: 'What you think Targie? (Target makes to leave) No need to dash off. (*Target stops*) Now you have paid us a visit. (*to Pug*) Do you want a bit of fun?'

Pug: (*salivating*) 'Yes.'

Flick: 'Pug wants to have a bit of fun, Target. How about you? (*Target says nothing*) Cat got your tongue? (*he and Pug laugh – the others giggle*) Well?'

Target: 'I gotta to go home.'

Flick: 'Cor blimey, it does talk! (goes up close to Target) You're a smelly little oik. You know that? Smelly... little ... oik. What you say to that? – Targie. (*no reply*) It's gone dumb on us again!'

'Bullet' makes a sudden movement at Target – who jumps – then walks away over to Goldie. Target weighs up making a dash.

'You thinking of leaving us again? Mummy Targie worried is she? (*looks at Target*) We haven't had any fun yet. Well Goldie, what do you fancy? (*he cocks an ear to Goldie who doesn't say anything – or says 'Don't know Bullet'*) Goldie wants me to twist off your ears. You got a wicked sense of humour haven't you Goldie! (*Goldie smiles/grimaces*) What's that Goldie? – Very slowly.'

Makes to go towards Target, who makes a run for it. 'Bullet' gets a hand to her – but she's away. 'Bullet' calls after her.

'See you tomorrow Target. Maybe I'll pay you a visit.'

Pug: (*after a pause*) Well if you can't take a joke once in a while....

Target: (*exasperated*) Oh...

Pug: ....you should stay away.

Target: It wasn't a joke!

Pug: It was.

Bounder: Knock it off Pug. Bullet was trying to provoke him.

Pug: No he wasn't.

Bernard: They're both as bad as each other if you ask me.

Target: And what about you lot! What are you as bad as?

Lucky: There was nothing we could do. He makes fun of us as well.

Target: It wasn't fun.

Lucky: Still wasn't anything we could do.

Whip: Bullet's Bullet, isn't he?

Pug: Wasn't he. Bullet's dead remember? And this Target killed him. Bullet never laid a finger on her. Let's get things right Bernard.

Target: He was going to.

Pug: (*sarcastic*) Oh yeah! 'Going to.' Who says?

Target: Me.

Pug: And that gives you the right to kill him does it?

Target: He was!

Pug: Well I think you might attack me – so I've got a right to kill you.

Flick: It's not the same Pug...

Pug: Why not?

Flick: (*to Target*) Look you knew Bullet didn't like you – so you should've kept out of his way...

Target: I don't want to spend my life like that! Keeping out of the way of humans is bad enough, now I've got to keep out of the way of dogs too!

Whip: You should stick to your own kind.

Flick: I'm trying to say something here.

Target: Well I thought after that on Wednesday – I'm not taking anymore. And since none of you was going to do anything about it – I'd have to do it myself. And I'm not sorry. Bullet was nothing but a thug and you lot were scared of him. So it was down to me.

There's a shocked silence. No-one knows what to say.

Flick: What you say about Bullet may be true....

Pug: It's a lie.

Flick: (*angry*) Stay out of this Pug. It might be true. But you should've taken no notice...

Target: But....

Flick: Let me finish for Pete's sake. We all knew Bullet was a bit cracked. But do you know why? I doubt it. Only Bernard, Pug and me knows about this. Bullet never talked about his upbringing but I'm going to show you something. When Bullet was little he was as gentle and, bright and lively and intelligent as any of us. It was his owner that ruined him. Go on Bernard, you remember Mr. Kitson.

Bernard tells a couple of dogs to position an old tv and gets himself a chair. He begins to play with 'Bullet' – played by Flick in such a way that 'Bullet' doesn't know how 'Mr. Kitson' is going to react.

Bernard: 'Come on Bullet.'

'Bullet' comes to him. He pushes him away violently.

'Come on. (*'Bullet' is unsure*) I'm not going to hurt you.'

'Bullet' races up to him. Violent 'play'.

Flick: As Bullet grew up, Mr Kitson began to get bored with him.

'Mr Kitson' turns on the tv and watches mindlessly. He eats as he watches. 'Bullet' wants to play. 'Mr Kitson' ignores him. 'Bullet' tries to get 'Mr Kitson's' food.

Bernard: 'Get off.'

Bullet retreats. Then comes again.

'Get off I said.'

'Bullet' begins to bark, getting in the way of the tv. At first 'Mr Kitson' ignores him. Then.

'Shut up.'

'Bullet' barks more. After a while, 'Mr Kitson' gets up, switches the tv off with irritation. Puts a lead on 'Bullet' and takes him out for a fast walk, tugging at 'Bullet' every time he stops to smell or urinate. They return home. 'Mr Kitson' switches off the tv. Once more 'Bullet' barks. 'Mr. Kitson' gets up and puts 'Bullet' out.

'Right, outside.'

He sits down and watches. After a moment, more barking. He ignores it. Then finally he opens the door and kicks 'Bullet'. 'Bullet' yelps and reels. 'Mr Kitson' slams the door and sits down. Gradually 'Bullet' transforms into an extremely savage dog, ready to kill anything which gets in his way.

Flick: That's what made him what he was. Mr. Kitson made him a right crackpot and then because he couldn't handle him, he just kicked Bullet out onto the street – (*to Target*) like your mother.

There is a pause – while they all consider what Flick has shown.

Bernard: (*ruminating*) Mm. I don't know Flick. It's all too easy to blame the humans.

Precious: Yes. Humans are nice.

Bernard: But, you see it doesn't hold water. Cause it was in Bullet's nature to be aggressive. It was because he was aggressive, Mr. Kitson couldn't handle him. I mean Bullet was a Doberman. It's his nature. Same for all dogs. Each has got to follow his own individual nature. I mean, take me – I'm not aggressive because I'm a St. Bernard. Not in my nature. My breed is very docile and I'm a slow – but deep – thinker. That's me. Whip's a Chihuahua – so you can't stop her hacking at your heels.

Whip: I don't hack at heels.

Lucky: Yes you do.

Whip: No I don't, dumbo.

Bernard: It's her nature...

Whip: (*to Lucky*) I'll get you after.

Lucky: Won't.

Bernard: And Target's naturally aggressive too, like Bullet. So they were bound to take a disliking to each other.

Flick: So then you're saying there's nothing anyone can do about it – killings are inevitable!!

Precious: Yes, Flick. And that's why we need owners – to keep us in order.

ACT TWO

Whip: But we haven't got owners Precious. Humans don't want us.

Precious: Mine does. She's still looking for me.

Whip: What makes you think you are so special?

Precious: I am. (*pause*) I'm specialer than you anyway.

Bounder: Pack it in you two.

Bernard: (*coming out of a deep think*) You see Flick you've raised a very interesting question there...

Whip: What was the question Bernie? So long ago I can't remember what it was.

Bernard: If it's in Bullet's and Target's nature to fight, is it inevitable they'll go on until one of them's killed the other?

Whip: Oh that.

Bernard: And don't call me Bernie. Bernard. And if so, can you blame them? Which implies personal responsibility.

Target: I'm not aggressive!

Pug: Huh!

Bernard: And being we don't have owners to control us – as Precious says – then we have to learn to control ourselves. (*looking principally at Target*) ...

Target: You should have told that to Bullet!

Bernard: We have to learn self-control. We must choose to control our natures. Instead of actually wearing a lead, we should each walk about imagining we've got a lead on.

Whip: Sounds stupid to me.

Bernard: I do it! Each of us can choose between good and evil. You can't blame circumstances Flick. It's down to us, individually. God gave us the choice.

Precious: Yeah.

Lucky: Let's go to the park.

Precious: Yeah.

Flick: No-one's going to the park.

94

Lucky: I want to go the park.

Flick: So what you're saying is, because we haven't got owners, we have to behave as if we did.

Bernard: Yeah. In a nutshell.

Flick: (*frustration*) But humans are the problem! They made us what we are! Look at Bullet! Look at how he was treated! Or at Target! She told us how the humans treated her dogs in Shortlands. Look at any one of us. You! We've been bred, our natures changed – sometimes out of all recognition by them. Then they train us, make us do what they want from the moment we're born. They train us so well we don't even know what we want. We think what we want is what we want. But it isn't. What we want is what they want us to want.

Bernard: Oh no...

Flick: Don't say oh no! Yes! Look, you said we should walk about imagining we've got a lead on. When we had owners they spent all their time training us not to need leads or chains around our necks. How did they manage that? Why didn't we all run away at the first opportunity?

Bounder: Because they fed us. We needed them.

Flick: (*irritated*) Well yes but that's only half of it – we could get food elsewhere. No, because they wrapped our brains in leads and chains. Then we come when our owners call – as if we wanted to. We don't have to imagine leads: they're already there in, in our heads.

Precious: But humans are kind! I would go – if I heard my owner calling.

Bernard: That still doesn't explain Bullet or Target. Target never had an owner.

Flick: But they still serve the Goodlanders' purposes. Bullet kept us divided among ourselves; and Target's killing Bullet doesn't change a thing but only goes to show how much we're supposed to need humans to keep us in order.

Bernard: I still think it's too easy to blame it all on the humans. Target should still know the difference between right and wrong. And killing dogs is wrong.

Flick – tosses away like a lost cause. Whip sniggers.

Bernard: Don't be like that Flick.

Flick: It's pointless arguing with you.

Pug: All this talk is all very well. The question is what we're going to do about him.

Flick: Nothing. Let her go.

Various dogs: What? You gone mad Flick? etc etc

Flick: What good will it do? (*She mooches away.*)

Pug: I think you've taken leave of your senses, Flick. (*to all*) I've said it before and I'll say it again. This Target is evil. And you can't get away from that. If we don't do something, she'll do it again when someone else says something she doesn't like.

Target: Bullet attacked me!

Pug: We've been over that. As Bernard says, if she can't control herself we've got to do it for her. None of us will be able to sleep safe at night otherwise.

Whip: Yes. Let's hang her now. (*Flick is jolted back to life*)

Flick: No.

Bernard: Look, supposing Target promised never to do anything like it again...

Pug: What?! You gone stark-staring... ? Promise?! She'd say anything.

Lucky: I've just thought. What are the humans going to do when they find Bullet? They'll go spare.

There is panic. Finally Flick establishes order.

Flick: Stop it all of you.

There is a moment's quiet.

Bernard: (*loudly*) Calm down.

Lucky: (*after a moment*) They don't know who did it. They'll put the blame on all of us. Oh dear.

Panic. Barking.

Flick: Quiet all of you. Do you want to bring the dog warden here?

Concentrated silence – they check to see if anyone's coming.

Bounder: Why don't we go and get Bullet's body and hide it somewhere?

Lucky: They might have found it already.

Precious: I'm not going anywhere near those bins.

Bernard: No. We shouldn't do anything suspicious. We should just behave ourselves and keep out of their way. Let sleeping dogs lie.

Pug: Bullet's not asleep. He's dead. (*looks at Target – malevolently*)

Whip: I know. Why don't we give Target to them?

Bounder: No we're not doing that.

Whip: Why not? We could take her to where Bullet is, tie her leg to a post or something, with a rope, then bark as loud as we can like we're having a scrap. Then before the wardens come, scarper so they only find Target and Bullet. She's still got the blood on her. Then we're all off the hook.

Pug: Yeah kill two birds with one stone.

Lucky, Precious, Pug and Whip converge on Target. Flick and Bounder try to intervene. Goldie doesn't know what to do. Bernard is saying...

Bernard: I think we should vote on it. I think we should vote on it.

Bounder: We're all under threat – even if Target is taken, they won't be satisfied. 'All dogs must be kept on leads', remember?!

Pug: Yes and who's to blame. She is!

Bounder: No. They brought in the dog warden and put up the notices before Target killed Bullet.

Pug: Rubbish!

Bounder: Isn't!

Lucky: What are we going to do? (*close to tears*)

Silence.

Bernard: (*with little conviction*) Maybe nothing will happen.

Lucky: 'Maybe'.

Whip: (*to Bernard*) Haven't you got any better ideas?!

Silence.

Lucky: I wish Bullet were here. He'd know what to do.

Precious: Yeah. Do you remember when those signs went up?

Whip: Put a sock in it, Precious.

Precious: No! Why should I! Everyone else can say things!

Goldie: Yeah let him speak! (*under breath*) Always telling dogs to shut up. (*look of surprise from Whip and others*)

Precious: Anyway, I was out doing a bit of sniffing, minding my own business and Bernard was with me – come on Bernard –

Bernard: Oh...

Precious: Come on, don't be lazy – and we were chatting about this and that when Bernard goes 'Someone's been round here. Humans.' And it was one of those notices.

Bernard ambles into the action.

Bernard: Someone's been round here. Humans. (*they see the notice*) 'All dogs must be kept on leads. By order.' Oh dear this means trouble.

Precious: Trouble Bernard?

Bernard: This means they aren't happy with the way we've been going on. Getting too rowdy. Oh dearo-dearo me. There's going to be trouble.

Precious: (*to them*) But I thought: (*to Bernard*) No it doesn't mean that Bernard. They don't mean us at all because they don't think we can read.

Bernard: What you talking about Precious, it's plain as the nose on your face what it means.

Precious: No, that notice is for dog-owners. Telling them to keep their dogs on leads. It doesn't apply to us, we haven't got owners. (*to them*) Silly of me, really.

Bernard: It says 'all dogs', Precious. Not 'all dogs with owners' All dogs.

Precious: (*to them*) Then Pug waddled up.

Pug: I don't waddle.

Precious: Yes you do, come on.

Pug: What's going on?

Bernard: Notice.

Pug: 'All dogs must be kept on leads. By order.'

Precious: Doesn't apply to us, does it Pug?

Pug: Course it does. It means we're going to get owners at last.

Precious: Does it?

Pug: Course.

Bernard: Means trouble, Pug. I tell you. It means trouble.

Pug: Rubbish. Goodlanders have decided to do something for us at last. Going to give us owners. We'll get beautiful leather leads and collars with metal studs in....

Precious: Beige fluffy ones. Oo!

Pug: I knew they'd see us right.

Precious: (*dancing up and down*) We're going to get owners. I'll get mine back again. She's been looking for me all this time! (*to them*) Then Bullet turned up. And do you know I was wrong. And Bullet saw it straight away.

Flick: (*as Bullet*) 'What's going on then?'

Precious: We're going to get owners and leads and...

Flick: 'Who wants an owner! You don't want one do you!?'

Precious: No.

Flick: 'Bernard? Pug – you don't want an owner do you?! (*Pug shrivels, and shakes his head*) Anyway where did you get this pea-brained idea from?'

Precious: (*pointing at notice*) There.

Flick: (*looks at notice – but can't read*) 'Yeah? So? What's that got to do with us, then, eh? Eh?'

Bernard: Seems plain enough to me, Bullet.

Flick: 'Yeah?' (*looks at notice – back to Bernard – to Pug*)

Pug: It says 'All dogs to be kept on leads. By order.'

Flick: 'Yeah, yeah. I can read.'

Bernard: Means trouble, Bullet.

Flick: 'By order'! Whose order? No-one gives me orders. I'm not wearing no lead for no-one. (*pause*) Shall I show you what I think of that.'

He sprays over it and laughs.

Bernard: I wouldn't do that if I were you, Bullet.

Flick: 'Yeah, well you're not me are you!'

He leaves. Precious sprays.

Precious: (*to them, triumphant*) See?!

Bounder: See what?

Precious: Bullet would have known what to do!

Bounder: Yeah, but what good did it do?

Precious: I don't know!

Lucky: He stood up to them, that's what.

Precious: Yeah.

Bounder: Spraying on their sign?!

Target: They weren't after him anyway. They were after me!

Flick: They were after us all! All dogs...

Target: They were!

Pug: You just got a chip on your shoulder, you. They liked you. They thought you were lovely.

Target: Then why did they come after me, and not you or you? I was just tugging this chip packet open outside the fish and chippy on Haffon's Way. (he does it) I wasn't causing anyone any trouble and then one of these new wardens...

Pug: Animal Welfare Officers to you.

Target: ...comes up and he's standing there in front of us.

Bounder and Target show it. Target has his nose in a piece of newspaper. 'The warden' strolls up to her. She looks up but takes no particular notice. 'The warden' stops. She looks at him quizzically. He smiles at her.

Bounder: 'There you go. Where's your owner then? Hm?'

He holds out his fist for Target to smell. She pulls back a little.

'Not gonna hurt you...'

He continues to offer the fist. Target sniffs it. He touches her and then moves his hand round her head towards the scruff of her neck. He makes reassuring sounds. Suddenly he grabs her.

'Got you. You little. . . In that van...'

Target bites his arm. He lets go in shock, holding the bitten wrist.

'Aah! I'll get you!!'

Target runs off.

Target: ...and if I hadn't have bit him he would've had me in the back of his van, and I've had had my chips instead of the packet.

Bernard: Yes but you must've been doing something.

Target: I wasn't.

Whip: You bit him.

Target: That was after.

Whip: But you still bit him. You asked for it.

Bernard: How do you know he wasn't going to give you some food or something?

Target: He grabbed me by the scruff of my neck, he was shouting at us.

Bernard: I still say you must've been doing something to get up his nose.

Target: I wasn't.

Pug: For once I've got to agree with her. That animal welfare officer was looking after our welfare. They were trying to do us a good turn. They don't like Targets and such like, any more than we do. They're on our side.

Target: A few minutes ago you were saying they 'loved' me!

Pug: Yeah, well I changed my mind. Goodlanders have got more sense these days..

Flick: They are after us all. You (*Target*) were just the first.

Target: (*thrown away*) Oh so it was just a coincidence was it?

Lucky: It's not just you anyway. They got that dog from number 37, 'cause she wasn't on a lead.

Flick: Why didn't you tell us about this before?

Lucky: I wasn't there. Goldie told me.

Flick: (*to Goldie*) Why didn't you tell us?

Goldie: I told Lucky.

Flick: Well tell us about it now.

Lucky: I want to tell it. .

Flick: I don't care who tells it – we just want to know.

Lucky: I'll tell it.

Whip: Big mouth.

Lucky: Stop picking on us.

Whip: I'm not. I pick on everyone.

Flick: Can we hear what happened?

Lucky: I'm going to be the animal welfare officer.

She adjusts her uniform then struts up and down.

Whip: That's nothing like one.

Lucky: It is!

Bernard: Quiet Whip.

Whip: I'll be the prissy dog from number 37 then.

Lucky: You were there Pug. And you Precious. You were looking for owners.

Pug: No I wasn't (*getting into position*).

Lucky becomes the warden.

Precious: If you want to get an owner, you've got to look beautiful, like me! (*he begins to tidy Goldie's hair.*)

Pug: I am beautiful.

Precious: No, you're not. You've got scabby skin.

Goldie: Oo there's an owner. Look (*pointing at Lucky*).

Precious: I think she's looking for me.

They all try to look beautiful.

Goldie: Hallo!

Pug: Look at them epaulettes! Cor! (*He makes his way towards 'the warden'.*)

Precious: Come back, Pug, you'll put her off. She wants me.

Goldie: She wants me.

Pug: No she doesn't. She wants me.

Precious: Doesn't. Me. (*to 'warden'*) Oo-hoo!

Pug: Got a longer pedigree than you, anyhow.

The 'dog from number 37' arrives in front of them.

Precious: Oy, get away.

Goldie: You've got an owner. Go on, get away.

A minor scrap begins which attracts the attention of 'the warden'. She moves towards them. the dogs show off to her.

Lucky: 'Here, doggie, doggie (*holding out fist to 'no.37'*).'

Goldie: That's not fair, she's got an owner.

Precious: Look at me!

Suddenly 'the warden' grabs 'no.37'.

Lucky: 'Got you. In that van'

She slams the door. The other dogs scatter.

Flick: (*to Goldie*) And what happened to her?

Lucky: Mrs. Pottinger went and reported her lost and then she found her and everything was alright. Wasn't she Goldie?

Goldie: Yes.

Bernard: I said those notices meant trouble.

Lucky: No she was alright.

Bernard: No...

Whip: What Bernie means is what if the dog warden had got one of them (*pointing to Pug, Goldie and Precious*)?

Bernard: Bernard.

Whip: No owner to 'find' you...

Precious: (*worried*) Ohh...

Flick: This is serious.

Bernard: I think we'd better all behave ourselves – that includes you Whip – until this trouble dies down.

Whip: That could be ages.

Bernard: No barking, no scrapping, no sniffing around chip packets, no waiting outside Butchers … just … do nothing … keep out of their way.

Bounder: No breathing! It's impossible!

Bernard: We don't have any choice in the matter.

Bounder: And if we don't?

Bernard: (*very gloomy*) I don't know.

Goldie: I do.

Whip: Who asked you Goldie?!

Goldie: Nobody.

Whip: Well go back to sleep.

Goldie: (*to Flick*) I heard!

Flick: What? What did you hear?

Goldie: It was when I was under the community centre over by the park. I was getting a ball out.

Whip: Boring!

Flick: Hold on a minute Goldie. (*goes over to Whip*) You open your mouth again without my permission and I'll stuff Pug down it.

Precious: Ugh!

Pug: What?!

Flick: (*ignoring them*) Now you shut it. (*to Goldie*) Now go on Goldie. What happened? (*she's still looking at Whip, who's got her head very low*)

Goldie: There was this meeting.

Flick: When was this?

Goldie: Just before the notices went up.

Flick: Show us what they said.

Goldie: (*organising them*) Pug, you be Mr Hurd; Lucky you be Mrs Gould; can Whip be in it Flick? She could be that horrible Norman what's-his-name who hates dogs…

Flick: Yes. She'll do him well.

Goldie: I'll be Mrs Willis who likes dogs. And Bernard you can be Mr Williams who was in charge of the meeting.

They set up a committee.

Bernard: 'Well we all know why we're here. We're all gravely concerned over the growing number of stray dogs in Goodlands. Who would care to speak first?'

Lucky: 'Well yes, Mr Chairman, I should like to say a word or two. Only last night there was a terrible racket outside my bungalow and I looked outside and what did I see but – it must have been half a dozen or so dogs – chasing round barking and careering all over the place. One of them even jumped over my garden wall and was scratching away at my front lawn. Most distressing. I mean it was past midnight. It kept me awake most of the night. And 'Lady' was upset too. And another thing, when I take 'Lady' out for a walk you get all sorts coming up, sniffing around and she doesn't like it and neither do I!'

Bernard: 'Yes, Norman.'

Whip: 'They want clearing off the streets once and for all. Fouling the footpath. You can't get from the supermarket to the car park without wheeling your trolley round their doings. Nothing but vermin. No use to anything, nor anyone. They want getting rid of.'

Bernard: 'I see. Yes Mrs. Willis.'

Goldie: '(*to Whip*) May I ask, do you have a dog yourself, Norman?'

Whip: 'No. Certainly not.'

Goldie: 'I thought not. Well I do and I'm a dog-lover. We have to be careful about generalising. There are dogs and there are dogs. To be perfectly frank with you I know some dog-owners who let their dogs foul the footpath, others have their dogs well trained. Then we have the stray ones. It's not their fault you know. We've let them down.'

Pug: 'With all due respect – through the Chair – we're getting off the point. However they got there, we're not concerned. The thing is they have to be disposed of.'

Lucky: 'If you mean what I think you mean, Mr Hurd, I couldn't be a part of that. I'm sorry. (*Pug indicates to speak*) I haven't finished. What we need is a dog refuge in Goodlands.'

Goldie: 'Hear, hear!'

Lucky: 'Then we could have them off the streets, and the strays could be looked after properly. There might even be people who would have them and care for them.'

Whip: 'That'd cost a lot of money...'

Bernard: 'Through the Chair if you please Norman. (*to Pug*) I'll come to you in a moment Mr Hurd.'

Whip: 'All I was saying was, it'd cost a lot. I know a fella with a van who could. pick 'em up, and bob's your uncle – end of problem.'

Pug: 'Norman is quite correct, so I don't think we should pretend to be horrified. Who's going to pay for a dog refuge? Then you'd need dog wardens or whatever they call them now. All costs money. Then irresponsible dog owners who didn't want their dogs would. Just set them loose in the sure knowledge the rate-payers would pick up the bill. The problem would just get worse.'

Bernard: 'Mrs Willis.'

Goldie: 'I still don't think it's right just rounding them up, Chair, and putting them down. It's barbaric.'

Bernard: 'Mr Hurd.'

Pug: 'We'll have to do it in the end. Why prolong the agony for them? Look I'm a dog-lover. I have two Rottweilers, perfectly behaved. We'd be doing these unwanted dogs a kindness. Really. Not to mention the relief it would bring to 'Lady', Mrs Gould.'

Bernard: 'The floor is yours.'

Lucky: 'I see what you mean but I couldn't go along with that. We fought the Nazis to stop things like that!'

Pug: 'They're only dogs; for God's sake!'

Bernard: 'Mr Hurd. Please. Language.'

Pug: 'Sorry. My apologies.'

Lucky: 'No offence taken.'

Bernard: 'Well. Time is getting on. Do we have a proposal to vote on? (*Pug indicates*) Mr Hurd.'

Pug: 'I propose we round them up and dispose of them. Simple as that.'

Discomfort from Lucky, Bernard and Goldie.

Bernard: 'Any other... proposals? Mrs Gould?'

Lucky: 'I suggest we put up notices saying that all dogs should be kept on leads and – employ an animal welfare officer. But not the refuge. That is too dear, I agree.'

Whip: 'What'll the dog warden do with them?'

Bernard: 'Please Norman, through the Chair.'

Lucky: 'We'd leave that to him.'

Bernard: 'Good. A vote: proposal one – to round them up and 'dispose' of them. Those in favour? (*Whip and Pug*) Those against? (*Lucky and Goldie*) Oh dear (*All look at him. He votes against*) Against. Right Mrs Gould's proposal? (*all vote*) Carried unanimously. I'm so pleased. Shall we retire to the bar?'

Flick: Why didn't you tell us this before?!

Goldie: Nobody asked.

Flick: Oh Goldie.

Bounder: It's alright they're not going to do anything. They voted against getting rid of us.

Precious: Yes. They're dog lovers. Goodlanders wouldn't do that.

Goldie: No, that's not all there was.

Bounder and Flick: What?

Goldie: Those two stayed behind after the others had gone, and Mr. Hurd told that Norman what's-his-name to get the van ready anyway. Because when there was more trouble Mrs. Gould and Mrs. Willis would come round to their way of thinking. And he said to be sure to make the back of the van air-tight. I don't know what he means.

Target: They are going to kill us with poisoned gas.

Lucky: Bullet. When they find Bullet they'll go bananas. They're going to kill us. Flick, they're going to kill us.

There is silence.

Whip: I'm getting out. I'm not sticking around. You lot can do what you like.

Flick: Calm down.

Whip: Every dog for himself.

He makes a run but Bounder stops him.

Flick: Stop it all of you. We've got to stick together.

Lucky: Yes we should split up. They can't catch us all. If we split up.

Target: No we should stick together and fight them.

Whip: What, you must be crazy. They'll mash us.

Precious: (*who by this time has found a rope and put it round his neck*) I've got a lead on. They won't touch me.

Bounder: Are you serious!

Precious: Come on everyone. Put leads on.

Pug: That Target's to blame for all this. Let's finish her now. Show the humans we can sort out our own trouble.

He goes for Target.

Target: You keep away from me Pug.

Flick: Stop fighting among ourselves.

Precious: (*who has found some more rope*) Here you are Goldie – Lucky. Put this round your neck. We'll tie ourselves to the pillars (*he's doing it*) then we will be on leads!

Goldie and Lucky begin to do it.

Flick: Stop doing that!

Lucky: Stop giving orders! You're not in charge!

Bernard has found some rope.

Whip: Yeah, you think you're the leader of the pack now Bullet's gone.

Flick: Bernard, stop doing that. Bounder, Target – get that rope off them.

Whip is now tying herself up too.

Bernard: Each dog has got to decide for himself Flick. We're all individuals.

Flick: Individuals! We're all dogs! We're all dogs!

Amid the melee, sound of radio receiver.

Radio: Come in A.W.O.3. North gateway to precinct rendered fully secure. What is your position? Over.

Goldie: (*very soft*) It's the dog wardens.

Warden: (*off*) Half-way down the South entrance. I'm sure they're in the central area.

All the dogs are absolutely still and frightened.

Probably lying doggo. (*he laughs*) Over.

Radio: Advance with caution A.W.O.3. A.W.O.7. bring up the extra men. We want them all, remember.

Suddenly a torch beam falls on the dogs.

Warden: They're here in the central area. Some of them have tied themselves up for us! Over.

Goldie: It's too late, Flick.

Flick: We didn't understand in time.

Goldie: Sorry.

Flick: It's not your fault Goldie. Not your fault.

Radio: Right. Have 'em.

The lights go – except torch which flashes across the dogs rushing about – much barking. Torch out. Suddenly, music from Pink Floyd's 'Dogs' is heard, very loud, starting at the point in the track at the echo immediately following the lyric 'Weighed down by the stone'.

LESSONS

Author's Note

This play was suggested by Kafka's short story 'A Lecture to the Academy'. It should not, however, be taken in any way as an adaption of that story. In my view, Kafka's and my own purposes are quite distinct, as are the characters of the respective Peters. Nevertheless, I would like to record here my debt to Franz Kafka and his extraordinary story. *G.G.*

Foreword by Chris Cooper

Lessons (running at 2 hours) is a play about education or, more specifically, a play which asks what is education, what is the relationship between class and ideology in schooling, and how far is education to do with the needs of the student and how far with society's requirements?

It was devised and written in the latter part of 1981. It opened in the first week of March 1982 for fourth and fifth year students (years 10 and 11), and ran in repertory until 1983.

The play was written and produced in a period when class antagonisms were clearly defined and felt. *Lessons* was created at the time of the Brixton and Toxteth riots, mass unemployment (which raised the question of what young people were being educated *for*) and Thatcher's election winning Malvinas/Falklands war.

In that sense it is a political play of its time and is rather didactic. The form and structure of the play is very Brechtian, and perhaps could even be viewed as a contemporary 'learning play'. Whether the play is any more successful in achieving its stated aim than Brecht was with his *Lehrstücke* is open to debate. It is noticeably different in form and content to the later work contained in this volume but is a useful and engaging introduction to Geoff's earlier work, demonstrating his skill as a writer and his confident manipulation of form to convey big and complex ideas.

However, as you might expect from a play in which an ape evolves into a human being in one generation, *Lessons* is also mischievously inventive and can engage and delight. There is plenty in it for production and adaptation today.

The central conceit of the play – that Peter Mann, an elderly academic giving a lecture with the assistance of the 'young actors' of the Cockpit TIE Team – works well and has huge potential for engaging the audience in a manner that would still be considered radical in mainstream theatre 30 years later. Furthermore, because the lecture is being dramatised for Peter Mann by the actors, the drawing back and forth of a curtain to reveal the stylised set pieces is a simple and effective convention that could lend itself to a less lavish and portable use of set design. And while the play was written to be played by only four actors, there are in total 20 roles that could be made available to a larger cast of actors or a youth theatre and which could be extended at key moments such as the expedition, on ship, at the docks etc and amongst the audience itself.

Any contemporary production, like the first, would however have to take care to focus on the tragi-comedy of the play. This is when it is at its most moving and human. Humour is critical to *Lessons*. It is part of the structure of the play and includes Peter Mann's on-going dialogue with the actors and production team as he delivers the lecture. It is central to the text too. To break free from the cage in which he has been cruelly imprisoned, Peter determines to become fully human, and ultimately succeeds,

> **Peter:**....as time went on I had learnt all that distinguished man from the apes: to be tolerant of other people's points of view, to rationally argue when I disagreed with something someone said, to value the unique talents of every single individual, to look with sympathy and concern on those less fortunate than myself. Scientists, as I told you, marvelled at my development.

The irony of this is deeply felt, as Peter discovers that the human attributes and sensibilities he has learned puts him in conflict with the human world and cannot comprehend why. This is his tragedy.

The 'chimping' of Peter Mann and the other performers is essential. Tag McEntegart (the original Production Manager/Lighting and Sound Designer) notes in a letter about the production that Peter's costume was a nightmare to get right but critical to the meaning of the play and that the chimpanzee behaviour was 'very well and sensitively done, not done for comic effect at all, but in fact the opposite...The actors had coaching from a dancer/choreographer.' Playing *Lessons* **not** for comic effect is the key to opening up this play for an audience to be engaging, useful and relevant.

Lessons was first performed at the Cockpit Theatre, London in 1982

There were two casts:
Harry Miller, Dave Swapp, Elsa O'Toole, Lynne Aston
Harry Miller, Dave Swapp, Margot Leicester, Anne Yuille
Writer and Director/Cockpit TIE Team Leader: Geoff Gillham
Designer: Marion Davies
Costumes: Vivienne Jones
Production Manager/Lighting and sound design: Tag McEntegart
Production Assistants: Richard Jarvis, Michael White
Schools Liaison Officer: Rachel Dawson

CHARACTERS (in order of appearance)

Peter Mann
(a group of actors who play the following parts from Peter's autobiography)
A large female chimpanzee
A young female chimpanzee
Lionel Shirley-Smythe (an explorer)
Salty (his aide)
A black porter
Fred (an old seaman)
Badger (a seaman)
Jimmy (a young seaman)
Captain Arkwright (ship's captain)
Mr. Appleyard (the owner of a variety show)
Docker
Miss Keilich (an animal trainer)
Susanne (a variety artiste)
Mr. Simpkins (her rehearsal pianist)
First chimpanzee (in the zoo)
Second chimpanzee (in the zoo)
Third chimpanzee (in the zoo)
Ms. Yvonne Yarrow (a psychotherapist)
Chauffer

PART 1

When the audience are settled, a spotlight comes on a small, quite elegant table with a wooden stool behind. On it stands a glass of water and a glass jug of clean water. The whole is to one side of the acting area. With hardly a pause Peter Mann walks from one of the entrances down to the table. He is carrying a small briefcase, slightly dog-eared, and a couple of books too large for his briefcase. He is dressed in evening dress which looks a little worse for wear but by no means scruffy. His shirt is white and perfectly starched. His bow-tie is discreet, but not white or black. Say, dark blue with beige spots. His shoes, though well-worn, are well polished. He is old but difficult to precisely age. His hair is on the long side, greying around the temples, but carefully groomed, growing down onto, out of, his forehead and bushy eyebrows. Hair also grows around his neck and up towards the cheek. His ears protrude through his hair, and his chin and lips are somehow pushed forward. In short, he has something of the facial features of a chimpanzee. His hands are somewhat hairy. He arrives at the table, places the books on it and the briefcase beside it. He adjust his shirt-cuffs.

Ladies and gentleman: It is not an exaggeration to say that I feel honoured to have been asked to come here this morning[1] to speak to you about myself, my education and my life. For it is without intention to flatter you that I say that to address a group of young people, such as yourselves, *is* one of the highest honours for an old man. Young minds learn; old ones never have. (*He runs his finger between the back of his neck and his collar.*) Now, before I start, I hope you will allow me to offer thanks to one or two people without whom this little talk of mine would have been at worst, impossible, and at best, shall we say, indigestible. So I would like to thank the young actors here at the Cockpit[2] who not only were so kind as to think my story one that would be of some interest to you but, in the capable hands of Miss Leicester[3], their producer, have

---

1 This should accord with the actual time of day: afternoon, evening.

2 First performed at the Cockpit, London. All references should be changed to the actual theatre performing the play.

3 Substitute the name of the actual director.

patiently and painstakingly rehearsed reconstructions of certain moments of my education. In this way you will be able to see what happened rather than hear it related, which can be, I know, extremely dry, not to say dull. Should it nevertheless prove to be so, let me say at once that that will neither be the fault of the actors nor of yourselves as witnesses, but rather of the story itself, the responsibility for which lies either with me or with life itself. And for which let me apologise in advance, should you find it dull. (*He takes a small sip of water.*)

Lastly, I should like to thank Mr. Stubbs[4], the Chief Education Officer, for allowing me to address you in the role of, how can I say, of a lecturer. Since I have no formal teaching qualifications, he could easily have prevented me from being involved with this project of the Cockpit Team, most particularly in speaking to you, and especially since its subject, is education and therefore one about which less enlightened men than Mr. Stubbs would certainly have insisted that only suitably qualified people could speak. However in the event, he waived this requirement and has kindly consented to my being here in front of you today.

(*He adjusts his shirt cuffs. He then picks up his briefcase, places it on the table, opens it and draws out a sheaf of tidy handwritten notes, places them on the table neatly, closes his briefcase, puts it back in its original position, and, for the first time, stands behind the table.*)

The Cockpit Team have asked me to give an account of the life I formerly lead as an ape. And this I shall now attempt to do, though I must confess my memory of that time is somewhat hazy. Were this all I had been asked to do, I should certainly have refused. There are, to be sure, eminent zoologists who know a great deal more than I on the subject. They have, after all – some of them – made a life's work of studying different species in the natural habitat of the creatures or in the (*slightest pause*) laboratory. However, the Cockpit Team also asked me to tell you something of how I made the transition from what I formerly was, to what I am now. In short, how I became a human being. (pause) So, at last, let us begin. With my beginning.

(*He walks over to the white curtain and draws it back towards where the table is. He speaks as he does so. Also as he does so there is the sound of exotic birds which continues throughout the scene. The light is beautiful. The acting area is, in fact, a white curtained box. On the back curtain is projected a painting in Rousseau style of jungle undergrowth – large fern fronds, beautiful birds and insects. In the acting area are three chimpanzees. A large female, and two younger ones, male and female. There is one large solid mound – a termites' hill – the action of this scene is described later, below. The female has an infant clinging to her fur round her belly – this cannot be seen at first. The prevailing*)

---

4 Omit this section, down to 'in front of you today', if not performed to school pupils. Otherwise change to the name of the actual Education Officer and Local Authority.

picture is one of unconscious, social being... but it should it should be performed as accurately as human actors can do. Peter watches the scene after his introductory remarks, much as one watches home movies – occasional remarks punctuating periods of shared quiet watching, impromptu.)

Please remember these are not real apes you are seeing. Actors only. Reconstructing my earlier former life. It would be impossible to bring real apes into the theatre, under the lights and so on, and expect them to perform as human beings can.

(The Mother Chimpanzee is eating fruit, in a relaxed manner. The Younger Female is watching the infant round her belly and occasionally the Mother. The Younger Male is grooming himself by the termite hill, back to the audience.)

These are just part of a group, you will understand.

(The Younger Female puts out a tentative hand towards the infant. The Mother pushes the hand away. The Younger Female whimpers briefly, softly. Pause. The Mother leaves her fruit to one side and lies back with the infant on her tummy. She looks at it and tickles it.)

(excitedly) There you are: see the tiny one? See him clinging on? That's me. Nearly three months old. *(a little ruefully)* He's only a dummy – I hope that is all right.

(The Young Male saunters over towards the Young Female.)

Oh-oh. Trouble! Brother wants to play.

(The Young Male jumps on the Young Female; they play-fight, she trying to get away. Young Male is pant-laughing. Young Female squealing but not enjoying it much. The Mother gets up after being knocked into and gives a dirty look to the Young Male. She walks away. She lies down again and grooms the infant, sucking the top of his head briefly. The Young Female flees the Young Male and sits again with the Mother. The Young Male looks across but decides not to follow. He turns away and goes. The Young Female who has continued to watch the infant, now begins to groom the other's back gradually during the following, working round to the region of the infant. The Young Male returns carrying three straight twigs about 6 inches long.)

Termites! I used to love them. Could sit for hours fishing for them.

(The Young Male sits by the termite hill, puts his twigs down. He rubs the hill above a hole with his index finger. He then selects a twig and carefully lowers it about 4 inches into the hill. He holds it there for a moment, then slowly draws it out.)

They grab the twig for dear life – with their mandibles – *(illustrates word with pincer-movement of his thumb and index finger)* Nothing like an angry termite in the season! *(he smiles)*

(The Young Male licks the termite off the twig and repeats the whole process again.)

I can only compare the pleasure of a juicy termite with my present delight at the first strawberry of the year. 'Firstness', if you understand my meaning. I do not eat termites now. (*He smiles*) I suspect it would be frowned on, in England at any rate. (*He has suddenly had his attention caught by the Young Female.*) Look at her! She wants to touch the tiny one. (*He giggles*)

(*The Young Female is now very close to the infant, grooming. She keeps darting a glance at the Mother, who is impassive, and accidentally-on-purpose grooms the infant. Since the Mother does not react, the Young Female nuzzles at the fingers of the infant. Then the infant gives a soft whimper. The Mother immediately pushes the Young Female away – but not hard enough – and cuddles the infant. The Young Female puts her hands on her head briefly. She then drops them, rocks to and fro a moment, whimpering softly. The Young Male collects a new stick. The Young female stares at the infant, puts her hands behind her back, lips pouting and rocks just a little. The Young Male continues fishing. He looks briefly across to the other two and then returns to his fishing. The Young Female puts out her hand again to the infant. No reaction from Mother, who now has lain back again, but looking at the infant. The Young Female grooms the infant again cautiously, looking, as before, at the Mother. She pulls the infant gradually from the Mother and holds it to herself. There is a quiet whimper from the infant. The Mother immediately takes the infant back, 'kisses' the infant's head then cuddles it close. The Young Female raises her arms in the air in surrender. Sound and lights fade.*)

Of course, I do not remember all this but it is much the same for any chimpanzee in the wild. But now comes my first contact with human beings. (*After drawing the curtain and returning to his place.*) I was captured on the Gold Coast, now called Ghana – they had a military coup there just before the New Year[5], did you read about it in the newspapers, see it on the television perhaps? – well that is by the way. Albeit, it was then called the Gold Coast. I shall show you *how* my capture took place in a moment. But I would like to say that although it may not look pleasant to you, and indeed, nor was it for me at the time, I do not regret, no not for one moment, that far-off day when fate saw to it that the paths of ape and Where was I? (*glances over to his notes*) Captured on the Gold Coast. Yes. The hunting expedition...(*he stops*) Oh. I must take my clothes off now. (*he begins to do so, explaining as he does*) This does not require an X certificate. You will see that decency will be preserved. (*he smiles*) But, an ape fully clothed, on the Gold Coast, would be anachronistic, not to say possibly a humorous, spectacle. (*he continues to undress*) A lot of fur, you see.

(*He does have, except for the balding spots where clothes have rubbed fur away, and a baldish rump.*)

5 Play written January, 1982. Any up to date reference to Ghana will serve (eg. problems with debt repayment, government policy etc.) The point is, he keeps up to date with Ghana and politics generally.

It is rare now that I remove my clothes in front of people.

(*He is carefully folding his clothes and hanging them over the stool and table.*)

I used to do quite often, to show those people who expressed an interest in the wounds I received at the time of my capture. The first shot hit me here. (*Shows scar on cheek.*) Quite enough I would have thought to have stopped me in my tracks. But the wound I received in the groin – just here – (*he shows the remains of a scar on the inside of the top of his left thigh*) – was, in my opinion, a quite needless addition. I had already been winged by the **first** shot – (*pointing to his cheek*) – but this – (*pointing to groin*) – was a **wanton** shot. (*Pause*) Certain idiots in the newspapers and sometimes, I regret, even in the scientific journals, used to say that my predilection for removing my trousers for visitors to my house, that this habit of mine, proved the fact that I was not a man, but still held to my ape-nature ... A **wanton** shot. The hands that wrote such things should have their fingers shot away, one by one. (*he moves a little, shifting his balance from one foot to the other*) For myself I shall continue to remove my trousers to whomsoever I please. And know that, for people such as yourselves to whom, although it may cause, sometimes a smile or even a little laughter which I know would be wholly without malice, such pointless acts of violence by grown men will be as beyond your comprehension as it is beyond mine. (*pause*) Be that as it may, (*he once more walks toward the curtain*) let us continue with the scene of my capture.

(*He starts to pull the curtain back, continuing to speak as he does so. This is the first time his rump is visible to the audience. There is the sound of gentle lapping water, insects; low, it continues throughout the scene. The light is low and has a reddish glow. On the back curtain is projected a painting of a tropical sea with a large red sun dropping below the horizon. To the left there is a clump of coconut trees and the edge of the land. There is sand in the foreground on which a rowing-boat is beached. Mid-ground there is an old-fashioned steamer, quite small by perspective. In the acting area there is a small bush, standing all alone, behind which are Lionel Shirley-Smythe, Salty and a black porter. They are all trying to hide or look as though they are not there. At least Lionel and Salty are; the black porter looks less than enthusiastic. Lionel is dressed in khaki safari gear with a pith helmet and neck flap binoculars around his neck. A fly swat in his hand. Salty is dressed less elegantly: long trousers, too big for him so tied round with a leather strap, but he has a safari-type jacket – somewhat too small and thus split in various places. He has a battered pith helmet and a grubby piece of cloth fixed at the back. He is holding a shot-gun and various accoutrements, a knife in his belt. The black porter is dressed in western clothes – very much cast-offs – but he doesn't look like a tramp. He's chosen 'convenient' clothes. He has no headgear. He has a massive pack on his back, hamper-type case and carries various implements – butterfly-net etc. Sweat marks are visible on all three men.*)

The hunting expedition was led by the intrepid explorer and zoologist, Lionel Shirley-Smythe. As you see, the party was concealed near the water's edge, behind the bush. They had taken cover to await evening drawing in, when animals tended to come down to the shore-line to drink. I cannot swear to the complete accuracy of this part of my account for of course I was not there,…at the beginning at least. But from the many accounts which have been written that I have subsequently read, of hunting expeditions, I daresay were Lionel Shirley-Smythe here now, he would not find it so far from the truth.

(*He is now back by his table. The three men look very obvious.*)

Salty: Do you think they'll be able to see us, Sir?

Lionel: Keep your voice down. They'll hear us. (*He looks out towards the forest. Salty does too. Whispering*) Have you loaded the gun?

Salty: Beg pardon, Sir?

Lionel: Have you loaded the gun? (*thumps it*)

Salty: Yes, sir. All ready.

Lionel: Good man. (*The Black Porter is moving trying to put the pack off.*) Tell the darkie to keep still.

Salty: Hey, keep still you. (*moving gun*) Or I'll blow your balls off.

(*The Black Porter keeps still, but looks sullenly at Salty.*)

Lionel: (*noting it, to himself*) Surly beasts.

Salty: What's that, sir?

Lionel: (*looking up*) Nearly dark, what? Shouldn't be long now, Salty.

Salty: No sir, you're right there.

Lionel: Oh, yes. (*pause*) Get in close to me man. Do you want to be seen or what? (*Salty gets in closer, with a slight clatter*). Sh! (*Salty tips hat in automatic apology. Long pause, Lionel and Salty intent on the undergrowth, the Black Porter uninterested, looks about generally.*) What's that awful smell? (*Looks at Salty, who in turn looks at the Black Porter.*) He been rubbin' himself in coconut oil again? Tell him to move over there. (*Pointing towards boat.*)

Salty: (*about to do so*) Won't the animals see him sir?

Lionel: Good God man. It's nearly dark. He's a black man, isn't he?

Salty: (*with a kick*) Over there. And keep your mouth shut and your eyes closed.

(*The Black Porter moves off into open space, sits comfortably and relaxed. He doesn't close his eyes.*)

Done, Sir.

Lionel: (*sniffing*) I can still smell it. (*He looks at Salty.*)

Salty: Me sir? I can't smell nothing.

Lionel: Anything. You can't smell anything.

B. Porter: Coming!

Lionel: What did he say?

Salty: Don't know, sir. Oy! What did you say, blackie?

B. Porter: (*pointing languidly*) Coming.

(*There is a general flap between Lionel and Salty.*)

Lionel: Get down, Salty

Salty: You want the gun, sir?

Lionel: (*looking wildly*) Damn it! I can't even see it. (*fetches binoculars up, drops them on the straps*) Pah! Not worth a curse. Here pass me the gun. You take the binox.

(*There is a general mêlée of binocular straps getting entangled with Lionel's pith helmet, which falls off. Salty picks it up, puts it on Lionel's head. The binocular straps are caught around the barrel of the shotgun, as Salty tries to look through them. Finally, they get settled again.*)

Any sign of it, Salty?

Salty: No sir. Not yet.

B. Porter: Will have smelt you a mile off.

Salty: Think we'll have scared it off, sir.

B. Porter: Comin' all the same.

Lionel: Doubt it Salty. Doubt it.

B. Porter: Juss ain't learnt to distruss the white man yet.

Salty: Cor, look sir (*without the binoculars*) there's a whole troop of them, coming down to the water.

Lionel: Where?! Where?

Salty: There, sir. Look. Whole troop of monkeys.

Lionel: Apes, Salty. Apes. No tails, don't you know.

(*He takes aim. Peter moves slowly, chimpanzee-style from the table across Lionel's line of vision.*)

Squeeze it gently, dear. Like woman's thingummy, what?

(*There is a loud bang from the gun. Peter squeals and falls with a roll. Salty and Lionel quickly reload.*)

Give him another for luck, what? I say, what a bag!

Salty: (*to the Black Porter who has sat fairly impassive throughout*) Get the net. Throw it over him. So he don't get away.

(*Black Porter gets the net.*)

Lionel: No chance of that.

(*He fires the second shot. The slightly moving Peter jerks and then is still but whimpers for a moment or two.*)

Damn good shot, though I say it myself.

(The three move towards Peter, Salty fairly gingerly; Lionel triumphantly but keeping his distance; the Black Porter matter-of-factly, with the net. He puts the net over Peter and secures it. He does various stages in advance of Lionel's instruction.)

That's right. Put it over him. Now turn him over on his tum-tum. That's right. Wrap it round. That's it. Tie the little chappie nice and securely. (*going over to Peter*) Once in the chops. Once in his goolies. Not bad, eh, Salty?

Salty: Not bad at all, sir. (*pause*) Do you think he'll live?

Lionel: Oh my word, yes. Good bit of buckshot up your braces never did anyone any harm. Come on. Let's get him back to the Steamer.

He sweeps off, followed by Salty, leaving the Black Porter to drag the net. He pulls it, from a longish strand of rope, a few yards.

Peter: (*breaking the scene*) That's fine thanks.

The actor playing the Black Porter drops his character.

B. Porter: Can you manage with...?

Peter: Yes. I'll be fine. Perhaps you'd close the curtains though for...

(The actor immediately understands and as Peter comes forward in the net, the actor closes the curtain.)

Lionel Shirley-Smythe was no ordinary person. He was indeed quite a remarkable human being. I should say, too, since sometimes such things matter, that he was later awarded by George the Fifth, a KBE – for his services to the Empire. I know such things mean little to you, nowadays, and I daresay you are perfectly right, but it meant a lot to him. At the time. He is dead now. Run down by a bus on a pedestrian crossing. Outside the House of Lords. (*pause*) But I digress from the main point. I cannot say that I recall much of my journey to the Steamer for I was only partially conscious. Which was probably just as well, for young as I was – I should imagine I was 3 or maybe 4 years old – I would have been fully capable of tearing the net apart. In which case I may have escaped or bitten an unfortunate porter. But, as I say, this did not happen since I was all but unconscious. And what consciousness I had, was not, at that time, preoccupied with escape but only with the red-hot needles that seemed to be probing the region of my private parts. (*pause*) I sometimes think what an irony it is that I entered this (*pause*) marvellous world of human society barely conscious of it and preoccupied with my own pain. It is strange, is it not? Be that as it may, I came to myself – and I should say this is where my own memories gradually begin – between decks on Shirley-Smythe's steamer.

One of the actors opens the curtain from behind and Peter gets down on the floor within the net. On stage there is a cage, raised up so that its top is some two feet above head height. It's mounted on a rocking-horse type mechanism which has a brake so that it can either be firm (as it is at this time) or sway gently to give the impression of a ship's movement (as it does later). Its design is as he describes later. There is the sound of a low, stationary ship's humming. On the back curtain is a projection of the inside of a ship's metal hull. Quite dark. There is a large porthole through which can be seen a bright blue sea and sky, and perhaps some palm trees on land. This is to one side, away from the cage. There are various cages and crates with animals in. Peter is some distance from the cage in the net. He lies motionless.

Lionel: (*off*) Where's my little chimpy-wimpy? How's your nice ca-age?! Coo-ee! I'm coming to find you! I've got my big gu-un!

A fly swat appears held horizontally like a gun. Peter stirs a little and is trembling.

I've got my bang-bang. (*chuckling delight; mock sinister*) I've got you cornered. Who won't get away, eh?!

Lionel suddenly appears and, military-style, points the fly-swat straight at the cage. It takes him some moments to register that Peter is not in the cage. The word 'bang' hardly escapes him although it forms on his lips. He turns very slowly to look for Peter. Peter moves and, trembling, half stands. Lionel is still pointing the fly-swat as he sees Peter. Peter looks at Lionel. It is obvious Lionel is terrified out of his wits. Lionel shits himself.

Oh! my God!

Peter begins to struggle with the net and Lionel very softly:

Salty......! (*trying to be calm*) Now stay there boy. Nice boy.

He backs out the way he came in. As soon as he disappears he can be heard screaming:

Salty....!

There is the sound of commotion and Salty arriving.

You haven't put it in the cage! And it's made me do a poo in my pants.

Salty: (*still off stage*) Sorry, sir.

Lionel: It's all very well being sorry. Get it in the bloody cage!

Salty: Sir.

He enters, followed by Lionel. Peter by now is struggling with the net.

Jesus Christ! (*he reaches for a short handled gaff, the length of a broom*)

Lionel: Language, Salty.

Salty: Beg pardon, sir. (*Salty advances gingerly on Peter who is showing fear-grin*) Stay ... Stay ... there's a good boy.

He whacks Peter on the head with the blunt end of his stick. Peter yelps and collapses. Salty whacks him again.

Lionel: Careful, Salty. Don't want him dead or damaged in the head. Worth a lot of money in London.

Peter is not unconscious, dazed only.

Salty: Come on, yer brute.

He pushes him towards the cage with his foot, and the gaff. Lionel watches; he won't be helping at all. With considerable effort Salty gets Peter to the cage.

Would you mind opening the door sir?

Lionel: No. You do it, you lazy sod. Should've done this when he was brought on board.

Salty: Sorry sir. (*He opens the cage door*).

Lionel: My pants feel really wet.

Salty: You want me to get you another pair, sir?

Lionel: No. Get him in there first. (*He swats him with his fly-swat.*)

Salty: Yes, sir. Excuse me, sir?

Lionel moves out of the way.

Come on you. (*he starts to heave Peter up into the cage*)

Lionel: Get him out of the net, Salty. Don't want it chewed to pieces.

Salty: Sir. (*he undoes the top of the net*) Stand away, sir.

Lionel moves further away; Salty prods Peter with the gaff.

Get in there, you.

He prods him again, harder. Peter squeals and bounds out of the net into the cage. Salty slams the door closed behind. Peter doesn't know what's happened, but is still, apart from the trembling.

Got you, yer bastard.

Salty sees that Peter has the long strand of the rope net still attached. He gives it a yank. Peter yelps. The rope comes free.

You cause me any more trouble and I'll put one of them pythons in yer cage to play with you.

Lionel: I think not, Salty. No need for that. We're not beasts, you know. Should try to be kind to animals.

Salty: Oh yes sir. Course. (*looks malevolently towards Peter*)

Lionel: Now come on. You can change my trousers.

Salty: Thank-you sir.

They go out. The sound fades as does the light except that falling on Peter.

Peter: I do not know if you have ever been in a cage – probably not – since it is something more reserved for animals than for humans like ourselves, but I can tell you it is not an experience I can recommend. The cage was in fact much smaller than this – after all I was considerably smaller, then, myself. It was much too low for me to stand in and too narrow to sit down in. So I had to squat with my knees bent. And further, since it was thought likely that for a time I would wish to see no one, and that I no doubt would prefer to stay in the dark, my face was turned towards the side with no bars – a locker was adjacent and made the fourth side like this – while the bars of the cage cut into my flesh behind. (*pulling his head round*) Such a method of confining wild beasts is supposed to have its advantages during the first days of captivity, and out of my own experience I cannot deny that, from the human point of view, this really is the case. But of course, ape that I was then, such human considerations did not so much as occur to me. And, of course, ape that I then was, I did try to escape. (*From here on, he acts as an ape, narrates as a man*). When I had sufficiently recovered from the blows to my head, I ran my eyes and nose over the boards in front of me.

He does so. He gives a howl of delight and plunges his fingers towards a crack.

There was a gap running right through the boards of the locker.

He struggles to get a finger-hold. Wildly he uses his mouth. Stops. Looks and thinks. Then tries again with his fingers. Fails.

I tried for an eternity to enlarge that gap. But neither my strength nor all the – admittedly limited – powers of reason that I then possessed, could enlarge it by so much as a hair's breadth.

He sits and looks at the gap apathetically for some while. Then, very measured.

For the first time in my life I could see no way out. (*pause*) No.. way.. out. (*Long pause, as he recalls the feeling.*) One of my most vivid memories of the time, for all I know it was that very night, is not anything that actually happened. It is a dream. Oh yes, even as an ape, I dreamt. I find it curious that some dreams can be more real, more vivid, have more truth than life itself. We remember dreams of childhood long after childhood has receded from our memories. Do you find that? I do. I should like to tell you about it, if you will permit me. I call it, in my sadder moods, my dream of freedom.

The back curtain displays a blur of colour – green then blue at the top. The light is very low at this point, except that falling on Peter in the cage. As the dream progresses the light illuminates wherever he goes and the projection gradually come into focus showing chimpanzees swinging freely through the tree tops.

I'm in my cage. It is night. And I hear sounds.

The clear call of whales communicating underwater is heard.

Deep beneath the hull of the steamer. Calling. Calling. I gently push against the gate behind me. (*he does so*) It opens. No effort needed. No, not so much as to flex a muscle in my back. (*he backs out*) I climb out of my cage. (*He is now standing by the cage. He listens.*) The whales say to me: 'You're free; you're free', and I say to the whales: 'I'm not. Give me the trees'.

The whale sounds give way to music from Messiaen's 'Quartet for the end of time' – 1st and 3rd movements – not the whole. The projection comes into focus.

And then, I can see the sky above me. The clear blue sky, not the ship's ceiling...(*he is practically dancing*) ... And then a great vine, like those in the forests, falls from the sky. You must forgive me ... (*A rope ladder drops slowly from the flies*) ... I'm not as nimble as I was ... please imagine this ladder as a vine ... (*he begins to climb*) ... And I climb. Up. Up. 'I'm coming back. Wait for me'. And there they are. Moving through tree-tops as free as the notes from a clarinet. My brothers and sisters and all the apes in the natural world. Wherever hands reach out, a branch is there. Where every landing is changed to taking off. Where every moment moves the next. Motion ... all is motion. 'Wait for me'... And then I see the land is moving away. I'm like a stone. The trees are moving away. (*pause*) Between us is the sea. And I knew, like you know in dreams, I could not jump so far.

The projection goes out of focus and disappears. He climbs down the ladder which goes away up into the flies again. The music fades and the distant sound of whales can be heard once more.

Too far. I surely should have drowned. I woke with...such a sense of loss. (*after a brief pause, he goes to the curtain and draws it across, speaking as he does*) But you know, after that dream I drew a curtain, so to say, across my mind. I knew that I could either hanker after some – illusory – freedom and pine away till I died, or live and concentrate on more pressing matters – simply to find a way out of my cage. And after all I was free; I mean did I have freedom with a capital F when I lived in the forest as an ape? I think not. Was I not then subject to the same blind and indifferent forces of nature that I venture to say that we are – you and I – as humans, as men and women? You will understand I did not think this way at the time; as an ape I was yet far from being able to consider things in their theoretical or philosophical aspects. No. Just find a way out. That I found one owes not a little to the inner calmness that settled upon me over those first few days on board the steamer...

He walks over to the curtain and draws it as he speaks. The back curtain has a projection on it similar to the previous below-decks background, except only there is no land to be seen through the porthole. There are a couple of wooden cases, perhaps an empty oil-drum nearest the audience. There are two crew-members sitting on them – relaxed and calm. There is the sound of steam engines, the clanking of the engine room.

...A calmness that was decisive to my finding a way out of my cage. And for that I have to thank in no small measure the calmness of the ship's crew. (*he is walking towards his cage*) They never did anything in a hurry. The slow foot-steps above my head pacing upon the deck; the slow drawing on the smoke in their pipes ... (*he is now inside the cage but facing forward through the bars*) ... and what gave me cause for hope, if that is not too strong a word, is that I turned through ninety degrees – no longer staring at the hopeless crack in the locker boards.

He closes the gate upon himself. Badger, one of the crewmen, plays a mouthorgan or squeezebox quietly, a mournful tune of some ship disaster. The other, Fred, is chomping on tobacco while he is carving a piece of ivory in the shape of a whale. Peter is idly picking at his fur, casting an occasional glance at the two men. His cage swings gently from side to side with the movement of the ship. Some time passes.

Fred: (*after a glance at Peter*) Cor blimey, seen him, Badger?

Badger: (*after a pause – he has been watching Peter all the time*) Wha?

Fred: Him

Badger: (*after a pause*) Oh. (*He continues to play.*)

Fred: Been at it since we came in. (*he continues to work*) Got fleas.

Badger: Yer.

Fred: Must have hundreds of 'em. (*pause*) Sure I've got 'em... (*he scratches*) ... off him. Bastard.

Badger: Animals have fur, have fleas. Fleas jump

Fred: Oh yeah. Even so. (*He scratches, unconsciously.*)

Jimmy comes in, breezy.

Jimmy: Fuckin' hell. Someone died? Can't yer play somethin' happy?

Not waiting for an answer, he heads for Peter, acknowledging Fred as he passes him.

Fred: All right Jimmy?

Badger, without irritation, stops playing and brings out tobacco and pipe and fills his pipe during the following.

Jimmy: (*to Peter*) Hello, sailor boy. Alright eh?

Peter looks at him with some interest. Jimmy pokes out his tongue at Peter who pokes out his tongue back.

Hey, did you see that? (*laughing his head off*) He poked 'is tongue out at us.

(*Badger has seen it and is amused; Fred hasn't.*)

Fred: Didn't

Jimmy: He did. (*turning to Peter again*) Come on, poke your tongue out. (*Jimmy pokes his out*) Come on (*cajoling*) ... poke your tongue out. Like Jimmy. Like this. Come on. (*frustrated edge*) Come on. Poke your tongue.

Fred: 'E ain't going to do it...

Jimmy: 'E will. Won't you, sailor? You'll do it for your Uncle Jimmy?

Much patient/irritated demonstrating. Then he turns away.

Fuck you then.

Peter pokes out his tongue which the other two see but Jimmy doesn't. Fred and Badger roar with laughter, slapping their thighs. Jimmy's put out. Peter is also hooting and slapping himself with excitement.

Fred: (*somewhat redundantly*) You missed it. (*to Badger*) Look at 'im now. Goin' mad.

Jimmy: (*enjoying it now*) The bastard. 'E did it on purpose. Oo look, he's shit himself. (*He laughs, not cruelly, but relieved to get the laugh back on Peter.*) Look, Fred.

Fred comes over to have a look.

Fred: (*enjoying it*) Dirty beast! Heh!

Jimmy: (*to Peter*) Come on, lick it up. (*to Fred*) They lick it up, you know.

Fred: They don't, do they Badger?

Badger: (*lighting his pipe*) Dunno. (*He watches without criticism.*)

Jimmy: Like cats. They lick it up.

Fred: 'Ow d'you know?

Jimmy: Just do.

Fred: You're 'aving me on.

Jimmy: Ain't.

Fred: Well, he ain't licking it up.

Jimmy: (*changing subject*) Hey, what shall we call 'im. Gotta give 'im a proper name.

Peter's now fairly still, but watching.

Fred: What about 'Fleamarket'? Gotta a lotta fucking fleas. (*laughter*)

Jimmy: Nah. A proper name. (*thinks for a moment*) Watchoo think, Badger? I know. Peter. Saw one once when I was in Liverpool...

Fred's gone back to his work.

Fred: One what?

Jimmy: One of these. This geezer 'ad dressed him up in proper sailor gear, you know, and got him to do tricks. Drinkin' tea, things like that.

Fred: Yeah?

Jimmy: His name was Peter.

Badger gets up easily, and wanders over to the cage.

Fred: What, the monkey?

Jimmy: Yeah, course.

Fred: Yeah, that's good, ain't it Badger?

Badger: (*He is slowly puffing smoke through the bars to watch Peter's reaction intently.*) Yeh.

There's the sound of the ship's bell for change of watch. The three men, without exchanging a word or a glance, gather their things together and leave. Peter follows their every movement and lingers on the place they left the acting area. The picture on the back curtain fades and the sound of the steamer finishes.

Peter: That was my way out. (*Opening the cage, moving towards the audience, drawing the curtain behind him.*) If these men could move about, freely, unrestricted by a cage, could come and go as they pleased, well then I had to learn to be like them. Not that any promises were offered, that, should I actually achieve the impossible, a beneficent hand would remove the bars from my cage. No. Emphatically not. Nevertheless, as I watched these men over the long days and nights of the voyage, the sheer accumulation of my observations impelled me in the one direction: I had to learn to be like them.

(*He takes a sip of water, and turns over notes without actually reading them.*) It was, as a matter of fact, very easy to imitate them. Once I had decided to do so. I learnt to spit in the very first days. I could soon smoke a pipe like an old hand; and if I also pressed my thumb into the bowl of the pipe, a roar of appreciation went up between decks – as I then thought – approval far beyond that deserved for so simple a gesture. The fact that I carried out this operation comparatively infrequently may account for the somewhat over-enthusiastic applause. But, in truth, the heat transferred from the bowl of a lighted pipe to the tip of one's thumb is not a physical sensation I would frequently recommend. I had no end of teachers, mentors and advisers. Some, I should say, were not as – how can I express it? – committed as others, and quickly lost interest in the rigors of teaching an ape. And I do not blame them, even now. Determined pupil though I was, there were some things I found extremely hard to master. For example...

He begins to go to the curtain, speaking as he does, open it, revealing the same scene as before with the exception that only Badger is sitting there, pipe in hand – staring at the cage. The steam engine sound has not yet begun. Peter wanders up to Badger, opens the cage and gets in, closing it behind him, at which point the engines can be heard as before.

...my worst trouble came from the rum bottle. The smell of it revolted me. Even now I decline it when offered and forgo many a delicious-looking trifle for fear it might contain the substance. But I forced myself to it as best I could. There was one man who came to me over and over again – alone or with friends – at any time of the day or night. He would post himself before me, pipe in hand, and stare at me – indicating Badger – like this – and then give me instructions. (*Peter's in the cage*)

Badger: (*laying down pipe and picking up an empty rum bottle*) Think yer can do it?

Peter responds eagerly to it.

I think you can. Watch. Yer take the cork out of the bottle.

He does so – every gesture exaggerated and slow-motion.

Like that.

He looks to Peter to see that he's taking it in, which he is.

Go' that? Take the cork out of the bottle, then lift it to yer mouth like this.

He brings the bottle right down then slowly lifts the bottle through a great arc to his lips – looking at Peter throughout. Peter squeals and scratches with excitement.

Then you lift the bottle like this – (*tilts the bottle*) – and put your 'ead back at the same time.

He does so again, exaggerated and slow. He freezes there for a moment. Peter suddenly goes quiet and watches intensely. With bottle held a little away from his lips but looking towards Peter...

Then glug ... glug ... glug. Yer drink it. (*he brings the bottle slowly down*) Aaah!
Lovely stuff. (*grins and rubs his belly to explain*)

*Peter jumps up and down making a hullabaloo, then leans exhaustedly against
the bars.*

Right, you try it.

*He bangs the cork in the bottle and walks over to Peter. He offers it and Peter
takes it immediately looking at Badger all the way. Badger walks back to his
seat and picks up his pipe – he doesn't light it. He looks at Peter who is looking
at him, awed by the task before him.*

Go on.

Peter looks at the bottle, then looks at Badger.

Go on.

*Puts the pipe in his mouth; he's going to say no more. He stares. Peter stares back
until finally, with trembling hand he puts his hand on the cork. Then looks at
Badger who remains calm and mute. Then looks at the bottle and pulls the cork
out – a surprise to him – and looks again at Badger but now with excitement
more at what's to come than what he's done. Badger, impassive, still watches.
Peter then lifts the bottle in exactly the same way as Badger did, puts it to his
lips, then immediately throws the bottle down in disgust.*

Damn yer! (*he looks at Peter who in reply grins and rubs his belly*) It's no good.

*Peter stops grinning and rubbing, and doesn't know quite what to do with
himself. Badger calmly lights his pipe and contemplates Peter for a few
moments. Then he slowly goes over to Peter and retrieves the bottle. Peter is still
holding the cork. He touches Peter's hand.*

Give us the cork.

*Peter does. Badger pushes it home into the bottle. He goes and sits down; lays his
pipe down. Peter watches, shamed.*

You take the cork out of the bottle. (*he does so, as before, with no frustration*)
Like that, yeah? (*he looks to Peter who is studying intently*) Then yer lift it to yer
mouth. (*he does so, again in a big arc, looks at Peter who again gets excited*)
Then yer put yer 'ead back and tilt the bottle at the same time. (*He does so.
Peter squeals and scratches.*) And you hold it there. (*he holds it longer than
before to emphasise the point*) Got that? Hold it there ... Then glug, glug, glug.
You drink it. Glug, glug, glug.

*Peter jumps up and down in excitement as if to explain that he's got it. Badger
brings the bottle down.*

Aarh! (*he rubs his belly and grins*) Lovely stuff.

*He looks at Peter who is leaning against the bars exhausted, looking pretty
drunk. Badger pushes the cork back in. Holds it to Peter.*

Your turn now.

Peter gives a look as if to say 'Not again!'

Yer. Don't practise, won't improve.

He walks over and passes the bottle which Peter takes. Badger walks back and picks up his pipe and puts it in his mouth and stares at Peter. He holds the bottle limply to one side for a few moments, not looking at Badger. Then suddenly, he brings the bottle up and confidently, but carefully, takes the cork out. He gives a quick look to Badger, then lifts it to his lips, then throws it down in disgust. Badger puts his head in his hands and rubs his eyes. Peter grins and rubs his belly. Badger looks up.

Yess... we know you can rub your belly, old friend.

He lays his pipe down and goes over to Peter. He retrieves the bottle, and tickles Peter with it, impassively. Looking at him.

Try again later, eh? (*Peter hands the cork through the bars, and touches him on the hand with it*) Yeah.

He takes it and puts it in the bottle. The ship's bell rings for the change of watch. Badger collects his things and goes out. The back picture fades and the sound of the steamer disappears.

Peter: Too often my lessons ended in that way. In abject defeat. (*he opens the cage, gets out and comes forward drawing the curtain behind him, talking as he does*) And to the credit of my teacher, he was not angry – a quality which to this day I still respect in teachers, at least towards their pupils – and I am sure I must have caused him much sorrow, especially when his determination caused such mirth amongst the other members of the crew. And, as the saying goes, much 'leg-pulling'. But, as I say, he persisted through the whole duration of the voyage. We both did. Not all the credit is due to him. After all, I watched him – and them – with the most eager attention. And without in any way wishing to appear to you as arrogant, such was my desire to lift myself beyond the confines of my ape-nature and my cage, that I can say without contradiction that another like pupil no human teacher ever found on earth. (*pause*) Yet I would wish to take nothing away from the patience and calm insistence that I should succeed. He perceived that we were both fighting on the same side against the nature of apes and that I had the more difficult task. Such teachers are gold dust, wouldn't you agree? (*after a brief pause, he turns nimbly away towards the curtain and stops before opening it, excitedly*) What a triumph it was then, both for him and for me, when one evening, before a large circle of spectators ... but let me show you for yourselves.

He pulls the curtain back and gets into position in the cage. As he opens the curtain the sound of a party in full swing can be heard – men only! – and the steamer engines underneath. The back curtain shows below decks but has painted on it human figures enjoying themselves, maybe men dancing with men, talking, drinking and so on, at a ship's party. Downstage of the acting area are Lionel and Captain Arkwright with glasses. Arkwright is also holding a bottle with which he tops up Lionel's glass from time to time. Lionel is no longer dressed in safari gear; he is dressed quite stylishly in Oxford bags, waistcoat etc.

He is sitting on a shooting stick and waving about with the ship's movement. Near them is a crate that's been covered with a white cloth on which stands a gramophone with a large horn. This is playing Caruso in an Italian aria. Badger, sitting a little way off from them, is smoking his pipe and occasionally swigging his bottle. Near – but not next to – Peter's cage there is another crate. On this are the remains of food and dead bottles – this should probably not look realistic food i.e. more in keeping stylistically with the pictures on the back curtain.

Peter: There was a ship's party, celebrating something or other...no, but see for yourself. (*he's now in the cage*)

Lionel: Excellent do, what, Captain Arkwright?

Arkwright: Yes indeed, sir. (*topping up Lionel's glass*) Capital, as you might say.

Lionel: Yes, yes. Very nice. (*pause...looks at Arkwright*) But I say old chap, do keep still. Keep moving about. (*Arkwright waves about in rhythm with Lionel*) That's better. Fine singer. Got to hand it to them.

Arkwright: (*catching up, but not enthusiastic*) Hoh yes, sir. Very fine.

Lionel: You know, you're a bloody good Captain, Captain. Decent chap.

Arkwright: Very kind of you to say so.

Lionel: No, I mean it.

There is a pause. Lionel unabashed, Arkwright feeling out of his depth in polite conversation. Lionel's look strays across to Peter who is grooming himself, unconcerned about the party, the moment Lionel's gaze falls upon him. Up to then he's been watching. Arkwright follows Lionel's gaze which returns to him.

Arkwright: Ugly brute.

Lionel: (*a contradiction*) Good specimen. (*he deliberately picks non-existent dust/fluff off his sleeve.*)

Arkwright: Oh yes. Good specimen. (*pause, retrieving lost ground*) Tell me, sir, as a natural scientist and an explorer, do you think we're descended from ... apes?

Lionel goes absolutely still and looks Arkwright in the eyes.

Lionel: Darwin! (*pause*) Huh! Are you trying to ruin my evening, Captain Arkwright? (*pause*) Keep still man; told you before. Are you seeking to get me annoyed, sir? In a word, are you trying to WIND ME UP?

Arkwright: No sir. Not on my life, sir.

Lionel: Are you sure?

Arkwright: No, I was, er...

Lionel: Very well. You may pour a little more of that spirit in my glass. (*Arkwright does so, relieved to serve*) Take Signor Caruso off the gramophone. He will scratch himself hoarse. Ha, ha, ha.

Arkwright: Ha, ha, ha. (*he takes the needle off the gramophone*)

Lionel: Let me explain something to you. Then you will be clear. I, sir, am a Christian, and an Englishman. Now then ... because one is a Christian one knows the truth. Because one is also an Englishman, one tolerates others who don't. Do you follow me? Now Mr. Darwin was an Englishman – I am sorry to say – but in putting forward his ridiculous ideas that human beings evolved from apes he showed himself most certainly not to be a Christian. Is this not so?

Arkwright: Oh yes.

Lionel: Therefore, his ideas are not true, but false. Q.E.D.

Arkwright: I don't have your learning, I'm afraid sir.

Lionel: No, no of course not. Well let me put it this way (*he wanders somewhat unsurely towards Peter's cage – who backs off at his approach – Arkwright follows with the bottle*) In the Bible you will find this unambiguous sentence: 'And God made man in his own image'. Nothing could be clearer. Look at the two of us. He poses in front of the cage. Do you see? Only one of us looks like God, what? (*pause*) Does this creature behind me look like God?

Arkwright: No sir. He's an ape.

Lionel: Quite so. (*he drops the pose*)

Badger: Learns fast, though.

Lionel: (*surprised, to Arkwright*) Who's this fellow?

Arkwright: Badger, sir. He's one all the lads have been joking about.

Lionel: Oh him.

Arkwright: Shall I tell him to move away, sir?

Lionel: No, no it's party-time! Let him have his say! Now fellow what profundity do you have to offer us, eh?

Badger: Just said, 'e learns fast.

Lionel: Yes? And what is that intended to imply? Hm?

Badger: Nothin', sir. Just sayin' 'e learns fast, that's all.

Lionel: Oh. (*to Arkwright*) I think I smell a Darwinian. (*to Badger*) Are you a Darwinian, Badger?

Badger: Don't know what that is, sir.

Lionel: Good. Good. Better not to know. You read your Bible though I hope...

Badger: Can't read, sir.

Lionel: (*losing interest*) Jolly good. Where's that bottle, Arkwright?

They both turn towards the chest by Peter's cage, just in time to see Peter reaching through the bars to grab the bottle Arkwright was holding.

I say, that's our...

Badger: (*authoritatively*) Leave him.

Lionel: Oh.

They do. The party chatter goes silent as Peter ceremoniously uncorks the bottle, lifts it in a wide arc, puts his head back, tilts the bottle and continues to drink until the bottle is drained; some of it pours on his face. He puts the cork back in the bottle. He then, with the most fluid of motions, tosses the bottle to one side. Then looking at the crowd.

Peter: Hallo, Peter. (*He is about to rub his belly when he collapses in a heap on the floor of his cage.*)

Lionel: I say!...

Badger: (*after a pause, lighting his pipe*) What's that sir?

Lionel: Think I'll pootle off to beddy-byes. Arkwright.

He goes. Arkwright looks at Badger, who motions with his pipe to Peter.

Badger: You off too, sir?

Arkwright: (*uncertain*) Yes.

He goes after Lionel. The back projection goes. Peter and the actor playing Badger get up; the steamer sound also goes. The actor helps Peter down, congratulating him quietly.

Peter: (*to the actor*) I hope I haven't broken the bottle again! Will you do the curtain?

Peter comes forward quickly, mopping any water from around him. The actor closes the curtain behind him.

Only water, this time. (*he smiles*) Now I know you will soon be wanting an interval – 'intermission' I believe is the word they use now – and I should say I need one also. Both of us, so to say, to stretch our legs. But I hope you will bear with me a moment longer for me to complete the first phase of my life among the humans. For it was when I first arrived in London at the then newly opened King Edward Vllth Docks that I learned a lesson that determined my career almost to this day. It was the day after we had had that party that we docked. I am afraid I was a little worse-for-wear, even groggy you might say. My aversion to rum had returned with a vengeance and my brief sally into human communication proved only too brief. I did not regain the power of human speech for some days after. However, my eyes and brain sufficed on this occasion. It had been snowing, for snow lay on the ground – a small sprinkling of perhaps an inch – this is fortunate for us since it is not easy in the theatre to simulate snow actually falling. I have seen it most effectively achieved, however, in the cinema. But this is by the way. I had of course never seen snow before and so experienced its cold long before I learnt its name.

He has moved over to the curtain and draws it back. On the back curtain is projected a dockside scene with its line picked out neatly by the snow. One can see dockers, packing cases on the wharfside, and various ships tied up, gangplanks down etc. On the skyline can be seen St. Paul's Cathedral. Low, beneath the discussion that follows, can be heard sounds of working – the occasional shouted instruction, boxes being banged about, maybe the occasional ship's steam hooter. But the most dominant sounds are of caged birds and other animals. In the acting area are several large cases and perhaps some unrealistic dummy cases/cages with animals in. There is an empty cage with its gate open for Peter to get into. It should be as small as possible. Lionel is standing by it, wearing his Oxfords. He has gloves and a scarf round his neck. He is facing a potential buyer (Appleyard) who is dressed in an overcoat and a businessman's hat. He's a 'self-made' man. He is just finishing looking at another cage.

Appleyard: To be blunt, Mr. Shirley-Smythe, this monkey's not worth a farthing to me. Far too scraggy.

Lionel: Well how about five guineas...?

Appleyard: (*laughing contemptuously*) Mr. Shirley-Smythe, I run a variety show not a home for dossors.

Lionel: No, no. Quite, quite.

Peter: (*to audience*) There were hundreds of boxes and cages. Suddenly I realised I was one of the hundreds; thousands even.

He quietly gets in his cage and closes the door.

Appleyard: No, send it to the zoo. No good to me.

A Docker arrives carrying another box, marked 'LIVE ANIMAL – WITH CARE'. He has a Docker's hook in his belt and wears a cap. He is dressed as a workman would be.

Lionel: Very well.

Peter: (*to audience*) I decided in a flash. The variety show. A zoo meant only another cage.

The Docker hits Lionel with the box he is carrying – Lionel standing in the way.

Lionel: Be careful you great oaf!

The Docker dumps the box with a crash and walks back towards the steamer.

Docker: Shouldn't be in the way.

Lionel: Now listen to me you... (*The Docker is gone.*)

Appleyard: (*looking at Peter*) How much do you want for this chimp?

Peter tries, through his hangover, to look intelligent and winsome.

Lionel: Oh Peter. Very fine specimen. Awfully nice nature.

Appleyard: How much do you want?

The Docker appears again carrying two big cages.

Lionel: Well, I was thinking ... shall we say, four hundred guineas?

Appleyard: Four hundred guineas!!!

Lionel: Shall we say pounds?

The Docker crashes the two cages down right next to Lionel. The buyer continues to inspect Peter while the following exchange takes place.

Now then, I've had enough of you. Can't you see these boxes contain live animals ... they're very precious.

Docker: You wanna unload them yerself, mate?

Lionel: You don't take that tone with me, my man.

Docker: (*going*) Oh get stuffed.

Lionel: (*calling after him*) How would you like to get reported?

Docker: (*turning and shoving his hook*) How would you like this stuffed up your jacksie? (*he turns and goes*)

Lionel: Well, really!

Appleyard: This animal looks like it's got a hangover.

Lionel: (*innocently*) Does it? Shall we say three hundred pounds?

Appleyard: I'll give you fifty.

Lionel: Come, come. Fifty?! This animal talks.

Appleyard: (*turns to look at Lionel as though he's mad*) Talks? It's a chimpanzee – not a parrot.

Lionel: No, no 'pon my honour he talks. Two hundred and fifty. (*dipping down to the cage*) Come on now Peter. Talk to your Uncle Lionel.

The Docker comes in carrying yet another cage. He sees Lionel, puts the cage down and watches with Appleyard.

Say Hallo for Lionel. Hallo Peter. Hallo Peter.

Docker: (*to buyer casually*) He mad, or what?

Appleyard: Says it talks.

Docker: Touched in the 'ead, more like.

Lionel: (*venting his frustration, to Docker*) Now listen, you ... Get on with your work.

Docker: (*not an apology*) Havin' a break.

Lionel: Don't you answer me back. I'll have you drummed off the dockside.

Appleyard: Mr. Shirley-Smythe, could we finish our business...

Docker: You wanna try it. They'll lock you up in a nuthouse.

Lionel: How dare you?! (*he looks around for the foreman*) When I find someone in authority...

Docker: I wouldn't if I were you, or I'll load your precious fucking cages back on the boat and call a stoppage throughout the docks.

Appleyard: (*ushering the Docker away*) He is a bit touched – all the sun, you know.

Docker: (*going*) Yeah, well 'e wants to be careful. (*he's gone*)

Lionel: (*to buyer*) Give them trade unions, they think they own the world.

Appleyard: Shall we wrap up this business then Mr. Shirley-Smythe?

Lionel: Probably one of those damned socialists too, I shouldn't wonder.

Appleyard: Shall we way seventy-five pounds?

Lionel: Good war's what they need. Give them a bit of character.

Appleyard: Seventy-five. (*taking his money out*) Cash.

Lionel: Oh very well. (*magnanimously*) Cash is hardly necessary. Gentleman's word and all that.

Appleyard: Buy with cash. Sell with cash. Only way to do business. (*He passes the money over, and puts a cross on Peter's cage.*)

Lionel: Pleasure to do business with you, sir! Well, must pop; chaps at the Club will be waiting. (*Proffers hand which the Buyer takes perfunctorily.*)

(*Lionel goes. Buyer looks at Peter who is proffering his hand, mimicking Lionel. The Buyer doesn't take it, but, smiling, says...*)

Appleyard: Good.

(*The Docker appears again, carrying another case.*)

Wouldn't mind stacking this cage on the back of my van over there, when you get a minute.

(*Puts a pound note in his hand. Docker puts his crate down. Tips his hat.*)

Docker: No problem.

Appleyard: Thanks.

They both go. Peter unlocks the gate of the cage as the back picture goes and the sound stops, and comes forward. He doesn't close the curtain.

Peter: What did I learn? That we are born one of the mass, but if you want a way out of your cage, it is up to you. You fix your eyes on one thing, neither looking to the left nor the right. And with hard work and determination you can open the cage and close the door behind you. Firmly and forever. That is what I learned that day. (*He goes over to his papers and tidies them, speaking as he does.*) Would you care for a short break now, say fifteen minutes? Then afterwards, with the help of my friends here, I shall tell you what happened to me and how I learned to be a man.

He motions them to go, and sips his water as they leave and only leaves when the audience has done so.

PART 2

As the audience returns into the theatre, Peter is waiting for them – eagerly, but with complete dignity.

Peter: Good. Good. I have not bored you overmuch then. (*looking across to the teachers*) or perhaps your teachers (*or usher/usherette, if in theatre*) have dragooned you back into the theatre. (*to the teachers*) Yes?

Depending on answer: 'Well that's good.' or 'Oh, I'm sorry to hear that. I shall go more speedily if I can'.

Now then, perhaps some of you have been wondering can it be true? That an ape can really, within one generation, become a man? The question is well asked. And, of course, in the normal way, and under, shall we say, ordinary conditions, my answer would be, certainly not. However, in my case, the conditions were in no sense ordinary; and because of the combination of my single-minded determination and some, one can only say, extraordinary teachers, my way cannot by any stretch of the imagination be described as normal. So that, with perhaps the occasional error in detail, the main events that I have showed you and will continue in a moment to do so, are entirely true; so God is my witness. As such my answer to your question as to whether it is possible, would be an unequivocal yes. Now then, up to now I have spoken of the invaluable education I received at the hands of humans but one could not say that this amounted to a formal education, such as one might receive in a school for example. It was haphazard, rather. Arbitrary. But now, having escaped the zoological gardens and thence another cage, my systematic education began. To be a variety performer. I should say that the variety show did not mean my immediate release from the cage – far from it, such a thing is to be earned – and at the training school I did remain in one for a while; but the more I learned, and the more I adapted myself to the requirements of human society, the less I needed to be constrained by metal bars. But, in the first place, as I say, a cage was still my lot, for, try as I might, I could not convince a soul of my absolute willingness to refrain from doing what might be expected from a wild chimpanzee; viz, running amok. What a delight then it was when what was most necessary to me was offered by way of my first course of instruction. (*with great relish*) Language! (*he starts walking towards the curtain*) Of course by the end of the voyage I understood most that was said to me – I could tell by the tone of voice, the relation of words to things, and so on. But to speak myself. That was a different matter.

He opens the curtain, revealing a cage with a loose padlock on the door; the door is open, waiting for him. The backdrop shows an area of cages and stables with various performing animals in them. There are also humans, slopping out, changing straw etc. None of them look particularly happy. When the scene starts the sound of the 'stables' can be heard, low in the background. Mr. Appleyard stands by Peter's cage immobile until Peter gets in, which he does now, closing the door behind him. Peter begins grooming but also glances towards Mr. Appleyard who is watching him with some interest. Mr. Appleyard looks briefly at his pocket watch. As he puts it away Miss Keilich arrives. She is a strong hearty woman, dressed in a long wide skirt, wellington boots with mud on, and a cardigan. She wears thick gardener's gloves. She takes large strides, and carries a small hessian sack by one hand.

Appleyard: Miss Keilich. (*offers hand*)

Keilich: Mr. Appleyard. (*taking it heartily*)

Appleyard: Here early.

Keilich: Oh Yes! (*indicating Peter*) This is the chimp? (*puts down sack*)

Appleyard: Yes. Answers to Peter. (*Peter looks to Appleyard*)

Keilich: (*inspecting all the while*) Does he now?

Bends, nose to Peter's. Breathes at him. Peter looks quizzically. She makes various 'chucking' noises.

Hallo, boy. (*more 'chucking' noises*) You're called Peter, yes? (*Peter looks to her attentively*) Peter. (*more noises until, to Appleyard*) Seems amenable.

Appleyard: How long to train him?

Keilich: In the basics? Six weeks, couple of months. Less, if he takes to it. (*to Peter*) Want to come out of your cage, Peter? (*Peter hoots and gets excited*) Understands alright.

Appleyard: Good. Good.

Keilich: (*getting started*) Now then, Peter, if you want to come out of your cage you have to learn to do as you're told.

Peter hoots. She moves across to her sack meantime, pulls out a large bunch of bananas. Before she turns round...

Peter: (*unmistakably, but very approximate*) Wa' (nt) o' (ne).

Miss Keilich stops in her tracks. Looks at Peter who is looking only at the bananas and pointing.

Wa' o'...

She looks at Appleyard, who is nodding to her.

Appleyard: Fella I bought it from said it talked.

Keilich: (*very intent, enunciated speech*) Want one.

Peter: (*looks at her and then back to the bananas, as before*) Wa' o'.

Keilich: (*grabs a banana from the bunch; brings it towards Peter*) Want one. (*pause*) Want one. Want. One.

Peter begins to imitate the sound, she prompting with great difficulty he finally utters –

Peter: Want one. (*she immediately gives him the banana, which he immediately devours, then equally immediately*) Want one. (*he looks hungrily towards the bunch*) Want one.

Keilich: (*she goes over and takes another banana and brings it towards him*) Want one please. (*Peter looks perplexed*) Mine. My bananas. Want one please.

Peter: Want one.

Keilich: (*brings the banana nearer but still out of reach*) Want one please.

Peter: (*stretching hand out ... noises ... and ...*) Want one.

Keilich: (*decisively*) So you don't want one!

(*Goes to put it and the rest in a sack. Peter kicks up a racket.*)

You do want one. (*pulls out banana*) One of my bananas. You want... one ... please.

Peter tries the new sound of 'please' – but clearly doesn't understand the concept. She helps him by repeating the word and the phrase. During this she explains, again repetitively.

This is my banana ... my bananas. It's your banana when I have given it to you. If you want teacher's banana you must say please.

Peter: (*finally*) Want one please. (*she immediately gives him one, which he immediately eats and equally immediately*) Want one.

Keilich: Please. Want one please.

Peter: Want one please.

Keilich: That's right. (*she doesn't give him one; to Appleyard*) Remarkable animal.

Peter: Want one please.

Appleyard: Could you get him to talk properly?

Peter: Want one please.

Keilich: (*getting a new banana*) Maybe. We shall have to see (*holding out the banana*).

Peter: Want one please.

Keilich: (*to Peter*) You don't always get just because you ask, Peter.

Peter: Want one please.

Appleyard: (*going*) Keep me informed of his progress will you?

Keilich: Of course, Mr. Appleyard.

Peter: Want one please.

Appleyard goes. She turns her attention back to him.

Keilich: You want one of my bananas? (*she holds it out*)

Peter: Want one please. (*He grabs it, accidentally biting the glove as he does so. He devours the banana.*) Want one please.

Keilich: (*without anger*) You don't bite people, Peter. Never bite the hand that feeds you. Understand?

Peter: (*he does, briefly, then looks to bananas*) Want one please.

Keilich: (*putting them away*) No more for now.

Peter: Want one please.

The lights fade, the actress playing Keilich freezes. Light remains on Peter.

It was very hard to understand 'my' and 'yours'. For chimpanzees, the fruit is on the tree. You simply eat what you need. However, it was not long before I grasped it. At least I thought I had.

The lights come on again on Miss Keilich.

Want to come out of your cage, please.

Keilich: (*pointing the difference*) No, Peter. It's your cage; not my cage. Yours.

Peter: (*having difficulty with the concept; avoiding the problem*) Want to come out of cage, please.

Keilich: Yes. Whose cage, Peter? Whose is it? (*points to him*)

Peter: (*pointing to himself*) Your cage.

Keilich: No. Not mine. Yours. It's your home.

Peter: (*explaining, pointing to his own*) My fur. My head. My banana skin. Your (*pointing to her*) sack of bananas. Yours (*pointing around generally*) Your everything. (*pause, puzzled*) Your cage. Please.

Keilich: If you want to come out Peter, you must say, 'I want to come out of my cage, please'. Understand? (*pause; Peter still looks puzzled*) I've given you the cage. It's your cage.

Peter: (*still not grasping it, changes tack*) Won't hurt anyone. Won't break anything. (*putting it mildly*) Very cramped.

Keilich: Yes we know about that. Want to come out of my cage, please. Come along now. You're not coming out till you understand, you understand? (*pause*) I'm waiting.

Peter: (*very reluctant*) Can I give you the cage back? Then it'll be your cage.

Keilich: No Peter. It's your cage. You can't give it to me.

Peter: Why not?

Keilich: I can see you don't want to come out. (*starting to go*)

Peter: (*quickly*) Want to come out of my cage; please.

Keilich: That's it! (*opening it with a key*) Easy isn't it. (*Peter is getting excited*) Ah-ah-ah. What do you say?

Peter: Thank you.

Miss Keilich opens the cage and stands away. Peter now becomes very hesitant.

Keilich: Come on. Come on.

Peter slowly makes his way out and looks round gingerly, takes a few more paces. He then gives a shriek of delight and bounds all over the place.

Right! Enough! Back in your cage Peter. (*he stops, considers it a moment*) Back in your cage. (*Peter goes back in rather sorrowfully*) Good. Whose cage?

Peter: My cage.

Keilich: Good boy. (*she comes over to lock it*) Whose cage?

Peter: My cage. Can I have the key?

Keilich: No. My key. Your cage. My key. When you've shown yourself responsible, Peter, when you've finished training then perhaps you shall have the key. Until then ... my key.

Peter: Yes please.

Keilich: Goodbye Peter.

Peter: Goodbye Miss Keilich.

The lights and sound fade and Peter comes out of the cage. He comes forward closing curtains as he does.

Over those first few weeks and months I learned quickly. With language now at my disposal my other trainers and teachers no longer needed the laborious process of repetition to teach me tricks and skills. They would explain my difficulties when such arose. To be honest, at first I somewhat flattered myself to think I had made good progress but it was not until Mr. Appleyard – who owned the variety show and myself of course – put me into the tender care of one Susanne, that I really saw the infinite distance I had to travel if I was truly to succeed as a performing animal. I say 'tender care' not without some irony, for in truth she was very strict. But in her field, to use a phrase I much like, she was at the top of the tree.

He goes towards the closed curtain but stops with an afterthought.

Now I should say that there is a small reference to sex in this scene at the beginning and also a little violence later on. I say this for the adults here this morning (afternoon) rather than for you for I know that young people enjoy to see them both on stage. But adults become a little bored at such things or even angry, and much prefer to see them respectively in brothels and battlefields. So hereby let me apologise in advance to any who so feel. And I would not include either of them at all were it not fundamental to my education as a human to learn to subdue the one and accept the other. I was still quite young at the time...

He draws the curtain as he speaks. It reveals a practically empty acting area, brightly lit. The back picture shows an old fashioned, cavernous ballroom – empty of furniture or people except for a tiny man (by scale) cleaning the windows up a tall ladder. In the acting area there is a non-real upright piano. In front of this, there is an (actual) piano stool.

...and it was often my habit while waiting for a teacher to arrive – if I was bored, that is – to play with my sex. No-one hitherto had minded, far less reproved me. I see now they put it down to my animal nature. So on this occasion (*he sits down*) I had a small hard-on – I much prefer the term to that flaccid technical term 'erection' which sounds more like what one would do to a tent or to a building than to oneself – and I was pinging it back and forwards, idly as one does. – Please don't strain to see; I am miming on this occasion, when Susanne came in.

Susanne comes in. She is an attractive woman probably of about 30, but carries herself severely. She wears a fur coat and carries a vanity case. When she takes her coat off she can be seen to be wearing boots, some smart jodhpur-like trousers and woman's military-type jacket. She wears gloves. She walks straight past him and places her vanity case on the piano stool and begins to remove her gloves.

Susanne: If that display of masculinity is meant to impress me, it doesn't. I am not impressed with puny penises. Stand up when I'm speaking to you.

Peter does so; she still hasn't looked at him. She takes her coat off and hangs it on a coat stand.

Your name is Peter?

Peter: Yes.

Susanne: You call me 'Madame'. (*she is opening her vanity bag*)

Peter: Yes, Madame.

Susanne takes a kind of cane from her bag and walks over to Peter. She whacks him in the groin. Peter screams and jumps away, clutches himself and whimpers.

Susanne: You don't do that again. You understand me, Peter. Neither in my presence nor out of it. And stop making that hideous noise. Anyone would think I hurt you. (*Peter stops whimpering but looks terrified*) Hands by your side. (*looks*) There, it's gone down now hasn't it?

Peter: Yes, Madame.

Susanne: Now then it's quite simple – if you want to be a beast you can go back to the jungle and be a beast. But if you want to be a performer with the Great Susanne, then you will put a stop to your bestial habits. Have I made myself clear?

(*Peter nods his head ruefully. Mr. Simpkins, her pianist, arrives rather flustered. He's an ageing, deferring man.*)

139

Ah, Mr. Simpkins.

Simpkins: I'm terribly sorry, Madame. I'm afraid I got held up in traffic. (*he hovers*)

Susanne: There are only two reasons for being late, Mr. Simpkins: one is the death of a close relative in which case you should send a telegram; the other is your own death, in which case you should delay that and not your arrival.

Simpkins: Quite, Madame. (*he still hovers*)

Susanne: Stop hovering Mr. Simpkins.

Simpkins: Your case is on my piano stool, Madame.

Susanne: Then take it off. You have hands, I presume; being a pianist.

Simpkins: Yes, quite, Madame, quite.

He places the vanity case on the floor with great care and sits down. Susanne whacks him with her stick across the back.

Susanne: Don't be late again, Mr. Simpkins. It's extremely rude. (*looking at Peter scornfully*) Like masturbating. Now then Peter, do you dance?

Peter: (*speaking very softly*) A little bit, Madame.

Susanne: Speak up.

Peter: (*clears throat*) A lit...

Susanne: Stand up straight. Don't slouch like a lout. Well?

Peter: (*standing up, speaking up*) A little bit, Madame.

Susanne: We shall see. Mr. Simpkins, a tango if you please.

The actor playing the piano mimes playing, while the sound of a piano in a large hall is heard on tape. It plays the famous tango, Fernando's Hideaway.

Watch me. (*she demonstrates imagining the partner – perfectly – the first four phrases*) And hold. (*she drops the pose*) Now you do it. (*sings*) And... one ...

The piano starts – Peter does too. He's not at all bad.

Stop!

Piano stops. Peter looks across, frightened.

That's terrible. (*showing stick*) You want my stick? You dance like a cripple in a shoe shop. Again. And ... one ...

Piano starts, Peter dances, trying hard.

Keep your head back! You look like a chimpanzee. (*in despair*) Stop, stop.

The piano stops.

You keep your head up (*pokes with her stick*) Tilted to one side (*stick again*) Contempt. So. (*she demonstrates head position*) Think of Mr. Simpkins. Anything, but look contemptuous. Isn't that right, Mr. Simpkins?

Simpkins: Yes, Madame.

Susanne: Very well. Again. And ... one ...

Piano starts. Peter fumbles and stops. The piano trails off.

Peter: (*bitterly disappointed and frightened at the same time*) Oh I can't do it.

Susanne: Can't? No such word as 'can't'. Won't. (*Takes hold of his fur and twists it. Peter squirms to take the pressure off.*) Stand still when I'm twisting your fur. Has a will of his own it seems, Mr. Simpkins.

Simpkins: (*without turning round*) Yes indeed Madame.

Susanne: (*ignoring him*) Do you have a will of your own, Master Peter? (*pause – she's still twisting*) Well?

Peter: (*bravely, under the circumstances*) I'm trying, Madame, honestly.

Susanne: (*she lets go of him with contempt*) Trying is not good enough. When I say you dance, you dance and continue to dance until I say stop. Now then what do you say?

Peter: I'm sorry, Madame.

Susanne: Don't give me your apologies.

She turns away and goes to her vanity bag – she brings out a coconut (without milk in it). She bangs it on Simpkins' head and it (the coconut) breaks in half. Simpkins, more in surprise than hurt, slumps forward causing a discord to sound. She puts half back in her case and places the other half on the floor away from Peter.

(*to Mr. Simpkins*) I took the precaution of draining it, Mr. Simpkins.

Simpkins: Thank-you, Madame

Susanne: Don't want to spoil the ivories. (*to Peter*) You like coconut, Peter?

Peter: Yes, Madame, if it's all right with you.

Susanne: It is. We have a saying, Peter, the stick and the carrot. Now then, which is it to be? Hm? (*before he can answer*) Now dance. With me. And ... one ...

Piano starts, Peter and Susanne dance – extremely well. They dance the whole tune through. She's not unimpressed, but this is not given to Peter.

And ... hold. Thank-you. (*Peter looks to her and then the coconut*) Not bad. (*picking up the coconut*) But not good either. Neither the stick nor the carrot this time I think. (*She puts the coconut away with the stick in her vanity bag. She turns round on Peter.*) And don't get any wild ideas of taking it by force. The last creature that tried to attack me was a jaguar. He made a very fine fur coat. (*She reaches down for her fur coat and puts it on looking at Peter all the while. She picks up her bag and gloves.*) Thank-you Mr. Simpkins. Tomorrow afternoon at three o' clock sharp. (*she starts to go*) Oh and that window cleaner was disturbing my teaching today, Mr. Simpkins. Would you ask him if he would be so kind as not to be here tomorrow afternoon, or tell him I'll break his little ladder for him. Good day. Peter.

And she goes. Simpkins goes tottering off towards the window cleaner...

Simpkins: I say ... excuse me ...

He exits – the back picture fades. Peter comes forward closing the curtain behind him.

Peter: She beat me less and less as time went by. Whether this was because she saw that I came to fear more her scathing disapproval when I failed than I did her stick; or whether my growing determination to become the most supreme assistant to her performance on the variety stage softened her a little towards me, I cannot tell. I do know that I never got so much as to lick the coconut, beyond endurance sometimes, and, at yet other times, plunged me to the depths of self-loathing that I should have thought myself remotely worthy of her coconut at all. But such is how an ape, struggling to be a man, thinks. And such is how artists and teachers of Madame's calibre teaches. Now I should like to show you the outcome of our act. I perhaps should not say 'our' act, for while it is true that the trade journals and the newspapers frequently had photographs of, and wrote much about myself, the theatre bills showed clearly that it was she who was the attraction: (*demonstrating big*) The Great Susanne and (*smaller*) Peter the Talking Ape. Moreover, it was she whom the audience applauded. She was indeed more beautiful than I (*smiles*) and danced superbly. Be that as it may, we performed for many years up and down the country in all the great theatres – many of them are closed now, alas – abroad to Europe and the United States. The act developed; we did – everything; singing, dancing, a great deal of patter to emphasise I talked – as if that needed proving! – oh, everything. We never ceased rehearsing, adding new things to the act; learning all the time. And then, what was to be her crowning achievement, she devised a mind-reading act. It was extremely difficult – it is, even for a complete human – to learn all the codes and signals that would convince the sharp examining eyes of the audience. At first it went extremely well, 'Susanne's' greatest success; and it should have been mine too.

He draws the curtain back as quickly as possible with loud, ongoing, applause. The acting area is more or less in darkness but it is set as follows: to the two sides nearest the front curtain are two ornate cut-out 'tabs' in rich velvet. In the acting area there is a small pedestal of the kind used by magicians to place their gear on; next to this there is a light high stool with a back. The back picture is of the backdrop to their act. This is not lit at the moment. Following directly on from the curtain being opened by Peter, there is a blackout. In the applause a follow-spot comes up on Susanne, receiving the applause; Peter is off-stage. She looks riveting – at least to the male eye. ((Feminists may not be so keen.)) She wears boots and black stockings. Her legs are completely exposed. She wears a one-piece suit and waistcoat in a rich black material, details picked out with black and white polka-dots. All with the crispness and smartness of a top class variety act. Her sexuality is most certainly present – but the act is not about her sexuality. When she speaks, she speaks with a non-specific mid-European accent. She motions with her hands as if to say 'no, you're too kind' and 'thank you., thank you very much.'

Susanne: No. You're too kind. Thank you, thank you very much, you are wonderful.

The applause dies down.

You really are a most kind audience. (*she looks serious*) And now I would like to show you a truly remarkable liaison between man and beast (*she smiles modestly*) or should I say woman and beast. (*she laughs artificially at the joke*) It is, ladies and gentlemen, rare enough between human beings. But between a woman and an ape, ladies and gentlemen, unique. And I refer, of course, to the art of reading minds. Now then if (*looking up to the electrician – the lights go up*) – thank you – if I invite Peter to join us...

She puts out her arm and Peter, dressed as a schoolboy (stereotype) walks on from the side towards her.

I shall commence this extraordinary telepathic encounter. How are you feeling, Peter?

Peter: (*feigning naturalness, well rehearsed*) I am feeling just fine, thank you Susanne.

Susanne: Good. I am very pleased to hear that. There you are, ladies and gentlemen, Peter is feeling fine. (*feigned sudden worry*) Oh, but are the waves of the ether clear this evening, Peter?

Peter: I am certainly hoping so. (*she turns in a dummy to the audience*) The audience here tonight is very warm and sympathetic Susanne.

Susanne: (*feigning delighted surprise*) Oh! He is so sweet, ladies and gentlemen! (*she moves to get a stool and places it down stage for Peter*) Indicating the stool ... Are you sitting comfortably?

Peter gets comfortable.

Peter: Yes, thank you.

Susanne: Good. (*turning to audience*) I shall now place this blindfold ... (*she gets it from the table*) ... over Peter's eyes ... (*She brings it forward to a member of the audience*) ... would you check it please? – so that he will be in complete darkness – is that a perfectly ordinary blindfold ... thank you ... There are no tricks, ladies and gentlemen ... (*she puts the blindfold over his eyes*) ... You can see nothing at all, is that correct, Peter?

Peter: It is. I can see nothing at all.

Susanne: Now then, is there a lady or a gentleman in the audience who would provide something from about their person ... from a handbag? ... anything at all. (*she elicits a response from a member of the actual audience*) Don't show it to me yet. What is your name, sir (madam)?...(*reply*) ... Now then sir (madam) would you give me the object, please. Thank you.

There is a low roll of a drum building to a slow crescendo. The lights dim except on Peter and Susanne ((follow-spot).

Now I am thinking of the object, Peter.

She is holding it up. Susanne spells the object out by emphasising key letters in the patter she carries on to build the mystery. Finally, Peter 'guesses' the object.

Peter: It's a ... (*whatever it is. The drum roll is completed.*)

Susanne: A ...(*whatever it is*) Thank you very much, ladies and gentlemen! You're too kind. (*gives back object*)

Peter: (*getting up*) Madame, madame...

Susanne: What an amazing and sensitive... (*seeing him*)

Peter: ...no more, please.

Susanne: Oh Peter, what are you doing? Are the ether waves disturbed? Sit down! (*normal voice, private*) We're not finished yet. Get back to your seat! Do you want to make a fool of me? Go back.

He does so as she sweeps on.

Now then, ladies and gentlemen, that was really too easy! Do we have another lady or gentleman? ... no, let us have a lady (gentleman) this time! Yes, sir (madam). What's your name? (*reply*) What a very unusual name! And have you come far to the theatre, tonight? (*reply*) Oh I am sorry! And do you have the object there? Thank you.

She takes it and holds it up. The lights dim again except on Peter and Susanne in the follow-spot in the audience. The drum roll begins again.

Now I am thinking of the object, Peter ... I have formed a *mental* image in my head. (*she speaks very clearly, giving special stress to key word as signals*) Is it *too warm* for you Peter? (*Peter is struggling*) The gentleman in the *back* row is going to *sleep*. (*She laughs. Pause. Then somewhat urgently.*) You'll send us all to sleep. (*she laughs, calmly but icily*) Don't you know? Who's a naughty boy?

Peter: (*blurting out*) A vanity bag.

The drum roll is completed.

Susanne: (*very calmly*) No, Peter. (*to audience*) I think we'll...

Peter: (*butting in*) A fur co ... No. A ...

Susanne: Don't guess, Peter. (*flustered, but covering as a professional*) I think, ladies and gentlemen, the ether waves are a little disturbed tonight. (*she laughs artificially*) This was a [naming whatever it is] Peter.

Peter: (*gesturing 'of course it was'*) Yes, yes a [whatever it is] I was just about to say that.

Susanne: (*less than covering*) Oh what a shame! (*smiling*) Let us try once more shall we? A most unique phenomenon, ladies and gentlemen – a mystery to our greatest scientists of the mind. Now then what is your name, sir (madam) ... (*reply*) And have you come far? ... (*reply*) Good, do you have an object, there? May I have it please?

Peter is straining to hear every word – she looks across to him to check he's getting the verbal messages.

Thank you.

The drum roll begins again. She holds up the object and looks as though she's thinking hard. The *picture's* in my head now. (*pause*) Clear as *day* now. (*Peter again is struggling*) Take your time, don't rush. Can you see the *back* of my mind, Peter? It's *definitely* there. At the *back*.

Peter squirms like a panic-stricken child.

Peter: Er... (*under breath, saying key words to himself, not all right*) Picture, head. Pic...

Susanne: (*on edge*) You've not been concentrating, have you? Mm? Listen to me, Peter. You'll get the *picture* one *day* – you can *back* that. *Definitely.* (*very sharp*) Won't you? (*she smiles grimly to audience*)

Peter: (*still more panicky*) Er ... picture, head ... (desperately) ... want to go to the toilet, Madame ... (*the drum stops*)

Susanne: (*very firm, but smiling*) Stay where you are. Isn't he a tantalising sweetie! (*to him*) Last chance. (*drum starts*) To get that *picture* one *day*, back in your brain. Definitely last chance. (*smiles to audience*)

Peter: (*desperate*) Can't do it Madame. (*drum stops*) Can't remember a single one.

He snatches off his blindfold and throws it on the ground, then looks at the object and declares what it is, in a plain act of defiance, then throws his cap down and stamps on it, then folds his arms.

Susanne: (*after a pause, smiling killingly*) Aha! You'll be sorry for this!

She walks calmly towards him, picks up his blindfold and his cap and puts them on the table. She turns towards the audience.

Well, tonight, alas ladies and gentlemen the truly remarkable and – delicate – art of telepathy has left our young friend. So let me leave you then with our world-famous dance...

Peter: I'm not doing the dance...

Susanne: (*smiling*) Our world-famous dance ... (*grabbing his fur and twisting it, out of sight of the audience, very low, to him – English accent back*) You will. (*she looks out to the audience smiling and takes up tango position*) Ladies and gentlemen – our world-famous dance.

Peter swings round to her and bites her on the offered (left) thigh on the other side from him. He stares at Susanne's leg.

Susanne: (*spontaneously from the bite, though more in surprise than pain*) Little runt!

She clutches her thigh and looks at Peter, ready to kill him. He runs off. She smiles to the audience. Music plays a jolly tune. She rushes off after Peter. The spotlight rapidly fades before she actually gets off. An actor draws the curtain across in the blackout. The lights rise quickly and Peter comes though the curtain. He is once more naked.

Peter: To this day I have not the slightest idea why I did it. Nor have I shown you the incident because I am proud of my behaviour. Far from it. It was – and I use the word quite particularly – beastly. But you grasp from this particularly unpleasant event of my life, I hope, the difficulty that I had in overcoming my ape nature even after all my training and lessons at the hands of true professionals. The audience, I should say, treated the whole thing as a huge joke; indeed they assumed that 'Susanne' had planned it all. But the truth seeped out, as truth will. The newspapers got hold of it and, well you know how the newspapers twist things – 'WILD APE ATTEMPTS HUMAN RAPE'. Mr. Appleyard saw to it that neither Susanne nor myself were available for comment and eventually the whole thing died down – except of course in scientific journals where learned arguments were thrown back and forth across their columns for months as to whether it was indeed possible that an ape could evolve into a human in one generation. I should say, in passing, that the argument was only finally resolved some seven or eight years ago when I was in a position to allow a full examination into my case history and achievements in human society. But to return to the effects of my outburst that evening. (*he goes over to his table*) You will permit me I hope to dress myself for the next scene while I speak to you. (*he does so – the actor playing Mr. Appleyard [out of character] helping him*) Susanne, of course, refused point blank to work with me, and indeed, we never even met again. I gather that, after a long vacation, she returned to the variety stage under another name, and with another accent. Her act consisted – a comedown I fear from working with primates – of swallowing snakes and such like. She did this for a short while; then one night, in Rotheram, she was swallowed by a snake on stage. It upset me for a week. (*pause*) As for myself, I was more fortunate. For that unprofessional behaviour I could have been sacked on the spot, but Mr. Appleyard once more took a hand (*he is now completely dressed*) in my development.

The actor stays where he is except at the appropriate moment to get an umbrella passed through the curtain to him. Peter continues to speak as he walks over to the curtain.

It was rare to meet Mr. Appleyard, although he owned us all. This was perhaps only the second occasion I'd met him in all the time since I'd first come into his possession on the London docks. Imagine, then, my thoughts when a week after the biting affair he asked to see me at the Zoological Gardens in Regents Park.

He opens the curtain. Just behind the line of the curtain, there are bars running the full width of the acting area, reaching as high as the curtain rail. The back-picture shows a boring brick wall. In the acting area are two chimpanzees – looking moth-eaten and extremely apathetic; on the floor beside them are a few

146

bits of uninviting half-eaten fruit; empty crisp bags and ice-cream wrappers that have been thrown through the bars. Desolation. When the action starts there is the incessant sound of pouring rain. Peter is outside the primates' house.

It was raining, I remember, and I hadn't brought my umbrella.

He is now back at the opposite side of the acting area to Appleyard, who puts up his umbrella as the sound begins. Peter is waiting like a youth outside the headmaster's study. Appleyard 'arrives'.

Appleyard: Hallo Peter

Peter: Hallo, Mr. Appleyard.

Appleyard: You'll be getting wet. (*Peter nods but doesn't say anything*) D'you know why I've brought you here (*indicating cage*) to talk?

Peter: No Mr. Appleyard.

Appleyard: You think you do, don't you? Mm? (*Peter doesn't say anything*) Well, it's not for that. (*Peter looks up*) Not necessarily. (*Peter back a bit*) I want you to look in that cage.

Peter: I don't think I can, Mr. Appleyard.

Appleyard: Yes you can. Just look. (*Peter looks*) What do you see?

Peter: A cage.

Appleyard: Yes. What else?

Peter: (*looking away*) My brothers and sisters. My kind.

Appleyard: (*correcting*) Were your kind. (*pause*) Speak to them. Go on.

Peter: Don't make me Mr. Appleyard. Please.

Appleyard: (*firmly*) Speak to them. (*pause*) Don't be afraid.

Peter: What shall I say?

Appleyard: I don't mind. Anything you like.

Peter: (*turns towards them*) Hallo. (*one of the chimpanzees picks up a piece of fruit, inspects it without interest, then apathetically chucks it away*) Are you hungry? ... My name's ... (*dawning – without joy – to Appleyard*) They don't understand English.

Appleyard: No. No. They're chimpanzees, Peter.

Peter: Yes. (*Pause ... he then brightens a little and tries some sounds and puts out a very gentle submissive hand towards them. Nothing happens at all. The chimpanzees are completely still, but not attending.*) Oh no. (*to Appleyard*) I can't remember ...(*trails off*)

Appleyard: Long time ago. (*Peter is staring at the chimpanzees*) Now I want you to listen to me Peter, because I'm going to tell you something. (*Peter looks at him*) Will you do that? Come under my umbrella – you'll be soaking. (*Peter comes over*) When I was a boy I had nothing. I was brought up in what you'd now call a slum. My father died when I was eight. And my mother brought up six of us. Plenty people out of work and those who got work earned a pittance.

And I said to myself, 'Tom, you're not going to waste your life away and never have anything.' Day after my father died I got up early and went and looked for a job. And I got one; mucking out the stables at the milk-depot yard, for sixpence a week. Three hours every morning. And I got muck in my hair, muck in the very pores of my skin and I must have stunk. And I daresay there were some who looked down on us 'cause I smelled of shit. But I didn't care what they thought. And do you know why? Because I could look at them in the eyes and say 'I've never asked for nothing from no-one.' And I saved every penny. Oh I had some set-backs! But, to cut a long story short, I became a buyer for a firm of importers of exotic animals. And with the knowledge I gained and the money I saved I started my own business. Now I own them all – the animals and the artistes alike. And I can buy anything I want. (*pause*) Do you understand me?

Peter: Yes.

Appleyard: I'm a self-made man. And I'm going to make you one too. I know your talent. I know your ability to work.

Peter: You're very kind to me Mr. Appleyard...

Appleyard: Not kind. Don't upset me. I'm a businessman.

Peter: Well what I mean to say is how can I go further without Madame?

Appleyard: (*sternly*) Yes. I was going to speak about that. I don't want any more of my performers broken by you. Am I making myself clear? Look at that cage again. How many creatures do you see in it?

Peter: Well, two.

Appleyard: In ten years, maybe less, it will be crammed to overflowing; and all the other cages. (*Peter is perplexed*) Why? Because the animal shows, the circuses, variety itself will be all but finished. Only the best and the strongest will survive. And when the zoos can't take any more the scientific laboratories will move in and do experiments on the rest. And why's all this going to happen? Because the public WILL NOT WANT TO KNOW and only THE VERY BEST will survive. Which are you going to be, Peter? (*he looks at Peter; he looks at the other apes*) It's as dangerous as living in the jungle, eh Peter?

Peter: I don't know if I'll cope.

Appleyard: Just have to learn to live in it, that's all. Don't need to go round biting everyone; know who to bite and when to bite them. But you do none of that, understand? (*he looks and sees that the rain has stopped – as has the sound; he brings down his umbrella*) Looks like it's stopped for a bit. (*he shakes his umbrella*) Walk with me. (*they walk slowly across the stage and back again during the following*) What's your greatest asset, Peter? (*Peter tries to walk and look like Appleyard, unconsciously*)

Peter: Er, I don't know.

Appleyard: Your ability to imitate. (*Peter realises he is imitating A's walk and immediately stops*)

Peter: (*modestly*) Well I have tried.

Appleyard: To imitate human beings. I'm going to get a new trainer – 'teacher' I think is a better term. When she's finished with you, you'll be the best in the field, and completely reliable. You'll still look like an ape, otherwise there'd be no point, but you'll behave exactly as a human being. They'll love you. If they don't, or you don't make the grade, you'll be in there. (*indicating cage*) No more tricks or dancing – you'll be an impressionist – a human impressionist. Cabaret, and then when we're ready ... television. Your own show. We'll call you Peter Mann.

Peter: Mr. Appleyard, I don't know what to say!

Appleyard: Don't say anything. Work harder than ever you've done before. I want perfection. Nothing less.

Peter: You shall have it.

Appleyard: (*looks up; sees it beginning to rain*) Come into my office tomorrow morning to sign the contract. Yes? (*puts up umbrella*)

Peter: Yes.

Appleyard offers his hand and they shake hands, just briefly.

Appleyard: Good. (*indicating cage*) Take a good look, Peter, before you go. And don't ever come here again, eh?

He goes. The rain comes heavier. Peter looks at the two chimpanzees.

Peter: Goodbye. Never again. (*he closes the curtain and the rain fades away*) I shall not linger on what I felt as I walked away from those cages and out through the turnstile. The pain I felt at the fate of my former kind was such that I had to lock it away deep in the recesses of my mind. Of course I knew that there was nothing I could do for them. For myself I had to concentrate my mind on achieving the last stage of my transformation. And this meant to root out the last vestiges of my ape nature, not simply be able to imitate human beings but in the very essence of my being – become one. While the determination to achieve this goal was mine every bit as Mr. Appleyard's – indeed, since his existence was in no way threatened by my potential failure, as was mine, I think now my determination was if anything stronger than his – he was very kind and found me a teacher of outstanding quality to oversee my final step to the way of humanity.

He walks across the stage and draws back the curtain. It reveals a spacious room. The back picture shows some of the interior of a room and through the windows, an elegant garden with trees etc., very beautiful. In the acting area is a couch that can be laid on, and a matching upright chair. There is a wicker bird-cage on a stand containing two canaries. There is the peaceful sound of canaries throughout. Yarrow is lying on the couch; she is snazzily dressed, but in casual wear. Peter walks in. Peter looks immediately at the canary – he doesn't see Yarrow. Yarrow leaps up.

Yarrow: (*urgently*) Yes?!

Peter: Er, Ms Yarrow?

Yarrow: (*completely calm*) Yes. Do call me Yvonne. (*she offers a sophisticated hand*)

Peter: (*nervously and trying hard*) Oh yes, thank you very much.

Yvonne: Yvonne.

Peter: Yvonne.

Yvonne: And you must be Peter-with-a-little-problem.

Peter: Yes. Rather a big one I'm afraid.

Yvonne: There are no big problems, Peter. Lie down here, will you, Peter. (*indicating couch*)

Peter: That's very nice of you. (*wants to please but feels awkward, semi-lies*)

Yvonne: No, lie comfortably. (*Peter tries to*) There that's better isn't it, Peter?

Peter: Yes – Yvonne.

Yvonne: Now just relax. Do you feel you want to close your eyes?

Peter: Well … not really

Yvonne: That's all right too.

There is a longish pause. Peter looks sheepishly across to Yvonne.

All right?

Peter: Oh yes.

Yvonne: Now what I'm going to do is ask you a few questions and see what the little problem is, eh?

Peter: Yes, thank you.

Yvonne: Then we'll see what we can do to put it right. All right Peter?

Peter: Yes. Thank you.

Yvonne: Now then I want you to think back to when you were a little chimp.

Peter: (*correcting*) Chimpanzee.

Yvonne: Very interesting.

Peter: Eh? (*beginning to sit up*)

Yvonne: (*quickly*) Just relax. (*he goes back*) Think back to when you were a little chimpanzee in the jungle. Are you thinking?

Peter: I can't remember very much.

Yvonne: That's all right. Did you like your father?

Peter: Er?

Yvonne: Were you, shall we say, frightened, of him?

Peter: Frightened? No. Why should I be?

Yvonne: Let me ask the questions, Peter.

Peter: I'm sorry.

Yvonne: That's all right. What about your mother? Did you like her?

Peter: Yes, I suppose so.

Yvonne: You don't remember her going off and leaving you...

Peter: Chimpanzees never do that, Miss Yarrow ... Yvonne. I'm sorry.

Yvonne: No. It's all right. So she smothered you with too much affection.

Peter: Chimpanzees never do that either – they do what any mother must do if an infant is to survive.

Yvonne: (*very disappointed*) Yes I'm sure. (*she takes the chair and sits on it, back in front of her – intently*) You see Peter, we're trying to find where your violent feelings come from – and if we're to find them we have to unlock the memories of your childhood, which of course don't want to come out. Do you understand me?

Peter: Yes. I think so, Yvonne.

Yvonne: And you're resisting me aren't you?

Peter: Am I?

Yvonne: Yes. Chimpanzees never do this, never do that...

Peter: They don't. (*sitting up*)

Yvonne: (*victoriously*) You see? (*indicating himself*) But we're going to unlock the cage of your mind and let these nasty things out – and then they won't trouble you any more.

Peter: I don't like cages, Yvonne. Horrible things.

Yvonne: (*sympathetically*) Yes. But you see we make our own cages, don't we?

Peter: Do we?

Yvonne: Yes, we make our own. Then we say to others: 'Don't put me in there; don't lock me up'.

Peter: Do you say that too?

Yvonne: (*put out*) Well no. Of course not. But I'm not on that couch am I?

Peter: You were though.

Yvonne: But I was just resting.

Peter: Ah.

Yvonne: (*after a pause*) Clever little chap aren't you?

Peter: Well I want to be human, like you.

Yvonne: Good. Good. Well we'll leave the questions for the moment and do a few tests. That all right?

Peter: Yes, Yvonne.

Yvonne: Now then I'm going to say something and I want you to say or do whatever you want. You understand me?

Peter: Yes, I think so.

Yvonne: Right. (*pause – aggressively*) All chimpanzees are vicious little beasts and should be put down.

Peter: (*hackles rise immediately – but controlling*) That's not true.

Yvonne: Oh yes it is – they're stupid, mean, ugly little bastards. (*she hits him very hard*)

Peter: (*about to go for her*) Say that again and...

Yvonne: They've got about as much brain as my little finger. (*Holding finger up. Peter goes for her. Dropping hostility.*) OK Stop. (*Peter stops, perplexed*) Oo now. You were getting very angry there, weren't you! Bordering on violence.

Peter: Yes – but you...

Yvonne: (*tutting*) You have to learn to be tolerant of other people's ideas. Apes may fight over things like that but not humans...

Peter: They'd never say them.

Yvonne: You're contradicting me again ... you see? Mustn't do that.

Peter: Oh I see.

Yvonne: You must say something like ... you may have a point there but, or, perhaps you're right, but I have always found such and such. Now when we've found out what your little problem is you won't get aggressive when someone says something you don't like. That'll be nice won't it?

Peter: If you say so.

Yvonne: Very good. 'If you say so' that's very good Peter. I can see you don't agree but – well, that was very good. (*pause*) Okay. I think we can leave it there for now. (*chirpy*) Same time next week? (*Peter's looking towards the canaries*) Is anything the matter Peter?

Peter: Er no. It's just that ... well Yvonne ... I was wondering why you kept them in a cage...

Yvonne: They like it in there. If I didn't keep them in there they'd fly away and get pecked to pieces by horrible rooks and mauled to death by those nasty cats. No, they're grateful to us humans, for keeping them safe. That's why they're singing. (*slight pause*) All right? (*smiles*)

Peter: Yes. Thank you.

Yvonne: Not at all, Peter.

Peter: Do you think I will be able to be human, then?

Yvonne: I have no doubt of it.

Peter gets up and comes forward to address the audience with great excitement. The actress playing Yvonne closes the curtain.

It was extremely hard – harder than anything I had yet attempted. Yvonne was endlessly patient with me. She never lost her temper except on purpose to test me, and when she hit me as she sometimes did we laughed about it afterwards. Because she'd only pretended and I would be taken in. But as time went on I had learnt all that distinguished man from apes: to be tolerant of other people's points of view, to rationally argue when I disagreed with something someone said, to value the unique talents of every single individual, to look with sympathy and concern on those less fortunate than myself. Scientists, as I told you, marvelled at my development. Despite my appearance which still, I admit, has something of the chimpanzee, they declared, with only the smallest number disagreeing, that Peter the Ape was no more and Peter the Man existed in his stead. Mr. Appleyard was pleased with my development too. Everything that he had said was possible, had occurred. Star billing at the very best cabarets; young girls assisted me; and then a television show all of my own: 'Peter Mann Human Impressionist'. People stayed in to watch me. And yet, with all the fame and razzmatazz that surrounded me at the time, nothing was so dear to me as the clear, pure knowledge: Never ever a cage again. So warmly did I embrace the ways of humanity, that as time went on, I less and less thought of myself at all. Rather, I found my attention more and more focused upon the problems of others, a feature unique to human beings, as I am sure you will readily agree. For example, only a week or so ago, I remember seeking an appointment with Mr. Appleyard to discuss one such concern that I had. He kindly agreed to see me, so I went to see him.

Peter goes to the curtain and opens it. There is the sound of an office typing-pool, telephone ringing occasionally. The backdrop picture illustrates this – a large efficient – not extravagant – office area. In the foreground is Appleyard's office wall and door into the main office area, through the large window of which can be seen the typing pool. There are Venetian blinds which at present are open. In the acting area, Appleyard is seated at an office desk on which there is a telephone and various office stationery. He is relaxed, going through papers. Peter comes in, somewhat agitated.

I knocked, I heard him say...

Appleyard: Come in, Peter.

...and I went in, closing the door behind me.

Appleyard: (*very warmly*) Peter. Going over to shake hands. How are you Peter?

Peter: Very well thank you Mr. Appleyard.

Appleyard: Good. Good. I enjoyed your show very much, the other week.

Peter: (*surprised*) Oh you watched it!

Appleyard: Oh yes! I did enjoy that impression of Dennis Healey [*or current Prime Minister*]. Drink?

Peter: Er, no thank you Mr. Appleyard. (*smiling*) I have the eyebrows for him I think! [*or whatever feature is relevant*]

Appleyard: Sure now. Small Scotch perhaps.

Peter: Er ... no thanks, if it's all right with you.

Appleyard: Course it is! Whatever you like. Now then what can I do for you? Not often we get the chance to chat. What's on your mind? You want a bit more money?

Peter: Er no. Thank you very much. (*Peter pauses, not knowing how to say what he wants to say*)

Appleyard: Well what is it then? Come on. We're old friends. You can say what you like.

Peter: Well ... I wanted to ask ... I mean ... do you still keep up the animal importing side of your business?

Appleyard: (*slight pause – much of his bonhomie disappears, but not sinister*) Why do you ask?

Peter: Well I thought you stopped it years ago, after we ... talked at the zoological gardens.

Appleyard: Yes...well...?

Peter: You see I have been given to understand that large numbers of chimpanzees and monkeys of various kinds are being used, how can I put it, for 'experimental' purposes.

Appleyard: (*more at ease*) And you're concerned about it aren't you?

Peter: I am rather.

Appleyard: Very naturally.

Peter: Do you still import animals?

Appleyard: From whose point of view are you asking, Peter? (*pause*) From an ape's or from a man's? Em?

Peter: (*in difficulty*) Er, as a human.

Appleyard: I thought so, Peter. (*he walks slowly as he speaks*) You need to understand this, Peter. You're quite right, such experiments do go on. You're quite right. But they're for the good of all humanity. Do you see? They sacrifice their freedom and their lives, some of them, for all of us – you included.

Peter: I can see what you are saying, Mr. Appleyard – I am sure you have a point there – but I do not quite see how subjecting them to nerve gases, or to poisonous bacteria, or to controlled nuclear radiation benefits either humanity or the chimpanzees.

Appleyard: (*very alarmed*) Who told you that?

Peter: You don't import animals – Mr. Appleyard, do you?

Appleyard: Peter, who told you?

Peter: One of your drivers was loading crates, with holes in, you understand, on a lorry, when I came to collect my salary last week. They reminded me of animal crates, so I asked him what they were. He said they were crates for the Ministry of Defence and, jokingly, you understand, he said: 'Do you want to come, Mr. Mann?' and laughed heartily.

Appleyard: I see. (*pause*) Well he was joking Peter. So you've no need to worry. I don't import animals anymore and I certainly don't send them to the Ministry of Defence.

Peter: Yes, Mr. Appleyard. Thank you very much. I knew I must be wrong. I hope I have not offended you in any way Mr. Appleyard – by my asking.

Appleyard: Not at all. (*moving Peter to the door*) Now you must excuse me Peter, I've a lot of work to do.

Peter: (*obliging*) Yes of course, I am sorry to take up your valuable time.

Appleyard: ('*pushing*') That's all right. Goodbye.

Peter: Goodbye, and thank you very much.

He exits. Appleyard's smile fades quickly. Lights go.

I was much reassured by my visit, as you can imagine – although afterwards I wished that I had thought to ask him what was in the crates, and why they had for all the world looked like breathing holes at the top. Albeit, these thoughts were to be banished from my mind that very night by new events which overtook me. Just when you think the cage of your ape-nature has opened finally onto the infinite vistas of humanity, and you stride confidently down to the water's edge to drink, life turns round and fires a bullet in your groin. (*pause*) I had just done a late night television chat-show, as they call it, at the BBC – rather boring to tell you the truth: they ask you questions and don't listen to your answers or ask you to tell them about 'funny things that have happened to you' and then pretend to laugh – anyway, as I was saying I was coming out from Broadcasting House when...

He goes to the curtain as he speaks and opens it. The back picture shows London city lights, extravagant buildings lit up, taxis, cars, red buses. The view is looking down a street. In the acting area is a cut-out of a black Mercedes car face on. There is a chauffeur in the driver's seat. When the scene begins traffic can be heard; the lighting on the car should be from above to cast shadow over his face.

I saw Mr. Appleyard's car with his chauffeur in it. I saw him when...

The chauffeur makes a gesture on the steering wheel. There is the sound of a horn of the car, although Peter has seen him already. To chauffeur, speaking through the car window.

Hello there! Mr. Appleyard here too?

Chauffer: No. He sent it for you.

Peter: (*leaning on the window*) How very kind.

Chauffer: Get in.

Peter does so. The traffic noise fades over the following.

Peter: Do you know I have only ridden in this car when he has attended (*The engine is started followed by the car moving off and up the gears then the sound is low. The chauffeur is not listening to him. Peter trails off...*) my performance.

(*pause*) You must be very tired. Long day for you. (*No reply. Peter, to business*) Does Mr. Appleyard want to see me then?

Chauffer: No.

Peter: (*sensing all is not well*) Oh. Well...

Chauffer: He doesn't want to see you at all, Mr. Mann.

Peter: How do you mean exactly?

Chauffer: You're finished. He doesn't want you anymore. (*Peter goes quiet, but dignified. Chauffeur makes a quick glance to check his reactions.*)

Peter: (*to himself*) Doesn't want me any more. He said only this morning he enjoyed my show. (*no reply from Chauffeur*) So where are you taking me?

Chauffer: (*unconcerned*) Anywhere you like. Home. Suit yourself.

Peter: So he asked you to collect me, so that you could tell me I am finished, is that right?

Chauffer: Yes.

Peter: I see. (*pause*) Did he give you any reason? (*Chauffeur looks in mirror and then turns wheel right*) I have worked for Mr. Appleyard practically all my life.

Chauffer: (*fed up*) Frankly, Mr. Mann, you've become a bit of a bore. No one's interested in you.

Peter: Did he say that?

Chauffer: No. I am.

Peter: Yes, well with respect...

Chauffer: Look, just think yourself lucky he hasn't sold you to one of them vivi-what-you-call-them.

Peter: ...sectionists. (*pause*) He has no dealings with them. (*Chauffeur looks across to him but says nothing. To himself.*) I've not been violent; I have completely mastered my ape nature; I like to think I speak and behave as a civilised human being. I have contributed to science. In some small way.

Chauffer: (*Bored, irritated with this catalogue*) Listen Mr. Mann. Don't think you're something special. You aren't. You're just like anyone else. When the squeeze comes some of the pips have got to pop out.

Peter: (*not been listening*) Take me to see Mr. Appleyard would you please. I wish to discuss it with him. We'll discuss it like reasonable men.

Chauffer: He's not here. He's gone away.

Peter: Where to? He never mentioned it to me. I saw him this morning.

Chauffer: (*sigh*) Some mothers. Thought you were supposed to be bright! He's away and he's said to me if you cause any trouble 'break his neck and say he had an accident'.

Peter: He didn't say that! Mr. Appleyard wouldn't say that. Stop the car would you please, I wish to get out.

Chauffeur looks in the mirror and brings the car to a halt.

Chauffer: I'll drop you home. I'm only telling you.

Peter: No thank you. (*Peter opens the door. Traffic noise begins.*)

Chauffer: Suit yourself. Oo Mr. Mann...(*he brings a brown envelope out from beneath the dashboard*) ...he told me to give you this.

Peter: What is it?

Chauffer: Hundred pounds. Cash.

Peter: No thank you.

Chauffer: Don't cause any trouble, eh!

Peter: Goodnight. Thank you for the lift.

He closes the door with dignity and walks away. The chauffeur puts the envelope in his inside pocket. The sound and lights go. Peter turns and comes forward. He starts speaking while the actor playing the Chauffeur gets out of the car [no door] and closes the curtain.

It was an unpleasant job for the chap to do. Particularly after a long and wearisome day driving around in London traffic. Curiously enough Mr. Appleyard had not gone away, as I afterwards learnt. That surprised me, but I suppose he must have been very busy. (*pause*) When I got out of Mr. Appleyard's car, I could not quite focus my mind – my age I expect – all sorts of thoughts, images, pictures...how can I put this so that you will understand my meaning? ...were speaking to me, saying 'Listen to me; Look at this' ... softly as though coming from a great distance – I hope you will not find me too fanciful – I know human brains are very rational things. (*he smiles*) And I was drawn to walk, would you credit it, to the zoological gardens which were at any rate quite near. Even as I walked it seemed quite absurd. The very place that most repulsed me drew me to it. Can you credit it! But I who had no more in common with an ape than you do, needed to look upon them once more. And as I walked (*he walks towards the curtain*) ...What a strange thing it is, is it not? – that I who at that moment was a free and full human being should need to know what those captive apes were doing now.

He draws back the curtain slowly and continues an arc round to stand facing them from his table. The light is very low. There is the silence of night. The back picture shows a night image – just discernable – and a full moon with some cloud. Up against the curtain rail are the bars, exactly as before, of the primates' cage. There are three chimpanzees. One is looking straight at Peter, another is looking out in the other direction. The third is gnawing, which can be heard live at the central bar. To audience, but very softly as a naturalist would speak when not wishing to disturb a creature.

I could not believe my eyes. Gnawing at metal bars. (*longish pause*) They knew I was watching them. They had clearly got my scent long before I reached their cage.

The ape on lookout furthest from Peter silently canters over to take the place of the one watching Peter. They all move round one, the one previously watching Peter moving to gnaw and the one gnawing moving to take the other's place. Peter moves closer, firmly but without disturbing them. The ape watching him speaks, the others continue with their important tasks.

Chimp: You've come back at last.

Peter: You speak ... like I do.

Chimp: Of course. (*pause*)

Peter: But you said nothing when I spoke to you... before.

Chimp: You don't think we let them know we understand. (*the far chimpanzee moves round*) Please excuse me. (*he moves to gnaw, the gnawer moves round*)

2nd Chimp: (*without anger*) You wanted to be human.

Peter: (*uncertainly*) I am one.

2nd Chimp: (*ignoring not rudely*) There are two kinds of human: those who put us in cages and those who are in cages themselves. Which are you?

Peter: Er, neither...

2nd Chimp: Oh yes. You don't need a metal cage any more. They've put the bars in here – (*he taps the top of his head*)

Peter: I don't understand.

2nd Chimp: No. But have a care, if you ever do.

Peter: (*after a moment's pause*) Do you think you'll get out?

2nd Chimp: Yeah. (*A silence falls. There is another change around.*)

Peter: And then I thought I heard ... (*the sound of whales is heard, quite softly*) ... from a long, long way off ... (*to the apes*) Goodnight.

They make no response. He begins to walk.

Those whales.

The lights come up on him as he comes back to his table. The actors remain in tableau at the bars. To audience.

I will not tax your interest longer with a summing up of what I've learnt over my long life. The actors have, anyway, spoken more eloquently than I ever could. As for my last encounter in the zoological gardens I must confess to being ill-equipped to judge its true significance. But, equally, I am confident that your quick and ... generous minds will judge it truly as you, no doubt, have done the rest of my story. (*pause*) That is all.

He bows slightly, and just a little embarrassed. He collects his notes together and puts them in his briefcase, picks up his books. As he starts making his way out, he sees the open curtain. Quietly to himself.

Oh.

He puts his books down and closes the curtain, oblivious of the audience, who may or may not be applauding. He picks up his books and briefcase and goes out.

DRESSING UP, STRIPPING DOWN

based on 'The Emperor's New Clothes'
by Hans Christian Andersen

Foreword by Chris Cooper

The play (running at 2 hours), written for Harlow TheatreVan in 1993, is based on the story of *The Emperor's New Clothes* by Hans Christian Anderson.

It begins with the Emperor in his underwear trying on clothes and demanding something new to wear for the Great Parade. His Chief Minister explains that there is no money left in the coffers. It is at this point that the Weavers appear causing the Emperor to call the guard.

> **1st Weaver**: Shall we wait for the guard?
>
> **2nd Weaver**: Or shall we tell you why we've come?
>
> **Emperor**: Er....
>
> **1st Weaver**: We can wait if you prefer....
>
> **Emperor**: No. I don't think they're coming anyway. (*they all wait a moment*) Bastards! They've cut back on everything.

Thus, realpolitik and a well-loved story are conjoined in biting satirical comedy about the state of British society. Once again the question of ideology looms large, by focusing on the seen and the unseen, and what people *choose* to see.

Members of TheatreVan had been sacked the previous November and were engaged in an Equity-backed dispute with their management. The Company took a lead role in the national TIE Crisis Campaign, and this production became very much part of it and other campaigns against the cuts which were laying waste to public services and to what was left of the TIE movement. Supporters and colleagues from all over the UK booked the play to perform in numerous community venues and gave financial and practical support to make the tour possible. Booking a performance of this play was an act of solidarity with the sacked members of TheatreVan and with the wider campaign against cuts.

The first time I saw *Dressing Up, Stripping Down* I found it extremely funny and disturbing. The play expressed how I was feeling and gave me an extraordinary insight into the cynicism of modern political life. I assisted in the organisation of two of performances in the North West, one for the Lancaster and Morecambe Trades Council and the other for a performance to Lancashire Women Against Pit Closures in Newton Le Willows. There amongst the uproarious laughter (for that is what it was), there were moments of absolute silence and knowing, rueful recognition.

It feels as though the play once again resonates with the age. At the time of writing there is again no money and while we are told that we are all in it together, the poor and most vulnerable are being made to pay for the debt created by the privileged. Once again we must ask what is seen and unseen, and why do we choose not to see that the Emperor is indeed naked?

The play was written for four actors but it could be played by nine, if not more. It is a versatile piece that was designed to be performed in any location required. The realisation of the production requires a focus on the objects – such as the clothes and the mannequin of the child. It is, in my opinion, crucial that any production should maintain this convention of the mannequin – not to distance us from the action but to bring us closer to it.

The way the actors deal with the challenge of the comedy in the play will make or break any production and there is no room for comment on the characters or for sending them up. Satirical humour can bring us into a relationship, sometimes an intimate one, with content that we might ordinarily be unaware of or choose not to see. This is because comedy gives us a different way of seeing.

It is also worth commenting on the typically bold and very important decision to make the actor playing the Emperor to actually strip naked. The laughter generated by all that has gone before makes the stripping possible and at the performances I saw the audiences were giggling even as they were they were thinking, perhaps even hoping, 'he's not really going to is he?' But this action brings about a fundamental turn in the play. The contrast between the nakedness and clothes is very powerful. When the Emperor returns to his chamber following his public humiliation he begins to weep uncontrollably, naked, before the audience. The laughter gradually dies as the weeping continues and even though the Chief Minister reasserts some control we are left feeling uncomfortable at the public disintegration of a man we had enjoyed ridiculing only minutes before. A very human dimension has entered the fray.

In this play we can discern another development in Geoff as a writer. While the political drive remains undiminished, the allegorical story form and the use of pantomimic asides to the audience engages the audience in a different way from a play like *Lessons*. The writer is not afraid to let us know he is enjoying the joke too! It is possible to see the influence of Edward Bond in moments like the weeping Emperor. We are seeing a paradox that is beyond direct address or explanation, that asks us questions of our own values.

There are two further sequences that capture this development further, the beating of the child (mannequin) for apparently destroying the washing on the line, and the unresolved confrontation with the Emperor at the end of the play. In this scene Trees (short for Theresa), the mother of the child who has exposed the Emperor's nakedness, beats her child over a prolonged moment of time, in a way which resonates with the earlier moment when the Emperor weeps. It is almost too much to take, but the prolonged beating makes the audience conscious of its own reaction and Trees is exhausted and traumatised by her rage that 'I can't afford new cloves.' And when the naked demented Emperor appears threatening Mother and Child with scissors demanding they too be humiliated by stripping, Trees refuses: 'Aw gawd. Someone should've done something before it got to this. Who let it get to this?'

The answer to that has to come from the audience.

A community theatre piece first performed in various venues around the country in 1993.

Emperor – Peter Milne
Chief Minister and 1st Tribune – Amanda Finney
1st Weaver, Dawn, and 3rd Tribune – Gill Parr
2nd Weaver, Trees [Theresa], and 2nd Tribune – Deb Williamson
Directed by – Geoff Gillham
Designed by – Alex Elliot and Tom Castle
Stage Manager – Tom Castle

Characters (in order of appearance)
(Emperor is male; other characters except where gender is indicated can be male or female.)
The Emperor
The Chief Minister
The Two Weavers
1st Tribune (Madge)
Trees [Theresa]
Dawn
Tree's child (a mannequin)
2nd Tribune (Jackie)
3rd Tribune (Tina)

There is an interval between Scenes 6 and 7.

1. The Emperor's Dressing Room

The Emperor, dressed in vest and pants and socks held up with garters, is surrounded by a mountain of clothes. The clothes show the influence of styles from throughout the twentieth century. He wears spectacles. He holds up clothes to himself or half tries them on, flings them down with dissatisfaction, muttering as he does so; 'no, no, no', 'terrible', 'oh that's no good' etc.

Emperor: (*holding a piece of clothing – to audience*) A long time ago, in a country far away from here, there lived an Emperor. The Emperor was so excessively fond of new clothes that he spent all his money on them.

He throws down the clothing.

Absolutely useless!

He goes to the door. Calls.

Chief Minister! (*to audience*) They might look new enough to you – Minister! – but when I say new I mean new, I mean brand new!

The Chief Minister enters. She is dressed in smart, respectable clothes. Late middle age.

(*to Minister.*) I positively must have some new clothes.

Chief Minister: Your majesty there's no money in the exchequer. You've spent it all on clothes.

Emperor: They don't last like they used to. I need something new.

Chief Minister: Wear some of your old clothes.

Emperor: (*picking up clothes, showing them, throwing them down*) Have you seen them! Look! You want me to wear these!?

Chief Minister: They're perfectly alright.

Emperor: (*still holding clothes to him*) Do you want me to look a joke in front of everyone? Perhaps – (*throwing the clothes down*) – you want me to go out in my vest and pants to the Great Parade.

Chief Minister: Your majesty.

Emperor: Or cancel the Parade?

Chief Minister: Y –

Emperor: What will our investors say?! What will the people say! If we cancel.

Chief Minister: (*in-take of breath*)

Emperor: Do you want our economy to go completely down the swanney?

Chief Minister: Wear your grey suit!

Emperor: I don't believe this.

Chief Minister: I'm quite serious your majesty. The sober tone will suit the mood of the country and impress our investors that there's no waste – even at the highest levels.

Emperor: My grey suit!

Chief Minister: I am leaving now. I have work to do. (*she exits*)

Emperor: (*calling after her*) Have you! I hope your brain drops out! (*to self*) Grey suit. (*opens door*) And don't you walk out on me! (*closes door*) I'm not wearing the grey suit. Not wearing the grey suit. What does she think I am! I'm the Emperor. (*opens door*) I AM THE EMPEROR. (*closes door*) I should get rid of her. That's what I should do. Chief Minister, huh! She's not running my affairs properly – that's the thing. Then she blames me. That's what she does. Says it's my fault. Doesn't say it – that's what she means. Disloyal self-server – that's what she is. And incompetent to boot. Expects me to carry the can. Well, we'll see about that. Oh yes. Grey suit. Wear your grey suit. It'll suit the mood. Well, it's not my mood. It's not the Emperor's mood. Not mine.

During this two weavers enter the Emperor's room, quietly but without secrecy. The Emperor does not notice them immediately. They are women dressed in men's clothes. It is unclear whether they are women pretending to be men, or women who are wearing men's clothes out of preference.

1st Weaver: (*with distaste*) A grey suit for the Great Parade?

2nd Weaver: (*ditto*) For an Emperor to have to put up with people like that.

The Emperor, seeing the two intruders, snatches clothes to hide his body.

1st Weaver: Wrack and ruin.

2nd Weaver: Unforgivable

There is a pause while the Emperor and the weavers look at each other.

Emperor: (*calling out*) Help! Guards! Intruders! Help!

Pause.

What are you doing here? Who are you? Have you come to kill me?

1st Weaver: Absolutely not!

2nd Weaver: Do we look like assassins?

Emperor: I don't know what an assassin looks like.

1st Weaver: Shall we wait for the guard?

2nd Weaver: Or shall we tell you why we've come?

Emperor: Er....

1st Weaver: We can wait if you prefer....

Emperor: No. I don't think they're coming anyway.

They all wait a moment.

Bastards! They've cut back on everything. It's terrible you know. You wouldn't think I was an Emperor.

2nd Weaver: Not the way they treat you.

Emperor: You wouldn't think I was anybody at all.

2nd Weaver: You're the king pin.

Emperor: Yes.

2nd Weaver: Without you – (*she makes a sound and gesture of everything falling apart*)

Emperor: Tell me, who did you say you were?

1st Weaver: We're weavers.

2nd Weaver: (*slight correction*) And tailors.

Emperor: Oh, I see.

1st Weaver: We've come to offer you our services.

Emperor: Where are you from?

2nd Weaver: If you would care for us to do so.

Emperor: Well yes, I would.

1st Weaver: Sijil.

Emperor: I don't think I know that. Were you one of mine? No matter. If you can make me some fine new clothes – in time for the Parade -

2nd Weaver: We can.

1st Weaver: The finest clothes you've ever seen.

2nd Weaver: That's what an Emperor should have on the day of his Great Parade.

Emperor: God! At last somebody understands me! You ought to be my government!

They laugh with him.

That's not a joke. My Chief Minister says – now this is a state secret – just between you and me, yes? –

1st Weaver: Yes.

2nd Weaver: Of course.

Emperor: She says there's practically no money in my exchequer.

Pause.

It's a problem, yes?

2nd Weaver: (*after a moment*) Well you know what Chief Ministers are like. There's always no money.

Pause.

1st Weaver: Let's not speak of money. But of clothes.

Emperor: Well I don't know...

2nd Weaver: Where there's a will.... the Parade...

Emperor: Yes I know...

1st Weaver: (*going, to 2nd Weaver*) It seems we were mistaken. Our apologies.

2nd Weaver: (*not moving, to 1st Weaver*) We're going to leave the Emperor in the lurch?

1st Weaver: We're not leaving him in – he said he doesn't want them.

2nd Weaver: He does (*to Emp*) don't you? (*to 1st W*) Grey suit?!

1st Weaver: He doesn't! Come on.

Emperor: I DO! I'll find the money. Somehow.

1st Weaver: (*ceasing to go*) Let's not worry about the money.

Emperor: I can't live without new clothes. I really can't.

1st Weaver: Yes, we know.

Emperor: It would be death. It you only knew how dark the world sometimes feels.

He slumps down.

2nd Weaver: (*after a moment, to 1st W*) He's in a bad way.

1st Weaver: That's why we came

2nd Weaver: (*to Emp*) Cheer up. We'll sort something out. More than sort. (*to 1st W*) Can I tell him?

1st Weaver: (gestures assent)

2nd Weaver: (*to Emp*) We're going to solve two problems in one. First. These clothes will be the most magnificent clothes, that anyone, anywhere, has every worn. Second. The clothes that we make have a unique property. They are visible only to those who are loyal to the wearer and those who are not fools.

Emperor: (*coming out of his lethargy*) You mean they're invisible?

2nd Weaver: No. They are visible only to those who are loyal to the wearer and those who are not fools.

Emperor: I see.

Silence.

2nd Weaver: With these clothes you will be able, at once, to expose anyone who is disloyal to you and clear them out of your court. Or dispose of them any way you wish. As for fools – the same thing. Everyone else will say: 'These are the most splendid clothes we have ever seen, or will ever see. May the Emperor live for ever.'

Silence.

Emperor: Can you do this?

2nd Weaver: (*to 1st W*) Bring the mirror.

The 1st W places the mirror quickly in front of the Emperor. The 2nd W brings the Emperor to his feet.

Can you imagine it?

Emperor: (*looking at self in mirror*) I can. Oh god I can.

2nd Weaver: (*looking at him in the mirror*) We can do it.

The Emperor goes to the mirror and embraces his reflection.

Emperor: New clothes. Fine new clothes.

1st Weaver: (*holding the mirror still*) The finest.

Emperor: The finest. I will dazzle them.

1st Weaver: You will.

Emperor: (*going to door*) Chief Minister! Chief Minister! (*to them*) Do you need to take measurements?

1st Weaver: We have. An experienced eye takes a man's measurements in a second.

Emperor: Yes that's right. I can see you're like me.

The Chief Minister enters.

Now then. These men are my new weavers –

2nd Weaver: And tailors.

Emperor: Yes. I want them given anything they ask for, in the way of materials, facilities –

Chief Minister: What are these two people doing in here? Who are you?

Emperor: I let them in. It's not your place to question them.

Chief Minister: But –

Emperor: Or me. You will simply do as you're told or you can resign your office forthwith and get blown up in a car for treason. Which do you prefer?

Chief Minister: I'm absolutely appalled.

Emperor: Fine, be appalled. Do you want to live or not? (*to the weavers*) Do you know what you want, in the way of material?

1st Weaver: (*passing a sheet of paper*) It's all on here.

Emperor: (*passing the paper to Minister*) Get it. Pronto. I want.

Chief Minister: (*looking at sheet*) Five kinds of silk! Gold thread!

2nd Weaver: Magnificent new clothes.

Chief Minister: (*to Emp*) We can't afford this!

Emperor: What's this, 'we'? It's my exchequer. Mine. (*to them*) See what I'm up against?

Chief Minister: Your majesty, we can't afford this – (*sotto voce*) we're in debt.

Emperor: Then borrow it for God's sake. What do you think the Bank's for?

Chief Minister: We're already in debt.

Emperor: Then borrow some more and raise some readies. And do it now.

Chief Minister: This is crazy, your majesty. With all respect.

Emperor: Forget the respect and raise the sums we need for these clothes, or I'll get rid of you and wear my Nazi get-up in the Parade! How would you like that? (*to them*) How much will you want for your fee?

1st Weaver: Eighteen thousand zjlapis.

Chief Minister: How much?

Emperor: (*taken aback*) That's a lot.

2nd Weaver: Not for what we can do for you.

Emperor: (*to Minister*) Get it for them.

1st Weaver: (*ditto*) In advance. If that's alright.

Emperor: (*ditto*) You hear that? See to it. Now get out.

The Minister leaves. The Emperor turns and gleams at the two weavers.

I feel so much better!

He does a little work-out.

1st Weaver: Well, if you will excuse us we'll get down to work immediately.

2nd Weaver: Patterns to design.

Emperor: (*stopping mid work-out*) Just between ourselves – it gives me a bit of a hard on just thinking about those clothes. (*finger to lips*)

1st Weaver: Good.

Emperor: We won't say anything about the invisibility thing, eh?

2nd Weaver: No?

Emperor: Catch the traitors and fools unawares that way.

1st Weaver: I think you'll find more loyalty and fewer fools if you do tell them.

Emperor: Do you think?

1st Weaver: Yes.

2nd Weaver: After all that's what you want...

Emperor: (*considers*) Yes. Perhaps you're right. Alright. God, I feel good.

He returns to his work out in front of the mirror. The two weavers leave.

2. Weaver's Quarters

The two weavers are assiduously working. The 1st weaver is at a loom. The 2nd weaver is at a table working at the designs. A wicker dummy stands in the room. There is no cloth in the room.

1st Weaver: (*continuing to work – to audience*) Within twenty-four hours cash had been raised, materials paid for and delivered to the weavers' quarters.

2nd Weaver: Who in their turn discreetly made arrangements to have the materials sent to Sijil together with their fees.

1st Weaver: But they worked, as you see, with the utmost diligence and long into the nights.

2nd Weaver: They hardly slept.

1st Weaver: But their loom was empty.

2nd Weaver: And their designs were nothing.

1st Weaver: Never did so much labour produce so little value.

2nd Weaver: Nothing.

The Chief Minister enters and stops at their door.

Chief Minister: (*to audience*) These are very shady characters. It's my opinion they are nothing more than cheap tricksters. I thought it right from the beginning. The first moment I saw them in the Emperor's chamber. Now I hear from one of the servants, ONE OF THE SERVANTS, that their clothes are supposed to be invisible to those who are disloyal to the Emperor or fools! Need I say more?

She listens at the door.

Well that's strange. I thought I'd find them flown the coop. Money, material, the lot.

She listens again. Then tries to look through the keyhole.

Agh! Can't see a thing. But it does sound like a loom. Perhaps they really are weavers. All I can say is, they'd better be good. Take them by surprise.

She goes in, suddenly, as if to catch them out.

Oh.

1st Weaver: (*placidly*) Come in Minister. How are you?

2nd Weaver: Bit late for you to be up and about.

Chief Minister: I've come to see how you're getting on with the Emperor's new clothes. (*looking around*)

1st Weaver: Be patient. No clothes yet.

2nd Weaver: We're only at the design stage.

As the minister approaches the design, the 2nd W neatly, but not secretly, covers her empty sheet with another.

Chief Minister: I would like to see that, if you don't mind.

2nd Weaver: (*professionally*) I'm afraid not. Working drawings. For our eyes only.

She places her hand and wrist on the sheet.

Chief Minister: (*to audience*) Very suspicious.

1st Weaver: (*still working at the loom*) Have a look at the material for the trousers if you like.

Chief Minister: (*Turning and taking a step or so towards the loom, stops. To audience.*) I don't see anything.

1st Weaver: Come closer. You can't see from there.

Chief Minister: (*rubbing her eye*) I have something in my eye. (*to audience*) There's nothing on the loom.

2nd Weaver: Can I help?

Chief Minister: No. It's fine. Thank you. (*to audience*) Now what? If I say I can't see anything on the loom they'll know I've rumbled them. Then they'll go to the Emperor and tell him I'm disloyal to him. I'll be out. On the other hand –

1st Weaver: Do come closer.

2nd M: Is it out?

Chief Minister: What?

2nd Weaver: Whatever you had in your eye.

Chief Minister: Oh. Yes. Yes it is, thank you.

1st Weaver: You'll see the quality close up.

Chief Minister: No it's fine. I can see it from here. (*to audience*) This whole thing is an elaborate hoax – I'm sure of it.

2nd Weaver: Well what do you think?

Chief Minister: (*to audience*) These two don't give you a minute to think. Part of their method. (*to her, sharply*) Just give me a moment. (*politeness*) Please.

2nd Weaver: No problem. Take your time. Just makes it difficult to concentrate on our work. Slows us down.

Chief Minister: (*to audience*) Hear that? Trying to make me feel guilty.

2nd Weaver: We don't want to make any mistakes, that's all.

Chief Minister: Yes – no. I shan't be a moment.

The two weavers look at each other and continue working.

(*to audience*) If these clothes are what they say they are then I'm either a fool or disloyal to the Emperor. Otherwise I'd see the material on the loom – (*casts a look*)

1st Weaver: (*to herself*) Dammit. (*she corrects a mistake*)

Chief Minister: (*avoiding being thrown, to audience*) – I've put up with a great deal to serve the Emperor. My loyalty is beyond question. It's not blind. But loyalty it surely is. And I'm certainly not a fool. Ergo, this is a hoax. And these two creatures are charlatans.

1st Weaver: (*exasperated, getting up*) I'm not doing any more. It's more than a man can bear. (*kicking the loom, to the 2nd W*) Look at this.

2nd Weaver: (*to 1st W*) Take it easy. She'll be gone soon.

1st Weaver: Tell the Emperor – I'm sorry the whole contract's off.

Chief Minister: (*to audience*) What's this? I think I've flushed them out.

2nd Weaver: (*to 1st W*) Just calm down.

1st Weaver: I'm through with it. Collect the materials together, and our money and return it to the Emperor, with our apologies. We promised nothing less than perfection to the Emperor and this is not perfection. I cannot work like this.

2nd Weaver: (*glancing to Minister*) I did say. (*to 1st W*) Now just leave this with me. For one moment. (*going to Minister*) Can I level with you Chief Minister? (*leading Minister out of earshot of 1st W*)

Chief Minister: Well, what is it you have to say?

2nd Weaver: I think – and correct me if I'm wrong – I think – you can't see anything on that loom.

The Minister surprised at the directness, says nothing.

Am I right? (*pause*) You don't say anything. Well I don't know which it is – whether you're disloyal to the Emperor or just a fool. Now don't say anything, because I know I'm right. If my colleague here wants to pack it in because he's not satisfied with the quality, that's fair enough with me. He's a craftsman. Perhaps you don't understand what that means. But – what I know in this moment – is about these clothes we are making and about you. And what I'm going to do right now – is go to the Emperor and tell him, about you. Because I'm holding you – and your arrogance – responsible. For what's just happened now. And then he and I are going to a nice busy pub and have a pint and a good old chat with the locals.

The 2nd W goes to the door.

1st Weaver: Where are you going?

2nd Weaver: Never you mind.

Chief Minister: Wait!

2nd Weaver: You want to come?

Chief Minister: No.

2nd Weaver: Well what is it then?

Chief Minister: There's no need for that. I shall see the Emperor myself and tell him the clothes are marvellous.

2nd Weaver: Are you telling me you can see them?

Chief Minister: Of course I can (*looking across the loom*) see them.

2nd Weaver: I don't believe you.

Chief Minister: I can.

2nd Weaver: You're trying to hide the truth. You're a liar. Out to save your bacon.

Chief Minister: (*going over to the loom, quite desperate*) I can.

2nd Weaver: What colour's the material on that loom then?

Chief Minister: (*as though crucified on loom*) What?

2nd Weaver: The colour?

The Minister doesn't know what to say.

(*to 1st W*) I'm going to see the Emperor.

1st Weaver: Take it easy. Maybe she doesn't know how to describe the colour. With two browns, three shades of grey interwoven with dark and pale lavender – it's hard to find one word that sums it up.

2nd Weaver: You've told her!

Chief Minister: Lavender-greyish-brown.

2nd Weaver: (*incredulous*) You told her.

Chief Minister: Exquisite combination of colours.

2nd Weaver: Now what do we do?

Chief Minister: I can see it. Really.

2nd Weaver: (*to 1st W*) What do you say?

1st Weaver: I think we should risk it. Give her another chance.

2nd Weaver: You're a very forgiving person, that's all I can say. Considering it was she put you off in the first place.

1st Weaver: I can put it right. (*goes back to the loom to examine the invisible cloth*)

2nd Weaver: (*to Minister*) You are a very lucky person.

1st Weaver: It'll take us some time though.

Chief Minister: Well, I'll leave you to it .... if that's alright?

The 2nd W goes over to the loom and the 1st W.

2nd Weaver: (*pointing*) You could take it back to there.

1st Weaver: Hm. I don't know. I almost prefer to scrap it and start all over.

2nd Weaver: You think?

Chief Minister: I'll be going then (*heading for the door*).

1st Weaver: (*to Minister*) Here. Wait. (*she goes to the table and scribbles a note*) We shall need some more stuff ordered. See to it would you? (*she passes the note over*) Can you read it alright?

Chief Minister: (*reading*) Oh god.

1st Weaver: Don't need to rush it through. Day after tomorrow will do. (*goes back to loom*) Well I suppose if I took it back to here .... might be able to salvage something.

The Minister leaves. The two weavers continue for a while to study the problem. Then the 2nd W returns to her table, lifts the sheet covering the first and begins to sketch.

Chief Minister: (*to audience*) What would you do in my position? They have me over a barrel. Of course there's nothing there. It's an elaborate charade. It has to be. But when you're with them, it's all so ... plausible. (*pause*) Should I blow the whistle now? Look, in my hand, another order for stuffs. This is going to cost a pretty zjlapi, let me tell you. A halt should be called now. But then the Emperor would dismiss me straight off and I'd get blown up in a car. I can't call a halt – even if the Emperor agreed, which he won't – that would be to admit to fraud right in the centre of the Emperor's affairs. That would be really good for the zjlapi! It's not even thinkable. Confidence is everything at times like this. So – this lot in here will have to be given the benefit. Which means – we'll all sing the praises of the clothes and publicise their magical properties. And hope for the best. If anyone perchance says the opposite we'll either say he's a fool or an extremist. And if needs be run him over in a car. (*looks at door*) Weave on weavers. I'll to the Emperor and tell him the clothes are going to be magnificent and have my press secretary put out a statement to the media. It's amazing what people will believe.

She goes.

174

3. Weavers' Quarters

As before. 1st W is at the loom, the 2nd at her table.

1st Weaver: (*working, to audience*) The Chief Minister did as she said.

2nd Weaver: (*also to audience*) As a result the Emperor's excitement with the new clothes grew as he imagined himself at the head of the Great Parade.

1st Weaver: He was relieved to discover –

2nd Weaver: although he scarcely doubted it –

1st Weaver: that his Chief Minister was neither disloyal or a fool.

2nd Weaver: He itched to try them on, or at least to view them.

1st Weaver: But something held him back. 'What,'

2nd Weaver: – he thought -

1st Weaver: 'If, after all, I could not see them?'

2nd Weaver: Then he thought...

1st Weaver: 'Since I cannot be disloyal to myself, it would mean that I am a fool.'

2nd Weaver: So he decided to play it safe.

1st Weaver: He summoned one of the people's tribunes

2nd Weaver: – whom he knows to be loyal to him –

1st Weaver: and asked her to go to the weavers' quarters to view the garments in the making.

2nd Weaver: Since the Emperor considered the tribune not far short of a fool

1st Weaver: – if she saw the clothes –

2nd Weaver: – then certainly it would be safe for him to do so.

1st Weaver: So the following day, the tribune paid a visit to the weavers.

The tribune enters. She knocks on the door and enters the weavers' quarters.

1st Tribune: Good afternoon. Are you the weavers the Emperor has employed?

2nd Weaver: As you see.

1st Weaver: We are. And who do we have the pleasure of addressing?

1st Tribune: I am the people's tribune.

1st Weaver: Good.

1st Tribune: I have come to see your work. I should like to see it.

2nd Weaver: You should have made an appointment.

1st Tribune: I don't see why.

2nd Weaver: It can be very disruptive. It's not like digging a hole in the ground.

1st Tribune: Well I'm here now. (*brief pause*) Would it be possible to show me what you've done?

2nd Weaver: (*vague gesture*) Over there.

The tribune gazes in the direction of the gesture.

1st Tribune: (*to audience*) I don't see them. (*to 1st W*) Where exactly? (*to audience*) I can't see them.

2nd Weaver: By the mannequin.

Tribune looks across to the dummy.

1st Tribune: (*to audience*) I'm not a fool –

1st Weaver: Go over, if you want.

1st Tribune: Yes thanks. (*to audience*) I'm not disloyal to the Emperor. After all, I'm a people's tribune.

1st Weaver: (*to 2nd W*) Leave off that and show her.

1st Tribune: (*to self*) Keep calm. Don't let on. If this gets out I'm finished.

The 2nd W has left her work, covering it, and moved across to the dummy.

2nd Weaver: Care for a closer look?

1st Tribune: Yes indeed. (*to audience*) I'd never have thought this would happen to me. It's not. Pretend I can see them. Yes.

She's strolls over and looks at the dummy intelligently.

(*to them*) Yes. Not bad. Not bad. What material's this?

2nd Weaver: Oh that's just off-cuts – thrown over there instead of (*to 1st, accusing*) in the bin.

1st Tribune: Ahh!

2nd Weaver: This is the stuff.

2nd W pretends to try to lift up a roll of material by the dummy.

Could you move your foot?

1st Tribune: Oh! My apologies!

The tribune moves her foot. 2nd W lifts up the invisible roll, brushes the footprint off and moves to her table. The tribune is in her way.

2nd Weaver: Excuse me.

1st Tribune: Sorry. (*to audience*) This is terrible! I can't see it at all.

2nd Weaver: Come over here. The light's better. See the texture.

Tribune comes over.

1st Tribune: Yes it really is lovely. Quite.... lovely.

2nd Weaver: That's gold in that. Real gold. See that? Glistens as the light catches it. This'll be the jacket and the waistcoat. On the waistcoat there'll be tiny flakes of mother-of-pearl stitched around the pockets with aquamarine edging – very fine.

1st Weaver: Nothing vulgar.

2nd: Weaver: The whole effect will be able to make the Emperor shimmer in the sunlight. It will be magnificent. Feel it if you want. Then you can tell the people you touched the Emperor's clothes on their behalf. (*taking her hand*) Come on don't be shy.

1st Tribune: (*shaking it off*) Take your hand off me!

2nd Weaver: Apologies. No idea you were so sensitive.

1st Weaver: He meant no harm. Would you like to see what we're making for the cloak? Genoa velvet with Persian silk lining.

2nd Weaver: Or I could show you the silk fabric for his under-garments.

1st Tribune: (*to audience*) These wretched weavers are conspiring to make me feel quite stupid. Well we shall show them I am not.

2nd Weaver: Yes, no?

1st Tribune: To be perfectly frank with you, I think that nice though the clothes are –

2nd Weaver: (*to 1st W, who also stops work a moment at the word*) Nice?!

1st Tribune: Nice though they are – they are far too extravagant. I think it's a hideous waste of money. How much is all this costing?! Must run into tens of thousands of zjlapis. Why, we could clothe half the populace with the money being spent on these. I think its fiscal madness. (*to audience*) See?

1st W has now stopped work and stood up. Neither seems to know what to say. There is silence.

Nothing against you but there you are.

1st Weaver: Oh dear.

2nd Weaver: Erm, we don't, er, involve ourselves in politics...

1st Tribune: Yes well I do. I'm a politician. And it's my function to look after the interests of the people I represent.

2nd Weaver: Wouldn't it be better perhaps to discuss it with the Emperor or his Chief Minister...?

1st Weaver: We're just weavers you see.

2nd Weaver: And tailors.

1st Tribune: I will. I will.

1st Weaver: You don't think the people will like these new clothes we're making...?

1st Tribune: I'm not speaking of whether the people will like them, but of whether we can afford them.

2nd Weaver: You feel you need to tell them?

1st Tribune: It's not a matter of whether I tell them or not. It's a question of principle.

2nd Weaver: Oh I see.

1st Weaver: We could make some for the people afterwards. Then everyone would be happy.

2nd Weaver: It seems such a pity to cause a ruck now. You yourself said, having seen the material, the people would like the Emperor's new clothes.

1st Weaver: And the money's spent now.

2nd Weaver: Why spoil people's happiness – they get little enough? (*pause*) For a principle.

1st Tribune: I'm going to see the Emperor anyway.

She begins to go.

Goodbye.

1st Weaver: You will tell the Emperor you saw the clothes and that they're coming on well, won't you?

She goes out of the door.

1st Tribune: (*to audience*) I really took a dislike to them. Very superior. Foreigners can often be like that. But I don't think they knew I couldn't see the cloth. Carried that off quite well. No, I'm sure they didn't know. (*she is about to go*) But wait a moment. I need to be clear in my own mind what this is all about. (*pause*) If I didn't (*sotto voice*) see the cloth (*normal voice*) that means that (*sotto voice*) I'm a fool or disloyal to the Emperor. (*normal*) If one thing's certain, I'm neither disloyal to the Emperor nor am I a fool. Therefore since I'm not a fool and not disloyal, I must have seen the cloth, even though I thought I didn't. Those two weavers in there didn't know I couldn't see the cloth because I did see the cloth and only thought I couldn't. Yes. That explains everything. Yes, I'm sure that's how it was.

She goes.

4. Weavers' Quarters

The two weavers are still working, but now they wield chalk and scissors, carefully marking out the pattern and cutting it out. No clothes or cloth are visible. The Emperor appears in a clean yellow oversuit and hard hat carrying a box with the words TOOL BOX written on the side.

Emperor: (*at the door, to audience*) I couldn't wait any longer. You know what it's like. Wanting them. Every time I think of those clothes my body screams. Gimme gimme. You know. It's been fifteen days since I last ... you know ... had new clothes. Not an hour passes when I don't think of them. (*pause – he begins to think of the clothes*) But I knew I had to take precautions. Hence this workman's outfit. I use it whenever I want to go about the streets incognito. Although there's no possible likelihood of my not seeing the clothes of course – just in case – I have devised a plan to make it appear that I've come in to check the electrics. Then if I can't see the clothes I can make a quick exit with no-one any the wiser. That's very unlikely of course but you don't live long as an Emperor if you don't keep an eye to the occasional googlie.

He enters the room.

(*accent*) Whatcha lads; come to check the plugs and that. (*to audience*) Christ! The clothes are invisible!

1st Weaver: (*welcoming*) If you've come to try them on – they're not quite ready.

Emperor: (*leaving*) Sorry mate, wrong room. (*to audience*) Aah!

2nd Weaver: But do come and see how they're coming on.

1st Weaver: (*to Emperor*) A certain agitation is always to be expected at this stage.

Emperor: (*to audience*) They've recognised me, shit. Pull yourself together. Maybe they haven't. Case of mistaken identity.

2nd Weaver: Come and see your trousers. Not finished off of course (*picking up the trousers and bringing them over*)

Emperor: (*to audience*) They have. (*to her*) I fink you've mistaken me for someone else.

2nd Weaver: Well anyway what do you think of the trousers? (*places them in front of the Emperor*) Oh the line is beautiful (*to 1st W*) don't you think? Really will make you look sexy!

1st Weaver: In a very discrete way.

Emperor: (*to audience*) Oh my god. I can't see anything at all. My Chief Minister saw them, even that idiot Tribune saw them. Am I the most stupid man in my own empire? (*to 2nd W*) I can't wear these!

1st Weaver: You don't like them?

2nd Weaver: We can scrap them, (*to 1st W*) can't we?

1st Weaver: Of course we can. If the Emperor doesn't like them. We can scrap everything we've done, order new materials, and begin again...

Emperor: No!

Silence. They look at him expectantly, the 2nd W still holding the trousers.

They're wonderful. They're ... magnificent ... trousers.

2nd Weaver: (*relieved, smiling*) It can sometimes take a moment or two to adjust.

1st Weaver: (*assuring*) Yes it can. With new clothes.

2nd Weaver: You see how the lavender blends into the browns and the greys here, and you see how I've cut it on the bias to emphasise the muscular energy in the thighs as you walk.

1st Weaver: That's perfection in the tailor's art. Believe me.

The 2nd W smiles a little, graciously, at the compliment.

2nd Weaver: What do you think?

Emperor: Well – they are the most gorgeous shades and er perfectly... cut. Do you think the bottoms are a little... wide?

2nd Weaver: Looking at them from there it might seem so but – I don't know – with them on and with the shoes, I think you'll find... (*gesture of 'just right'*)

Emperor: Yes, you're probably right. I haven't seen the shoes.

1st Weaver: Show him the jacket.

The 2nd W puts the trousers down.

2nd Weaver: Here, put your box down.

She takes the tool box from the Emperor. She takes the Emperor's spectacles from the top pocket and gives them to the Emperor.

Spectacles.

Emperor: Oh yes. Ha!

He puts them on.

1st Weaver: (*to audience*) And the weavers showed the Emperor each item of clothing, describing each piece in loving detail, explaining where work was still to be done and what that would be, and finally engaging the Emperor in discussion on the finer points which of course he was able to do since the weavers between them guided his every thought by the subtle descriptions and hints they gave him as they displayed the non-existent clothes which all their days and nights of labour had produced. The Emperor was there for over an hour. And, strange to say, although the Emperor in reality saw nothing at all, he actually began to believe he did. And from the centre of his being a deep thrill of anticipation began to run through his whole body.

Emperor: (*to audience*) But the Emperor still needed a final assurance. (*to the weavers*) These are truly the most wonderful new clothes I have ever had made for me. That is beyond question. (*to 1st W*) But tell me, when they're finished, do you really think that everyone will admire them when they see me in them in the Parade tomorrow?

1st Weaver: I really think that's beyond doubt.

Emperor: Do you? Really?

2nd Weaver: From what I hear everyone's talking about them. The press, people in the street, the pubs and clubs – even in the ladies and the gents.

Emperor: (*uncertain about the last*) Are they?

2nd Weaver: That's where you hear the real word. You should go sometime. Incognito.

Emperor: Yes... I will perhaps.

1st Weaver: You have nothing to worry about. Tomorrow you will be seen in all your glory and the clothes themselves will beggar all description.

Emperor: It's so good to hear you say that.

1st Weaver: Now – we have much to do before tomorrow midday – so if you'll excuse us we need to get on.

Emperor: Yes of course. I have taken enough of your time. Thank you both very much. Thank you. One thing before I go. I don't know how you feel about the patent...

2nd Weaver: Not for sale. Sorry.

Emperor: No, I was wondering, if everything goes well, we could develop some copies for everyone of importance. Perhaps even some cheaper mass-produced ones for the people. Exports even. Where I lead others wish to follow.

1st Weaver: Well we can think about it.

2nd Weaver: Yes we can talk about it after the parade.

Emperor: God. I'm so pleased I met you. I feel quite – rejuvenated.

He picks up his box and leaves. The two weavers begin work again.

5. Weavers' Quarters

The same. The weavers are putting the final touches to the invisible clothes. The 1st W is brushing the dummy with a clothes brush. The 2nd W is carrying coat hangers with invisible clothes to a rail and hanging them.

1st Weaver: (*to audience*) The night before the Parade the weavers worked without sleep.

2nd Weaver: (*ditto*) The lights from their quarters shone into the darkness outside. Beacons of industry.

1st Weaver: Final trimmings were added, each garment ironed and pressed.

2nd Weaver: And neatly set out in readiness on the mannequin and on hangers on the rails.

1st Weaver: In the morning – expectation was everywhere in the air. The Emperor rose early, as young children do on Christmas Day.

2nd Weaver: To say he was eager to dress in the new clothes and to walk the streets of his capital in them

1st Weaver: would be something of an understatement.

2nd Weaver: You would have to reach for the crudest of sexual comparison

1st Weaver: to even approach a description of his

2nd Weaver: heat for the new clothes.

1st Weaver: As for his Chief Minister,

2nd Weaver: reconciled to

1st Weaver: – embracing even –

2nd Weaver: the fraud at the centre of the Emperor's affairs,

1st Weaver: she was gratified to see that the zjalpi has been strengthening

2nd Weaver: to a remarkable degree

1st Weaver: on the news of the creation of the miraculous new clothes,

2nd Weaver: and, this morning, was surging on the world's currency markets at the prospects of their display by the Emperor in the Great Parade.

1st Weaver: So, at midday sharp, the Emperor, his Chief Minister....

The Emperor in stylish casual wear and the Minister enter and come through the door.

And his whole retinue –

2nd Weaver: You will have to imagine them if you will.

1st Weaver: – arrived.

2nd Weaver: At the weavers' quarters. (*he closes the door*) Bit of a squeeze.

Emperor: Is everything ready?

1st Weaver: Everything.

2nd Weaver: (*to Minister*) Morning.

Chief Minister: Good morning to you.

1st Weaver: Let us begin. (*she moves towards the dummy*) Will you see the new clothes before we try them on? Here is the jacket which you saw yesterday before completion. Notice the a la mode lapels and collar picking up from the pale lavender sheen of the jacket itself –

Emperor: Oh it's quite magnificent. I don't know what to say. (*pointing*) And the gold ... Sumptuous.

1st Weaver: But not gaudy.

Emperor: Oh no. Gorgeous without being gaudy.

1st Weaver: Quite.

Emperor: (*to Minister*) Don't you think?

Chief Minister: Quite, your majesty. Phenomenal. Magnificent.

2nd Weaver: (*to audience*) And all the Emperor's assembled retinue agreed and said,

1st Weaver: (*ditto*) 'Gorgeous. Phenomenal. Magnificent. We've never seen such a jacket.'

2nd Weaver: Although of course they could see nothing at all.

1st Weaver: (*going to a hanger and pulling it out*) And these are the trousers, also of the finest ficuna wool –

Emperor: I love the line of them, the cut. I can't wait to put them on.

During the following the 2nd W displays the items on hangers.

1st Weaver: (*to audience*) But before he did the two weavers showed him each item of clothing and described the colours, the textures, the patterns and the styling so that everyone in the retinue could picture what they could not see. Of course they all assumed that the Emperor and the Chief Minister could see the clothes. As a result, each member of the Emperor's retinue concealed from every other that he or she could see nothing but a naked mannequin and empty hangers in the weavers' hands.

Emperor: Don't tantalize me any longer! Let me wear them!

The Emperor undresses like a man in the grips of sexual passion, grunting with pleasure and anticipation and praising the new clothes.

The whole outfit is beyond words. Intoxicating! Ravishing! (*to Minister*) Don't you think?

Chief Minister: Yes I do. Quite stunning.

Emperor: That's the word, stunning! Dazzling! Ravishing! Oh words!

He is now standing as we saw him before, socks, vest and pants, and spectacles (somewhat askew).

(*calmer, eyes closed*) You may dress me in them.

1st Weaver: Everything will need to come off.

2nd Weaver: Your underwear, the socks.

Emperor: (*open eyes, uncertain momentarily*) Really?

Chief Minister: (*to audience*) Jesus Christ.

1st Weaver: We've made the most captivating under-garments a man may wear.

2nd Weaver: Pure silk. Tulle. With satinette support where it's needed.

1st Weaver: Very sensuous against the skin.

2nd Weaver: Look. (*she moves to the work table and picks up an invisible pair of shorts*) Like white silver. (*pause*) And a singlet to match.

Emperor: (*deeply moved*) Oh yes.

He looks at the Minister.

Aren't they just... (*he looks back at them*)

Chief Minister: (*to audience*) I just pray the zjlapi holds up if he goes out in these.

Emperor: (*to Minister*) What do you think? Shall I wear them?

Chief Minister: (*a gesture which is a mixture of resignation, being hanged for a sheep as a lamb, and 'yes, go on'*)

Emperor: (*to the weavers*) They're beautiful. (*to the retinue, with authority*) Very well. Let everyone turn away while we disrobe myself. No-one shall see the imperial penis or the imperial buttocks or for that matter the imperial nipples.

1st Weaver: (*to audience*) And everyone did turn away.

2nd Weaver: (*ditto*) Except the weavers.

Emperor: You two may just avert your eyes.

The Emperor removes his socks, vest and pants.

Pass me the shorts.

The 2nd W brings them to him.

The material is so light.

2nd Weaver: That's the beauty of it.

The Emperor puts them on.

Emperor: Very nice. (*moment*) Singlet.

2nd Weaver: Singlet.

1st W gets it from the table and passes it to the 2nd who passes it to the Emperor.
Singlet.

The Emperor puts it on.

Emperor: Tucked in?

2nd Weaver: I think not. Better loose. How do you feel?

Emperor: Perfection. Oh what a Parade it's going to be!

2nd Weaver: Well, I think we'll put the outer garments on first!

Emperor: What? Oh yes!

Chief Minister: May it please your Imperial Majesty if your court turns round again?

Emperor: Yes, you can all turn round.

1st Weaver: (*to audience*) And they did. There was an unmistakable sound from the retinue of a sharp intake of breath –

Chief Minister: (*turning round, intake of breath*) Huh!

1st Weaver: (*as before*) – as they saw the naked Emperor standing before them –

The Emperor basks in his glory.

– which on the outflow of breath simultaneously became 'how magnificent'.

Chief Minister: (*simultaneously*) How magnificent. (*to audience*) The Titanic sinking before you could not be worse to witness! And yet. (*she looks around the retinue*) And yet. Everyone in the retinue is as steady as a rock. Are the clothes after all visible to everyone but me? This is incredible. Stay calm. Yes. I must not betray myself. (*to Emperor, uncharacteristically sexily*) If I were younger, majesty, I could really find you quite ... arousing.

Emperor: (*looks at her a moment, then to the weavers*) What's next? Socks?

2nd Weaver: Socks it is.

The 1st W fetches the socks.

(*to audience*) And item by item the weavers dressed the Emperor with the invisible clothes. There. That is everything. (*she buttons the cloak*)

1st Weaver: (*bringing mirror*) Would you care to see.

Emperor: (*looking, gleaming*) Dazzling.

2nd Weaver: And everyone applauded (*they do*) and repeated the Emperor's words.

Chief Minister: Dazzling.

1st Weaver: (*to Minister*) Have you bought the crown?

Emperor: The crown. My god yes. Where's the crown?

The Minister brings the crown and hands it to the Emperor. He places it on his head. He stands looking in the mirror.

(*to 1st W*) You don't think it overdoes it? Not a distraction is it?

1st Weaver: No. The crown sets the clothes off beautifully.

2nd Weaver: Just so. (*she picks a fleck off the cloak*)

Emperor: Truly magnificent.

Chief Minister: Shall we begin the Parade?

Emperor: (*formal*) Be it known that it is our wish to bestow on these weavers our highest honours. They shall henceforth be known as The Imperial Court Weavers and Tailors. Their patents shall be ours. (*normal*) Yes. My people await my new clothes.

He exits followed by the Minister and the retinue.

1st Weaver: (*to audience*) For their part, quite forgotten, the weavers changed their clothes and quietly left their quarters in the Emperor's palace.

2nd Weaver: Even as the Parade got underway they were boarding the plane for Sijil –

1st Weaver: – their work done.

They both leave.

6. Park overlooking a Street

There is the sound of military bands and crowds milling about, whistles, rattles etc. Two women, one with a child, enter. They are looking for a vantage point to see the parade.

Dawn: Ere you are Trees. Over ere. Should be able to see i from ere.

Trees: Coo I ope so. Ain't dragging Joelly any furver. (*to child*) Ere you are darlin. Where's your Smar'ies. (*to Dawn*) Any sign of im yet?

Dawn: Nah juss bans.

Trees: Muss cost a mint to pu this lo on. (*to child*) Come ere Joelly. Don go wandrin off. Ge lost in this crowd. (*to Dawn*) Only come ou for er and she ain't the least bi interested!

Dawn: I know.

Trees: Coo look at em. Swea pourin off em.

Dawn: Poor fings.

Trees: Yeah! (*to child, picking her up*) Dyou wanna see the soljers? See their uniforms? See the one wiv the big drum? (*to Dawn*) She ain't intrested!

Dawn: Cos she ain't a boy.

Trees: Well I ain't a boy bu I could get interested in one of em!

Dawn: Trees!

Trees: No couldn't you though?

Dawn: (*laughing*) The kid.

Trees: She don understan. (*putting her down*) Do ya darlin. (*kisses child*) Look at er – more intrested in the grass! Ope she don grow up to be a sheep or somefing.

Dawn: (*laughs, then*) It's the crowds. Bi overwhelmin for em.

Trees: Ow much dyou fink they spen on this lo?

Dawn: Qui a bi.

Trees: I read they spen over ten fousand zjlapis jus on is cloves.

Dawn: Terrible init. An all this lo.

Trees: Wish they'd spend ten fousand zjlapis doin up the estate!

Dawn: Yeah. Make a diffrence wouldn i. Tell you there ain't the money but they ain't stinted themsels on this lo.

Trees: Oh no. Well when they wan somefing they jus find the money don they?

Dawn: Same wiv tha air show in June. I mean, wha good's that to anybody?

Trees: Yeah. Still it's somefing for the kids. And their dads! (*to child*) You alrigh Joelly?

Dawn: She's ever so good isn she.

Trees: (*to child*) Whas tha darlin? No ain't go no more. Wha did you do wiv the ones I give you? (*still attending to child, to Dawn*) Dawn, wha you reckon abou this invisibility lark?

Dawn: (*an in-joke*) Don you know that's why Rita Yallop stayed at ome!

They both laugh.

Trees: Didn wanna ge found ou!

Dawn: (*through laugh*) F I'd been as stupid as er I would've come for the trea!

More laughter. Trees shushes.

Trees: Shu up Dawn! Someon'll ear.

The laughter quietens.

(*more seriously*) You'll ge us taken in.

Dawn: Has to be a joke doesn i. I mean you can't make invisible cloves can ya.

Trees: Well I wouln've fought so.

Dawn: There you are then.

Trees: Yeah I know bu why did they pu i in the papers then?

Dawn: (*a statement*) Ya don blieve everyfing you read in the papers do ya.

Trees: No I know.

Dawn: Probably one of them hypes.

Trees: (*briefly looking to child*) Maybe they're expecting a protest or somefing.

Dawn: Wha, extremists?

Trees: Yeah, could be. Or demonstraors of some kind – you know.

Dawn: Well I ope I ain't ere.

Trees picks up her child. The Tribune enters.

1st Tribune: Got a good view I see.

Trees: Yeah i's nice ere.

1st Tribune: Lovely day for it.

Trees: Yeah some of them bansmen were sweain somefing terrible.

1st Tribune: This your kiddie?

Trees: Joelly.

Dawn: You're a Tribune aren't you.

1st Tribune: Yes. Everything alright?

Dawn: (*lying politely*) Yeah.

1st Tribune: I'm pleased. What do you think of the Parade?

Dawn: Oh it's good. Ain't i Trees?

Trees: Yeah. Bu we reckoned –

1st Tribune: So do I. Costly though.

Trees: Yeah, we fought tha, didn we Dawn?

1st Tribune: I've nothing against the Emperor having new clothes but let me tell you – I think the government's spent too much on them. Far too much. I mean there are people out there who are without jobs –

Trees: (*indicating Dawn*) Her Del's ou of work –

1st Tribune: That's what I'm saying. What's good enough for Peter is good enough for Paul. I think the government should be setting an example.

Trees: Thas wha we were sayin. Our neighbourhood's geing pretty rundown. No repairs and tha. All tha kid's playground stuff gets smashed up. Nofing for the older ones to do.

Dawn: They're bound to turn to vandalism and delinquency and tha.

1st Tribune: (*losing interest*) Yes that's right I think the Emperor should be coming soon. Can you see?

They all look.

Dawn: Migh be.

1st Tribune: (*still looking*) I touched the material you know.

Dawn: Did ya? What was i like?

Dawn and Trees look at each other as though something were sorted.

1st Tribune: It was beautiful I do say that. Shame that the weavers were from abroad. It's not as if we don't have excellent weavers of our own. Longing to be given a chance.

Trees: Two ain't going to make much diffrence.

1st Tribune: No I've got nothing against them.

Trees: (*to Dawn*) Joelly's gone to sleep now!

Dawn: It's all the runnin around earlier.

1st Tribune: (*excited*) Look there they are!!

There is an increase in crowd noise.

Dawn: Look Trees there e –

Trees sees the Emperor almost simultaneously.

Dawn:

& (*to audience*) Wha!

Trees:

1st Tribune: Aren't they the most magnificent clothes you've ever seen!

189

Dawn:

& (*to audience*) E ain' go no cloves on. Shi!

Trees:

1st Tribune: Don't they quite take your breath away!

Dawn: Be'er not let Trees know. She can see em. Christ Trees!

& (*looking to each other, then to audience*)

Trees: Be'er not let Dawn know. She can see em. Christ Dawn!

Dawn: Aren't the cloves fantastic Trees?

Trees: Ou of this world.

1st Tribune: I told you they would be!

Trees: Yeah they're beauiful (*to child, waking her*) Come on lovely, wake up, have a look at the Emperor. (*she raises the child onto her shoulders*) Can you see? See his lovely new cloves?

Dawn: (*to audience*) Then the child said,

Trees: (*to audience, voice of a child*) 'Bu e's go nofing on.'

A moment – as though the child had peed down her mother's neck. The cheering rapidly dies away.

(*covering*) Just ear wha the little monkey said!

Dawn: (*ditto*) Children! (*looks to the Tribune*)

1st Tribune: They talk nonsense, don't they.

Trees: (*bringing child down*) Where's those Smar'ies?

She searches wildly for the Smarties on the child's person.

(*to audience*) But the child kept repeating it. (*to child*) No e's not, Joelly. (*to Tribune*) I'm sorry abou this. (*to child*) Now be quiet now or you'll ge a smack.

Dawn: (*who has meanwhile looked again*) Trees...

Trees: Wha?

Dawn: (*whispering*) Joelly's right the Emperor ain't go nofing on.

Tribune exits.

(*ditto*) E's naked! Look!

Trees: (*she looks, sees it*) Be quiet Dawn. Ovver people will ear.

Dawn: (*to audience*) But it was too late. People nearby had already heard the child.

Trees: (*ditto*) And were repeating what she had said.

Dawn: At first in whispers.

Trees: But then louder.

Dawn: And more quickly.

Trees: Till everyone in the crowd

Dawn: Was saying

Trees: What they knew to be true –

Dawn:

and 'The Emperor is naked. The Emperor is naked.'

Trees:

Trees: Until the child's words reached even the ears of the Emperor. (*to child*) Oh Joelly – wha ave you done?!

She picks up her child in her arms, not roughly, more in anguish.

Dawn: (*to audience*) And when he heard them at that moment he knew that the child's words were true –

Trees: (*ditto*) But he, and the procession, kept on going

Dawn: As though nothing had happened

Trees: Except for one part of his anatomy

Dawn: Which by shrinking and retreating into hiding

Trees: Exposed the truth to all about the Emperor and his new clothes. (*to the child, deeply worried*) Oh Joelly, you've really done i now.

The two women go.

7. The Emperor's Dressing Room

The Emperor enters, naked except for his crown and spectacles.

Emperor: (*to audience*) How the Emperor got through the ordeal of the Parade, he did not know. Something in his training ... upbringing ... perhaps in his class, kept his legs moving along the route of the Parade as though nothing out of the way was happening. Lesser men would have broken cover, run to save themselves from the thousands of eyes that stared unbelieving at the spectacle of their naked Emperor. Perhaps it was because he did not run that people did not fling over the crash barriers and chase him out of the streets and out of the land altogether. Or perhaps it was their training, upbringing, or their class. Or perhaps it was plain, human pity.

The Emperor takes off his crown and indifferently puts it down on a chair. He then begins to cry until his whole body shakes in convulsions of anguish. After a while the Chief Minister arrives outside the door. She is carrying a mug of cocoa with a saucer on top.

Chief Minister: (*to audience*) The Emperor exposed to the eyes of the world! The country utterly humiliated! The zjlapi's going to be crucified when the markets open tomorrow! Well, those two – and Sijil – will know very soon this assault shall not go unanswered. We shall protect the Emperor, our country, and the zjlapi as a mother protects her child.

She knocks on the door and opens it. She goes in. She takes in his state which has now subsided – but it is plain he is in a severe state of shock.

I've bought you a hot drink. (*she puts it down*) Come on now.

She gets a bathrobe for him and puts it round him, takes him to the chair, moves the crown to the floor and sits down. She picks up the cocoa. She gives him the mug. All of these actions are carried out with effortless efficiency.

Drink this while it's hot.

He holds the mug but doesn't drink.

Emperor: I'm finished.

Chief Minister: You've had a bad shock. Now come on, drink this.

She brings the mug to his lips and holds the handle so that he drinks a little, without interest on his part.

Emperor: It's all over.

Chief Minister: (*gently*) No it's not.

Emperor: (*beginning to tremble*) I wanted to dazzle everyone with my magnificence. Everything's dust. Grey dust.

Chief Minister: Now don't talk. Get that down you and then we'll get you to bed. Things will look much better tomorrow. We can sort things then. (*trying to get him moving*) Come on, drink that.

She gets him to drink a little. He is still shaking.

Emperor: (*passing it to her*) I don't want anymore.

Chief Minister: (*putting the mug down on the saucer*) Come on then, let's get you into some pyjamas and into bed.

She gets him up and begins to take him out.

Emperor: I feel very cold. I think I've caught my death.

Chief Minister: (*momentarily panicked, then gently*) No you haven't. It's just the shock. Get a good night's sleep. All this will look very different in the morning.

They are gone.

8. Restaurant

A table with 3 chairs. On the table is an individualised coffee filter draining into a cup. Ideally the Tribune we saw earlier – 1st Tribune – should be seated at the table with the filter coffee. But she may enter at the point indicated in the text below.

2nd Tribune: (*to audience*) It wasn't only the Emperor who suffered as a result of the exposure of the Great Parade. For their part, the people were shocked at what had happened. Of course as they do they carried on their daily lives in the normal way. But you could feel something was changing in them. At this moment however it was as if they needed time to let the enormity of the event sink in. No such luxury was afforded to the Tribunes. One of them after all had supposedly seen the clothes in advance. She, like the Chief Minister, stood in danger of being discredited before the whole population.

1st Tribune sits down at the table by the filter coffee.

So the following day the three senior tribunes met (*– she stirs the cup as she walks towards the table –*) to decide what they should do in the restaurant where they liked to meet. This one (*pointing to self with spoon*) was steaming inside.

1st Tribune: You should try one of these. They're very nice.

2nd Tribune: (*coming to sit down*) Cold before you ge it. Prefer tea.

1st Tribune: Is there any milk Jackie?

2nd Tribune: (*sitting down, pointing to a plastic individual container*) In the po there.

1st Tribune: I prefer cream actually.

2nd Tribune stirs tea and drinks it. 1st Tribune checks the coffee and puts the lid back on.

Where's Tina?

2nd Tribune: Be ere soon.

1st Tribune: (*after a moment*) How are things at work?

2nd Tribune: (*non-committal*) Alright.

A moment... 1st Tribune checks coffee again.

1st Tribune: Ah there we are. All through.

She removes the filter, puts it neatly on the lid, opens pot of milk, pours it in. During this 2nd Tribune takes out a packet of cigarettes and a lighter.

I do wish you wouldn't smoke.

2nd Tribune: (*taking no notice*) Public place.

1st Tribune: (*not pushing it*) Quite.

She puts the milk pot in the filter.

Keeps things tidy. No sense in giving the waitress extra work.

3rd Tribune enters, somewhat hurried, comes over, puts briefcase down as she's speaking.

3rd Tribune: Sorry I'm late. Jackie. Madge. (*going to counter*) Just get a tea. Be with you in a moment.

1st Tribune: (*calling after her*) You should try a Costa Rica filter coffee, Tina. They're very nice.

3rd Tribune: (*off*) No tea's fine for me. Quicker.

1st Tribune smiles politely to 2nd Tribune. 3rd Tribune returns with a tea – no spoon.

1st Tribune: I do like this little corner.

3rd Tribune: (*Putting tea down, not drinking. She sits down between them.*) Right shall we get started? Now I think you will agree that the Emperor's Chief Minister has a lot to answer for with respect to the deplorable fiasco that passed for this year's Great Parade. Not only is it an outrage that people – including children – had to witness the Emperor's state of undress, but also that the whole country in his person has to, has had to, suffer such embarrassment – I might almost say – humiliation. The Chief Minister's bungling throughout this whole sorry affair has produced the lowest ever level of the zjlapi against all other major currencies. She has to take responsibility for that. I also understand that the two weavers have skipped the country and no doubt gone to ground living on their immoral earnings – while the Chief Minister did nothing whatever to prevent it. I'm very angry. And I know the people are. (*pause*) I want us, if we can, to find a common position so that the whole country can know our views on the very serious situation facing us all. Well what are your views? Any comments.

1st Tribune: I do think we shouldn't call them weavers. They are terrorists.

2nd Tribune: Oh do me a favour!

1st Tribune: No I'm perfectly serious. I don't think we can lay it all at the minister's door. Those two came here from Sijil deliberately and specifically to carry out theft, sabotage and mayhem. And if you ask me they've pretty well succeeded.

Pause.

3rd Tribune: Right, anything else?

2nd Tribune: It's a mess. A total mess.

2nd Tribune: The thing –

and

3rd Tribune: I've gotta say –

3rd Tribune: Sorry Jackie go on.

2nd Tribune: No if I can jus say. I fink that we ave to do some straight talking. I mean Madge wen to see the stuff, didn't she. –

1st Tribune: Oh –

3rd Tribune puts a restraining hand up.

2nd Tribune: No you did. You said you seen it. Then it turns ou nobody can see nuffin.

1st Tribune: So you're saying it's all my fault!

2nd Tribune: No look wha I'm sayin is – you should've said then the thing was a con. Then we wouldn't be in this mess.

1st Tribune: I thought I saw them!

2nd Tribune: That's jus grea init! You fought you saw em. Ain't you seen a man's body before? E didn't ave NUFFIN ON.

1st Tribune: I didn't see them on him – (*making to go*) If we just came here for a slanging match Tina – I thought we were –

3rd Tribune: Sit down Madge. Please. Jackie's got a right to say what she thinks. And she's said it. So now perhaps we can move on to discuss what we are here to discuss.

2nd Tribune: I ain't made me poin yet!

3rd Tribune: Jackie please. Madge, will you sit down please. We're going to move on.

2nd Tribune is silent. 1st Tribune is still standing.

Madge, please.

1st Tribune sits down.

I don't want us to be her till eleven o'clock tonight. Can we just focus on one thing.

1st Tribune: I make no apology for showing loyalty to the Emperor.

2nd Tribune: (*fed up*) Aw gawd. Go and ge yourself another Costa Rica fil'er coffee.

3rd Tribune: (*firmly*) Our position on the present situation.

1st Tribune: Well if you ask me I think we should support the Chief Minister all the way. I don't think Tina we should be seen to be scoring political points. I think at a time like this the country wants to see us rallying behind the Emperor – not thumbing our noses at his Chief Minister.

2nd Tribune: I don't agree!

1st Tribune: Well you may not. But I'm saying what I think at this present juncture and you'll kindly let me finish. (*pause*) We have to say quite clearly to the Sijilian government that we will not tolerate its nationals coming over here what amounts to stealing from the Emperor and trying to destabilise our economic and political institutions.

3rd Tribune: But Madge, I don't disagree with the substance of what you're saying, but the Chief Minister has to take responsibility for letting them get away with it.

1st Tribune: I don't think so. These were very skilful operatives. No-one suspected anything. It's unfair to single out one person and say she's to blame.

2nd Tribune: Are you a people's tribune or a member of the minister's staff?

3rd Tribune: Jackie, can we not have personal attacks. (*to 1st Tribune*) Alright, so what are you suggesting we do? Ask the Sijilian government to extradite them for trial here on charges of subversion, fraud, what?

1st Tribune: Well yes I think so. And they should return the money that they stole and Sijil should compensate us for the damage to our national life.

2nd Tribune: I think this is sheer madness! You think Sijil's goin to agree to tha! You don't even know if their government ad anyfing to do wiv it! They'd probly say it was a freely enered-into business contract agreed by bof par'ies! They even said the cloves were invisible. Wha ya goin to do if they say no? You'll ave a soddin war on ya ands! 'Stha wha you wan?

1st Tribune: There has to be international order.

2nd Tribune: Well it's a funny way of ge'ing in it! Look Tina I wanna say somefing. I think there should be no action on the weavers.

1st Tribune: No action!?

2nd Tribune: No. I don fink they're to blame. I don't even fink the Chief Minister's to blame. I fink the Emperor's to blame. He decided it. He told the chief minister e was goin to ave em.

3rd Tribune: You don't know that –

2nd Tribune: Tina, e's the Emperor. It was im tha wan'ed the cloves. It stands to reason.

3rd Tribune: Jackie, I'm going to have to stop you there. We can't develop a position on the basis of your suppositions –

2nd Tribune: It stans to reason Tina!

3rd Tribune: I'm sorry, I can't agree with your approach to the thing – I agree with you on many things, you know that, but I'm sorry it would be completely irresponsible for us as tribunes to ... go along that path.

2nd Tribune: (*to both*) Our job as tribunes is to tell people the truf. Ain't you learnt anyfing. Hasn't this whole business taugh us anyfing?!

1st Tribune: Oh grow up Jackie.

3rd Tribune: (*very firmly, cutting across 1st Tribune*) No. Your suppositions.

2nd Tribune: Oh Christ.

3rd Tribune: (*gentler*) Jackie. We have to take a position the people will support. You know that. Can you imagine how popular we would be if we attacked the Emperor?

2nd Tribune: (*also softer*) People out there ave ad enough. People wan cloving themselves. Why should they go on paying for 'is? I really fink we should call on the Emperor to abdicate –

1st Tribune: What nonsense! Tina, I'm going. (*she gets up*)

2nd Tribune: Well effin go then!! I'm talking to Tina.

1st Tribune: Tina. It's up to you. Either I go or you stop this nonsense now.

There is a brief pause.

3rd Tribune: I'm sorry Jackie. I've already said no. And that's it. Our unity is more important than anything. (*pause*) Whatever you say I can't go down that path.

1st Tribune sits down. 2nd Tribune looks at her empty cup.

Alright. It's obvious that we have very different opinions on this matter. And that's healthy, and as it should be. We've had a good, frank, discussion. But I think we all agree that it's important that we have a united position on it. At times like this people don't want us divided among ourselves. They want strong leadership. They want to know where we stand so that they can get in behind us. So what I suggest is this. We say that we do (*to 1st Tribune*) consider this matter a breach of international law, and that therefore we (*to 2nd Tribune*) negotiate with the Sijil government to extradite the two (*to 1st Tribune*) alleged terrorists but we say nothing about compensation (*to 2nd Tribune*). Secondly we call for the resignation of the Chief Minister – (*1st Tribune bristles*) I know Madge, we are all having to give some ground. Now should she do so – which I think could well be on the cards – it is possible that the Emperor may ask one of us to take on that responsibility -

2nd Tribune: I'm definitely not having that. Our job is to represent the people. We ain't in a career structure to become the Emperor's ministers!

3rd Tribune: Just hear the proposal out. If that should happen, thirdly, we then persuade the Emperor – explaining to him the people's feelings on the matter –

2nd Tribune: We do that anyway! He don't take any no'ice!

3rd Tribune: We bring pressure to bear on him, as his Chief Minister, to curb his excessive fondness for new clothes – something which I think he will be ready to see the good sense of after yesterday – and ensure that he governs the country in a fair and just manner.

1st Tribune: We could even organise a public subscription for his clothes for next year's Parade. Then people will have to pay only according to what they can afford.

3rd Tribune: Well we can look at the details later Madge. I know this doesn't satisfy any one of us completely. But I think it's a strong position and one which will gain a lot of support out there.

2nd Tribune: I'm not putting my name to that Tina. I appreciate wha your tryin to do. Get unity and tha, but...

3rd Tribune: (*winking to 1st Tribune*) Madge get us some more teas or whatever you want. (*puts money on table*) Just want a private word with Jackie. That alright?

1st Tribune: (*getting up*) What do you want?

3rd Tribune: Same as before.

1st Tribune goes.

Look Jackie, we call on the Emperor to abdicate – do you think he would? Because I don't. Look in here (*she taps her stomach*) I know you're right. But he isn't going to abdicate so what's the point pointing the finger?

1st Tribune: (*off*) How many sugars Jackie?

3rd Tribune: Madge. I'm talking to Jackie. (*to 2nd Tribune*) You'd have to bring the people out on the streets. To force him to step down. And what if he digs in and says he won't? Then what are you going to do? You're talking chaos Jackie. Chaos. (*pause*) And you don't even know if they would. I'm not sure they care that much. Are you? What if only a few did? Enough to cause a reaction but not enough to get what you want. Can you imagine that? You can't play with people's lives like that. (*pause*) Look if one of us could become Chief Minister we could have a lot of influence on how the country's run. But we've got to get into power – otherwise we're just bleating on the sidelines.

2nd Tribune: I'm not putting my name to it Tina.

3rd Tribune: OK so what are you going to do? You want to go tell everyone what you see to be the truth? What you think should happen? You want to try and bring out the crowds?

2nd Tribune: Tina, the Emperor's insane.

3rd Tribune: (*resigned*) Well that's a matter of opinion. (*calling*) Madge. You can come back now. Let's finish the meeting off.

1st Tribune returns balancing the three drinks. She puts them down. She makes room with the used cups.

Leave that.

She does.

Right I'm putting the proposal.

1st Tribune: Same one?

3rd Tribune: Yes.

1st Tribune: I agree.

3rd Tribune: Jackie?

2nd Tribune: No. I don't.

1st Tribune: Well that's very nice!

3rd Tribune: Well it's obviously got my vote. It's agreed. Are you going to stand by the decision Jackie or not?

2nd Tribune: I dunno. Ave to fink about i.

3rd Tribune: (*cold, not threatening*) Yeah do that. Good. Anything else? (*a moment*) I'll keep you informed of course. Meeting closed.

3rd Tribune gets up, picks up brief case.

1st Tribune: There's your tea there.

3rd Tribune: No it's alright Madge. Got to dash. (*to 2nd Tribune*) Let us know what you decide, eh?

3rd Tribune exits. 2nd Tribune is getting up.

1st Tribune: You don't want to talk Jackie?

2nd Tribune briefly looks, without expression, at 1st Tribune.

I'm sorry it's turned out like this. It is for the best.

2nd Tribune: Seeya Madge.

She exits.

1st Tribune: (*to audience, as she goes through her coffee routine*) What Jackie doesn't understand is that you have to compromise in life. No-one ever gets everything they want. You have to be realistic. It's no good being idealistic about things. There has to be a little give and take. (*sotto voce*) Jackie doesn't give anything. She wants the world to be perfect. (*normal*) Well I'm sorry but the world just isn't like that. Ordinary people know that. I mean they don't want to get rid of the Emperor – they wouldn't have even noticed the Emperor was in the nude if that little child hadn't piped up! And they'll soon forget about it too. Just something that happened. Take my word for it, most people are perfectly happy with the Emperor. And anyway, what would they do without him! Run their own lives? They've got quite enough to do bringing up their kids and going out to work every day. Well that's my opinion anyway.

She goes.

9. Back Garden and Kitchen

A washing line extends from the door to a pole above a patch of grass that passes for a back garden. In the kitchen is a table and a couple of chairs. Her clothes and those of her child are strewn about the kitchen. The child is sat in the garden, playing. The door is open. Trees enters the garden carrying shopping in plastic carrier bags.

Trees: (*to audience*) The people were agitated by the experience of the Parade. But since the tribunes seemed to have the matter in hand, and no-one called upon them to do anything, they thought – or hoped – everything would turn out alright. Besides they knew of the Emperor's excessive fondness for new clothes and, on reflection, they thought it was just one of those 'accidents-waiting-to-happen' that you hear so much about now. So in the days that followed they carried on living as best as they could, trying to make ends meet in difficult circumstances.

She looks at the washing line.

Oh no. Where's the washing gone?! (*a moment*) Joelly, where's the washin? As someone ad it? (*not waiting for an answer – anger rising*) Some piss-po' as nicked it! (*to child*) Oo's been ere! Joelly I'm speaking to ya. (*going to child*) Joelly! (*taking hold of child's arm*) Oo's been ere? (*to audience*) And the child said – (*child's voice*) 'The emp'ror.' Don't talk such wet! (*shaking the child*) Someone stole this washin. Now I wanna know oo it was! (*child's voice*) 'The emp'ror.' (*she slaps the child behind the knees*) Don say that. (*child's cry*) Yer should've been watchin. (*more slaps and cries*) Little bugger. Jus been playin while someone steals the washin. (*more slaps and cries – it becomes almost continuous until the beating ends*) Stop screamin! Where joo fink I'm goin to find the money to buy ya new cloves eh? Why didn you call ou for Dawn or someone?

Dawn enters the garden.

Let em take em and do a runner!

Dawn: Wha you doing Trees. Leave er alone.

Trees: (*still slapping*) Mind your own business Dawn.

Dawn: Wha she done?

Trees: (*to child*) Don try to ge away when I'm speakin to ya!

Dawn: Trees leave er! You'll urt er!

Trees: Some bastard from aroun ere stole all the washin – and she jus sits ere playin.

Dawn: That's no cause to it er like tha! Stop it Trees. (*she tries to intervene*)

Trees: (*still hitting, to Dawn*) Can you bring my cloves back? –

Dawn: (*still trying to stop Trees*) Ittin er won't.

Trees: – if you can't do tha let me bea my child wivou your inerference.

(*child's voice, desperate*) 'It was the emp'ror.'

Dawn: (*not listening to child*) Trees!

Trees: Piss off Dawn!

Dawn: You're crazy.

She manages to get hold of Tree's hands. The child falls.

Stop it!

Trees: (*voice of child crying*)

Dawn: (*goes to the child, picks her up*) Alrigh now lovely. It's alrigh. Mummy's very upse. All over now. Les rub them legs. (*She soothes the child. Still holding the child, to Trees who is recovering.*) Wha go into you Trees?

Trees: It was me big wash. I can't afford new cloves. I ain't even go proper shoes for er to wear when she starts school.

Dawn: I'll lend ya some money...

Trees: Then she says it was the emp'ror and .... She sees emp'rors everywhere now .... since the parade. Past a joke Dawn. (*pause*) Come ere darling – pass er to me Dawn. (*Dawn does. To child.*) Mummy's sorry. (*kisses child*) Mummy loves ya. It weren't your faul.

Dawn: Joo wanna come back for a coffee? Take i easy for a bi?

Trees: No its alrigh fanks. Gotta sor this shoppin. Fanks Dawn.

Dawn: Well if you're sure .... I'll ave a word wiv Del. We'll ge some money for ya someow. An I've probly got some stuff the kids ave grown ou of.

Dawn goes. After a moment, Trees with the child in her arms heads into the house.

Trees: Come on let's ge inside and sort this shoppin eh?

She goes in to the kitchen with the child and is about to put her down and go back for the bags when she sees the clothes on the floor.

Wha's....

She puts the child on one of the chairs, facing away from the door, and picks up the nearest piece of washing, one of her tops. It is cut to shreds.

Wha's.....

She picks up other items including the child's. All are cut.

Oh my gawd. (*in disbelief, to child*) Ave you done this? (*to audience*) And the child said, very quietly – (*child's voice*) 'No.'

Not knowing what to do she goes out the door and brings the shopping. As she returns towards the back door, the Emperor enters from within the house and stands still, looking towards the door. He is naked. He is covered, including his hair, with grey dust. There is also mud on his body, especially on his knees and backs of the forearms. He wears, in the manner of an ammunition belt, a heavy canvas sash over one shoulder and across his body. Round his waist is a similar belt with a holster. In place of bullets, the sashes carry model bombers and fighter planes, missiles and missile-launchers, army trucks, battleships and submarines etc. He is wearing goggles such that his eyes cannot properly be seen. There is a trickle of dried blood from his nose, and one from the corner of his mouth. There are torn clothes caught around his feet that have dragged with him. He is holding a large shiny pair of scissors by one handle and one blade – like a knife. There is blood on his hand. Trees enters the kitchen with the bags and closes the door behind her with her foot. Then she sees the Emperor and jumps in fright. The bags fall.

Trees: (*to audience*) The child said, (*child's voice*) 'Mummy!'

She goes towards the child to pick her up.

Emperor: (*before she gets to the child*) Stay there.

Trees: (*She stops. Under control.*) Wha are you doin ere? Who are ya? Ave you come to kill us?

Silence.

Emperor: Depends on you.

Pause. He motions with the scissors.

Strip off. (*to child*) And you. (*pause*) Now let's see you with no clothes on.

Trees: Who are you?

Emperor: Do it!

A silence. Trees is angry, but controlled. She makes the decision to go to the child.

I said stay where you are!

Trees picks up the child and stands with her.

Do as you're told! (*he threatens with the scissors*) Call out for help and – (*pause*) Get them off.

Trees: No. I won take my cloves off. I wear cloves to keep me warm. And sometimes maybe to look as nice as I can. And my child wears em for the same reason. No. I take them off to go to bed. Or to ave a barf... I take them off to make love. But wha I don do – wha I won do – and my chil won do – is take em off cause you tell me. You got tha? I won'.

Pause. There is no shift in either of them, although the Emperor doesn't speak.

(*gentler*) Look, I dunno wha's wrong wiv you. I ain't no exper bu I fink you must be sufferin to do fings like this. Bu I can't do nuffing about tha. Bu I can't let you do this to my kid or anyone else's wivou' tryin to stop yer. And if tha means I'm going to ave to try and kill yer to stop yer – tha's wha I'm gonna do. Cause I can't let ya do it.

The Emperor says nothing.

So eiver ge on wiv it or ge ou a my ouse. OK? (*to audience*) Oh gawd. Someone should've done somefing before it go to this. Who le it ge to this.

She looks to the Emperor, who continues to stand with the scissors in his hand.

(*shouting, but remaining still*) Dawn! Dawn! Dawn! Come ere! Dawn!!

The Emperor does not react to the calls.

Plays written by Geoff Gillham
(all except those below are unpublished)

Year	Title	First performance
1977	*A Sense of Justice*	Benwell TIE
1979	*Ways of Change*	Cockpit TIE
1980	*The First Casualty*	Cockpit TIE
1981	*Rise and Fall*	Cockpit TIE
1982	*Lessons*	Cockpit TIE (Trentham 2011)
1983	*Semmelweis*	Cockpit TIE
1983	*Antidote to Dreams*	Wolsey TIE
1983	*Crossing*	Action PIE*
1984	*Embryo of Death*	Cockpit TIE*
1985	*Not Extraordinary*	London SCYPT Individuals Group
1985	*Questions Arising in 1985 From a Mutiny in 1789*	Action PIE, Wales
1988	*When Sleeping Dogs Awake*	Belgrade TIE (Trentham 2011)
1988	*Under the Dictatorship*	Actors' Group
1989	*The Crunch*	[with Ibrahim Ngozi] Commonwealth Institute TIE
1990	*The Twisting Path*	[with Brian Bishop and Nigel Gilkes] Belgrade TIE
1990	*The Cultivated Wilderness*	Spectacle Theatre*
1991	*Logos*	Duke's TIE*
1992	*Chain Reaction*	TheatreVan
1992	*Goya's Diary Fragments*	TheatreVan
1993	*Dressing Up Stripping Down*	TheatreVan (Trentham 2011)
1994	*Getting to it*	Big Brum TIE Co*
1994	*The Partridge Dance*	Theatr Powys*

1995	*Bone-cage*	SCYPT Theatre Cooperative (Trentham, 2011)
1997	*The Kiss (The Moment)*	Noor Al-Hussein Foundation Performing Arts Centre (Jordan)* (Trentham 2011)
1999	*Eating Cactus*	SCYPT Theatre Cooperative*
1999	*Asylum*	Big Brum Youth Theatre
2000	*The Silent Witness*	Penygraig Drama Workshop*

Plays written to commission are indicated by an asterisk [*] after first production

Published plays

| 1985 | *Questions Arising in 1985 From a Mutiny in 1789* | Redington, C. (Ed) (1987) in *Six T.I.E. programmes* Methuen (First perfomed by Action PIE, Cardiff) |
| 2011 | *Geoff Gillham: six plays for TIE and youth theatre* | Trentham Books |

Articles (an attempt to put together a list of published writings)

Report on Condercum School Project	1974 (unpublished)
Drama and the Integrated Curriculum	1977, Young Drama 5(3)
Drama, Art and Emotion	1978(?), London Drama
What's Happening when Children are Experiencing Drama	1979, Schooling and Culture 4
The Construction of Theatre Images	1980, *SCYPT Journal* 5
The New from the Old – the present state of YPT	1981 *SCYPT Journal* 7
'Restoration' by Edward Bond – a review	1981, Newsline (24.7.81)
'Truth is No Defence' – an examination of the Theatre's Act (1968)	1983, *SCYPT Journal* 11
Sexual Politics against Art, and Vice Versa	1984, *SCYPT Journal* 13
The Peterloo Massacre, 1819	1986, *Marxist Review* 1 (7)
Unsuitable for Children	1988, Belgrade Theatre Broadsheet; re-pub NATD Broadsheet 15(1),1997
What Life is For – An analysis of Dorothy Heathcote's 'Levels' of Explanation	1988, TEJ 1; re-pub *SCYPT Journal* 34, 1997
The Playwright and History in the Soviet In the Soviet Union	1988, TEJ 1
The Death Agony Goes On	1991, TEJ 4

'Education and Dramatic Art', by David Hornbrook – a Review	1991, *SCYPT Journal* 21
The Theatre We Need	1991, TheatreVan Newsletter
The Rigidity/Flexibility Contradiction	1992, (with Chris Cooper) *SCYPT Journal* 23
The Value of Theatre-in-Education	1994, *SCYPT Journal* 27
Notes on a Curriculum for Living	1995, *SCYPT Journal* 30; re-published NATD Broadsheet 15 (1), 1999
The Unity of Culture in a Divisive World – Pt 2	1997 SCYPT Journal 33 Spring
The Unity of Culture in a Divisive World – Pt 1	1996 Summer, SCYPT Journal 32
Grasping the Nettle Where it Stings Most	1998 in A Head Taller – developing a Humanising Curriculum through Drama NATD publication
Pax Project: A Multi-layered Approach to Peace	2000, CARE International Building and Social Reconstruction in Bosnia And Hercegovina
The Significance of Culture in the Development of Human Beings	2000, NATD *People in Movement* (co-authored with Chris Cooper and Ian Yeoman) 2000, in *A Handbook of Materials on Theatre-in-Education*, SCYPT publication

Teachers' Packs

Prometheus	1989, for Actors' Group, London
Black and Blue	1988, for Duke's TIE Co., Lancaster